CW01022431

'This is a wise and beautiful book. Like some of th
humanistic tradition (Carl Rogers, R.D. La
Spinelli), Laura Barnett has a talent for makin
theory understandable to everyone without sacrificing complexity and depth.
She adds to this tradition a very precise consideration of the importance of
the body and transgenerational issues. As a vivid but modest presence in the
book, she demonstrates in her very attuned handling of delicate material the
book's three interwoven themes. Holding theory lightly and combining a very
distinct personal voice with compelling vignettes, she invites us to confront
the mystery of being human.'

Betty Cannon, *PhD, Professor Emerita, author of* Sartre and
Psychoanalysis *and founder of Applied Existential
Psychotherapy*

The Heart of Therapy

This thoughtful and heartfelt book develops two main themes: the healing power of a compassionate understanding towards ourselves and others, and the ways boundaries are set within and around various areas of our lives.

It examines how we live these boundaries, how they impact us, and what it takes to live these with deeper satisfaction. This book also addresses: shame and rage; the impact of trauma; the power of parental messages, spoken and unspoken; and transgenerational burdens. A theoretical chapter summarizes the author's integrative, phenomenological approach: it brings the insights of a body-focused trauma therapy and a systemic lens to an overarching Existential perspective. Numerous vignettes, case studies and client-therapist dialogues illustrate reflections on life, philosophy, therapeutic modalities and practice.

This book will be a thought-provoking read for trainee and practising counsellors and psychotherapists, or anyone looking for self-reflection on their own practices, life, and ultimately, what it means to be human.

Laura Barnett is an existential psychotherapist with a strong interest in trauma, including transgenerational trauma. For 20 years she worked as a psychotherapist, supervisor and trainer in the NHS. Since retiring from the NHS, she has been working from home, in Lewes.

The Heart of Therapy

Developing Compassion,
Understanding and Boundaries

Laura Barnett

Routledge
Taylor & Francis Group

LONDON AND NEW YORK

Designed cover image: © Getty Images

First published 2023
by Routledge
4 Park Square, Milton Park, Abingdon, Oxon OX14 4RN

and by Routledge
605 Third Avenue, New York, NY 10158

Routledge is an imprint of the Taylor & Francis Group, an informa business

British Library Cataloguing-in-Publication Data
A catalogue record for this book is available from the British Library

Library of Congress Cataloging-in-Publication Data
Names: Barnett, Laura, 1953– author.
Title: The heart of therapy : developing compassion, understanding and boundaries / Laura Barnett.
Description: Abingdon, Oxon ; New York, NY : Routledge, 2023. |
Includes bibliographical references and index.
Identifiers: LCCN 2022051615 (print) | LCCN 2022051616 (ebook) |
ISBN 9781032428253 (hardback) | ISBN 9781032428277 (paperback) |
ISBN 9781003364504 (ebook)
Subjects: LCSH: Psychotherapy. | Compassion. |
Boundaries (Psychology) | Self-perception. | Therapist and patient.
Classification: LCC RC480 .B275 2023 (print) |
LCC RC480 (ebook) | DDC 616.89/14–dc23/eng/20221122
LC record available at https://lccn.loc.gov/2022051615
LC ebook record available at https://lccn.loc.gov/2022051616

ISBN: 9781032428253 (hbk)
ISBN: 9781032428277 (pbk)
ISBN: 9781003364504 (ebk)

DOI: 10.4324/9781003364504

Typeset in Times New Roman
by Newgen Publishing UK

To Baba

and

To my children, my children-in-law,
And all my grandchildren,
With love and gratitude.

Contents

Acknowledgements

As the idea for this book originated from a client-related dream, my first thanks go to my clients without whom this book would not have come into being.

I would also like to thank all those family members, colleagues and friends who were prepared to read various draft chapters of this book with a critical eye: Alina Barnett, Clara Barnett, Rowan Barnett, Linda Beton, Kathryn Burton, Cyrille Cahen, Joylyn Charles, Karen Frances – who, with Gudrun Langner-Fahlisch, was first to wade through very early chapter drafts – John Harris, Melanie Lockett and Annabel Roditi. Their questions and comments proved invaluable to me: consensus gave their feedback additional weight, divergences reminded me of the importance of personal, hence subjective, engagement with a book of this kind. Final decisions have had to lie with me, for better or for worse.

Over these last five years, this book has bridged my personal and professional lives. It has integrated many of my personal dialogues: my dialogues between philosophy, life and practice; between body, mind, emotions and spirit; between different forms of therapeutic modalities and their practice; dialogues with colleagues and friends; and of course with clients. These have impacted on the format of this book, where the numerous concrete examples serve as either illustrations or starting points for reflections.

To contact all the clients I would have needed to approach for consent to publish would have been impossible and, in many instances, inappropriate. Most of the vignettes, therefore, are composite cases: each inspired by clients who shared similar histories, traits, ways of being and/or issues. Many relate to my time working in hospital with people who had been affected by a cancer diagnosis or had been in Intensive Care.

Where I was able to get in touch with some former clients, I was moved by their willingness to allow me to use part of our work. To them I am most grateful.

Further thanks are due to those who contributed indirectly to this book. First of all to my mother and step-father for helping to develop my lifelong interest in psychotherapy, for showing courage in questioning psychotherapeutic dogma, finding their own way, and enabling family discussions of that journey and its impact. To the therapist who first taught me the power of the very word 'compassion'; to all the wonderful supervisors who have accompanied, challenged and supported me along the way.

The existential therapists who have inspired me are too numerous to mention, and most know who they are. Among the Sensorimotor Psychotherapy faculty, special thanks go to Janina Fisher who gave of her time so generously, answering my long list of questions over a number of lunches, when I was her assistant on the level 1 training, as well as to Kekuni Minton and Tony Buckley from whom I benefitted variously, as student and assistant. I feel deep gratitude to the now sadly defunct International Systemic Constellations Association Easter Intensive courses at Bernried and Kochel, and most especially to Christine Blumenstein-Essen. My thanks also go to Professor Betty Cannon and Natasha Synesiou for the very strong validation they both offered me in their reviews of this book for Routledge. And to Grace McDonnell at Routledge who responded so swiftly and helpfully to all emails and, with her assistant Sarah Hafeez, saw this book through the various stages of the publishing process.

My last thanks go, once again, to my clients who have nourished my reflections on theory and practice over the years, and taught me so much about people and life.

Introduction

Dream

I sensed, as I woke up that morning, that it had been a night rich in dreams; yet it had left me without any images or recollection of its adventures. Instead, a thought had come to me with the intensity of Truth: "compassion, understanding and boundaries are the heart of therapy, they are the heart of life". While I have long considered all three to have predominant roles in therapy and in good interpersonal relations, I would never have singled them out in this dogmatic way. Maybe it was the prospect of seeing Mark later that day that had made me stop and ponder the statement, rather than dismiss it out of hand as mere nocturnal 'Truth'-mongering. Mark was a client I was finding particularly challenging because of my need with him to hold the tension between the man and his terrible suffering at the hands of others, and the great suffering and hurt he himself had inflicted. I do not usually take my work home but it seemed to me that my dreams that night must have expressed my struggle with this tension, and that maybe they carried a message that was worth my listening to.

This was almost five years ago; reflecting on these three words started me on a personal and professional journey. I am now struck by how fundamental these have become to my existence and my work. The dream awoke my curiosity, it channelled my thinking, my observations and my reading; it helped me to articulate different perspectives for myself and it is out of these that this book has emerged.

It would be absurd for me to argue that compassion, understanding and boundaries are all that is required, either in therapy or in life. Yet I can vouch, from personal and professional experience over these past five years, that they offer a helpful light to work and live by. What is more, they can help to develop and enhance those other fundamentals which we need to thrive – such as love, acknowledgement, respect, trust, freedom and meaning.

While we cannot change what happened in the past, we can change our attitude towards it and some of its ongoing impact on our lives. With greater understanding and compassion and better boundaries, we can learn to live

DOI: 10.4324/9781003364504-1

with ourselves, our past, the world and others in a more satisfying way – with less shame, anger, or guilt, and with greater self-worth and equanimity. Rather than examining these concepts abstractly, I have tried to show through examples their interconnection at work within the context of our lives. The vignettes are not about my skills as a therapist or at times my lack thereof; they seek to illustrate certain experiences, my clients' and my own.

In the first six chapters, I look at the multiple ways boundaries are set within and around so many areas of our lives, and how these impact upon us. I explore boundaries as they manifest themselves in the dimensions that frame our human existence. We are all embodied – and I don't simply mean that we all have bodies, but that we relate to ourselves and others, we live through our bodies, we even feel and think through our bodies. And as we are embodied in space and time, we live with both spatial and temporal boundaries. I also consider what it takes to live some of these boundaries more satisfactorily, what commonly gets in the way of our doing so and how we can overcome those obstacles. And I show through numerous examples how understanding – of ourselves, of others, of the context of our beliefs, actions and interactions – is paramount in developing (self)compassion.

And where better to observe all the above than in our relations to our parents, whether alive, long dead, or of whereabouts unknown? This is the focus of Chapters 7–12.

Chapter 13, Understanding, clarifies the theoretical underpinning of the whole book. In this chapter, I argue that we understand through four intricately interconnected means: our minds, bodies, emotions and what is other than those yet inseparably and intimately connected to them (call it spirit/soul/life force). And I illustrate through vignettes how each of these has an important place in therapy. This chapter represents a personal integration of my various therapy trainings and interests.

'Heart' is the name of the concluding chapter.

As I do not expect any specialized knowledge of therapy, there is a glossary to explain certain terms and summarize some of the main concepts explored in this book. And rather than a full bibliography, I have listed the principal books I have consulted when writing.

Chapter 1

Spatial Boundaries

We react variously to space – to height, depth, vastness, narrowness, closeness, distance and infinity, and we all react differently. The awe-inspiring sight of the infinite, starry heaven evokes deep existential anxiety for some, a sense of wonder, comfort and belongingness to others. Vastness and height can be elating but can also trigger agoraphobia and vertigo; the narrow space that offers security to some feels claustrophobic to others. Different people have a different felt sense of personal space: I had an acquaintance who liked to stand 'in my face', well no more than 5 centimetres from me, and I would back off until I was literally up against a wall. Our reactions to space are embodied: in the face of vastness, height, or narrowness, we may feel hot, cold, sweaty, clammy, dizzy, lightheaded, heavy, we may experience constricted breathing, an expanded chest, butterflies in our stomach, the feeling that we could fly. Our physical reactions to space also take place at an emotional, mental and spiritual level. Agoraphobia and claustrophobia, for example, are classified as 'mental health' issues, wonder and awe at the heavens would be considered as belonging to the spiritual realm, closeness and distance to the emotional; yet, we experience space as a whole and are affected by it in all dimensions of our existence at once.

If I were to ask you to bring your attention back to yourself, would you have a sense of how much space you take? Where is the border of your personal space? If you were to put a piece of string or draw a line all around you to represent that border and imagine that someone were to step over it, what would that be like? Is it mildly annoying, do you let or welcome that person in, or do you feel invaded, do you feel like pulling the drawbridge down, closing the shutters, barricading yourself in?[1] Would it depend, and if so, on whom, when and what? And what about the metaphysical boundary of the furthest distance of all, which fills us with awe: the boundary of what, if anything, lies Beyond? Does it feel the most remote boundary of all or the closest to you, within you even?

These experiences of spatial distance and closeness embody our fundamental boundaries to the world and others. They are linked to so many

DOI: 10.4324/9781003364504-2

questions: where do I begin and end? Where do others begin and end? What lies beyond this horizon? Where am I safe and secure, where do insecurity, risk and danger threaten? How close will I allow you to come? Can I trust you? This is my boundary, will you respect it? Can I trust you to respect it? Might you try to test it gently and, with my consent, help me expand it; or will you overstep it, invade it and do me violence?

In the following example, it is the felt impossibility of sharing the same space as his mother that brings Tom to therapy.

Tom and Jess's father had left when they were young; their mother had always been there for them. However, already as an older child, Tom was very conscious of not having his own space. His mother would come into his room in his absence to hoover and tidy his desk – despite his repeated requests to leave his desk alone, and when he was there, she would also "barge in" on him without knocking.

Tom's mum was very protective of both her children, but Tom was the apple of her eye. She would pile food on his plate, while serving small portions to Jess and herself, with the result that he became very overweight. She would put him on diets but worry that he was not getting his sufficient dose of nutrients and "push milkshakes" onto him. Meanwhile, Tom would be worrying about her. When it came to university, he felt unable to leave and entrust her care to his sister, so commuted great distances from home, foregoing any university life. After university, he continued to live at home.

At the age of 26, when Tom came to see me, he was alternating between feeling angry, lost and depressed; the situation with his mother had become unbearable. He told her that for the foreseeable future, when she was in Sussex, he would have to go to their cottage in Cornwall, and when she went there, he would have to go back to Sussex – he and she could not share the same space. Despite the luxury of being able to choose between two homes, this was a rather constricted way to live his life, and it depended on his mother sticking to his rules.

The situation is clearly a complex one – the father leaving them when Tom and his sister were young, the mother's feelings, the mother–son mutual protectiveness, the mother's preferential treatment of one child over the other, Tom feeling alternatively angry and depressed, etc. Tom's situation lends itself to a number of possible therapeutic explorations. However, for the purposes of the present reflections, more unusually, I would like to highlight the issues around physical space and boundaries.

As he was growing up, Tom had had trouble holding onto his own personal space and privacy: there was no lock to stop his mother barging into his room; even the personal boundary of his body had felt under attack as his mother overfed him, then tried to shrink him while pushing milkshakes onto him. This invasion of his physical boundaries was having repercussions on his sense of self and agency. He grew up not quite knowing where his and his mother's space began and ended, where he himself and his mother began and ended. When Tom decided to live at home, who was keeping whom safe and secure in this relationship? Was either succeeding? And if so, at what cost?

'This is my boundary, will you respect it?' was a major issue for Tom, and it was not surprising that he was having trust issues about entering into a relationship. Nor was it surprising that he felt disorientated within his blurred boundaries. Boundaries have a physical quality and demarcate space, yet they have a strong emotional impact: we may feel lost or insufficiently held when they are blurred or too loose; we may feel trapped, suffocated, or in a straightjacket when they hold us too tightly or rigidly; when boundaries are repeatedly invaded or melt away, we may lose our sense of self. On the other hand, when boundaries are erected into a wall, the relationship is distant or confrontational, as people become estranged, alienated, or solipsistic, each living in their own bubbles. Such relationships do not simply develop between parents and children, they occur between partners, or even between ourselves and the rest of the world.

At no time in recent history have spatial boundaries and their impact been the object of so much worldwide discussion and scrutiny, and so widely put to the test, as during the Coronavirus pandemic. Had 'lockdown' been a human experiment on how spatial boundaries can affect our sense of safety and well-being, as well as our relationship to ourselves, others and the world, it would have breached all the ethical guidelines! The very words chosen to define this period metaphorically reflected the forceful, physical act of power that setting such boundaries on a whole country represented (lockdown, 'le confinement', etc.). In addition, depending on people's personal histories, these words in themselves had the power to evoke memories, sensations and emotions of being locked in, locked up, confined in a tight space, etc.

What this boundary 'experiment' highlighted, as we might have guessed, was the high levels of anxiety, boredom, claustrophobia, depression, frustration, insecurity, panic and violence that many suffered at being thus confined to the very restricted world of their own homes and the people in it – or else its total loneliness. When that home itself was intolerable or unsafe, this made for a form of torture. But lockdown highlighted yet again how different we all are: for there were those for whom this period of constricted physical boundaries was an answer to their wildest dreams, a period of safety and relief from the torture of having to go out into the world. This boundaried way of living, this self-isolation, thus came in a whole spectrum of mood colours. There was the dark grey, or black, of the misery of being alone with oneself – or with the person(s) one lived with, cut off from whatever offered support and meaning to one's life; there were the restful colours of relief and peace and every shade in-between.

We need boundaries to give ourselves a sense of security and protect ourselves from invasion; and each of us has a different sense of where they need to place these boundaries to feel most secure. It is that *personal* sense of safety which was thwarted in lockdown, when governments dictated our spatial boundaries and deprived us of our freedom to choose their distance and flexibility.

Yet, setting the boundaries we would wish for ourselves may feel difficult: for setting a limit is tantamount to saying "no" to someone. Learning to say "no" calmly without feeling embarrassed or guilty, yet in such a way that the other person really hears it, is central to satisfying human relations.

Cathy's in-laws had moved nearby a year ago and now liked to 'come and help' regularly on a Friday evening: "you and Tim'll be tired at the end of the week, so you can put your feet up, grandad can read the children a story and I'll cook us some dinner" was how her mother-in-law had first offered. Unfortunately, the reality was far from this relaxing picture: grandad couldn't get the children into bed, let alone listening to the story, and granny kept complaining about not finding various implements or ingredients and left a trail of mess in the kitchen – washing up clearly had not been part of the deal! More often than not, it was grandad who had his feet up with his sherry, while Cathy or Tim were dealing with the bedtime rituals. Cathy felt increasingly frustrated, especially as in the last few weeks her mother-in-law had started making little digs at the way she ran her house. Although Tim could see the chaos these visits created, he was not prepared to do anything about the situation: "Well mum and dad are doing their best to help, we can't just turn them away". Cathy would often lie awake imagining conversations with her mother-in-law in which she tried to ask her to stop coming on a Friday, or ruminating over what she would say to her the next time she made an unpleasant remark. Cathy felt completely stuck: she was finding the situation intolerable and didn't see how she could put an end to it without seriously upsetting her husband and his parents.

I asked Cathy whether she would be prepared to try some experiments marking out boundaries with her arms and hands. Demarcating space to the side and front of herself with arms rounded, not outstretched and hands curved inwards, she was able to gain a sense of space in which to breathe and quietly feel herself be the competent mother and runner of the household that she was. From this position and thinking of how she might address her mother-in-law, Cathy experimented with her fingertips touching, then with her hands further apart, facing first inwards, then outwards:

C. That feels strong and fingertips touching feels more secure; but with my hands facing in, I don't feel able to address her, and palms outwards feels too aggressive.

She tried palms up in an offering position.

C. This feels like I'm giving, and I sort of want to do that too, but that's not the main thing I'm trying to say.

While one hand palm up and the other arm outstretched with her hand in a stop sign felt confusing. In the end, she settled for her left arm rounded, quite close to the body and protective of her stomach area and the other, a little further forward, in a stop sign. From this position, Cathy felt she could address her mother-in-law and stand up to her jibes politely but firmly. And by turning the 'stop' hand over into an offering position, she could tell her parents-in-law that a weekly Friday evening wasn't working for her and Tim, and that they would like to think of a better way for them to see each other. We practised with her standing, in these positions, with her feet firmly but not rigidly planted. The aim was not to have her speak to her mother-in-law with her arms and hands like that! Rather, the idea was to practise how that felt physically, mentally, emotionally when she stood in that posture, both protecting her sense of space and standing up for herself. She could then remind herself of the felt sense of this posture before speaking.

Next session Cathy reported back jubilantly that she had first tried this out with Tim and they had come up with a compromise suggestion together, which she was then able to express confidently and politely to her in-laws: they could come and babysit sometimes – the children would be more likely to behave when their parents were away. And it would be really lovely for Tim and her to go out together. Also they could have a flexible arrangement whereby the family would go to them for a meal at the weekend or they would come over for dinner. The in-laws turned out to be relieved by her suggestion, as they could see that their 'help' was being rather ineffectual, which made them feel deskilled as grandparents.

If you tried the hand positions described above as you were reading, you may have got a sense of each of these, though you might have experienced them differently to Cathy. For your felt sense is personal to you.

The difference between effective and ineffective boundary setting does not lie primarily in the words used: it lies in *the clarity of the intention* and *the way in which it is communicated*. Clarity of intention is the first hurdle at which so many attempts at boundary-setting fall: where would you ideally like the boundary to be, what would be acceptable and what would feel unacceptable or even intolerable? If you are not clear about this with yourself, how can you communicate it clearly and with conviction to others, and mean it? As most of our communication is non-verbal, our tone of voice, body postures, movements and gestures will have repercussions on how our attempt at boundary-setting is perceived and received by the other. It is clear that standing rigidly, looking fierce, raising a hand brusquely, jabbing or wagging a finger and speaking in a loud tone are likely to be perceived as aggressive. Whereas looking up with a childlike pout, standing hunched, or shifting from foot to foot will send a message of being a pushover. Sometimes, I find it difficult not to smile when clients, practising saying "no" wordlessly, through their stance and hands alone, start by peevishly leaning back in their chair and waving their hands. If, on the other hand, we stand in a relaxed but firm position and feel the ground under our feet, trying to keep our body aligned, yet not too rigid, the tone of voice we will use to express our boundary is more likely to sound firm, grounded and assertive. And the hand that comes up to say "no" or "stop" will be clear and firm, not wishy-washy or aggressive.

The beauty of trying these experiments is that they confer a felt sense of calm assertiveness that enables us to know what we wish to say and then communicate it effectively. And because this sense is embodied, if we pay attention to our experience of it – to our posture, to where and how we feel it in our bodies – we can learn to reconnect with it. Of course, there will always be some people who take offence, however tactful and reasonable the request, and some who are unable to take no for an answer... In both these cases, we need to decide whether the priority is to protect ourselves at the expense of their feelings, or to make them the priority at the expense of our own needs – either way, the choice is ours. Setting different boundaries can have a major impact on our lives.

Maggie was one of life's helpers: at home, she looked after her elderly father; at work, colleagues would ask her to help them out with this and that piece of work "you don't mind, do you? You're so quick at this". At Church, Maggie regularly helped at Sunday school and played the organ; she was also called upon to help with flower arranging, cleaning and gardening when people on the various rotas had dropped out.

Maggie's breast cancer diagnosis had come out of the blue; now the treatment was over and she was left with a sense of unreality about all that she had gone through over the past 18 months. One thing she was certain about was that she wasn't prepared to carry on as before.

We sought to understand what underpinned Maggie's need to always help others and we questioned the boundaries she had set in different areas of her life. To her surprise, as she quietly but firmly scaled back what she was prepared to do for her father, work colleagues and people at Church, she remained valued and, what's more, was treated with greater respect.

Maggie realized that exploring her boundaries was helping her discover what was most meaningful to her and felt most 'urgent'. She was beginning to articulate her own needs, wishes and priorities and to explore different avenues, now that she had freed some space and time for herself. When she heard herself mention voluntary work as one such possibility, she laughed – old habits die hard, but this was one she was going to kick!

It is clear how Maggie's difficulty in establishing boundaries with others had had repercussions on the boundaries of her own life's possibilities. By being open to all and sundry (father, church, colleagues, friends), her boundaries had closed her off to whole realms of possibilities for herself.

Maggie and I spent a long time exploring her giving; but how we receive is equally important. Some people are good at both giving and receiving, some can do only one of the two gracefully and others can do neither. Too much, or the wrong sort of giving, like the inability to receive gracefully, is uncomfortable for the person at the other end. Whereas receiving with gratitude can feel like a gift to the giver: it offers them the sense of feeling valued, as well as the possibility of expressing their appreciation, love, or friendship. Receiving gracefully and gratefully requires a boundary that can open to the other and welcome something of them in.

Some boundaries that could be drawn as parallel, horizontal lines embody power dynamics. The English language is rich in expressions of relative height – such as 'look up to', 'down upon', ' down one's nose at', 'put on a pedestal', 'put down' – which describe embodied, interpersonal dynamics of power, hierarchy, admiration and contempt. These expressions are stylistically referred to as metaphors, yet they are more than that: they are quite literal. If you are mindful of your posture and the direction of your glance, I suspect you will notice changes according to whether you are addressing someone you respect, admire (someone you look up to), or whether you are addressing someone whom you despise, find somehow disgusting or creepy. And in the presence of the condescending and haughty, do you stand up to them, shrink, or hang your head?

Whether we admit it or not, a height and power boundary is inherent in the therapeutic enterprise. While both therapist and client have to abide by a set of general therapeutic rules (confidentiality, time and place boundaries, etc.), the client also has to abide by the therapist's own rules, in particular regarding cancellations and payment. In addition, there are therapists who believe that their theories give them the expertise and the right to make theory-based interpretations about their clients and assert them to be True. That too, I believe, is a form of horizontal boundary expressing a power differential. This is further exacerbated if the therapist views the client's disagreement with that interpretation as 'resistance' and hence to be further interpreted away. Yet, even when the therapist gives the client the power to end therapy when they wish and seeks to make therapy as collaborative as possible, a joint endeavour, still there remains some power differential. The very fact that one person is consulting another over their problems or suffering, and investing hope and faith in their ability, experience, wisdom (real or fantasized), confers a certain superiority upon that other.

Hannah was sitting in front of me, looking dejected. She said that whenever she thought of her line-manager she felt defeated and hopeless and now it was impacting on her life and she couldn't face doing anything, let alone going back to the office. In fact, she added, if I were to ask her to pick up the pebble on the small table beside her, she wouldn't be able to summon the energy to do so. I acknowledged her sense of hopelessness and defeat, the effort it must take her to get out of bed every day and how, in this state, it must feel impossible to relate to colleagues, let alone to her manager. I suggested she observe her posture, the dejected way in which she was sitting here with me, her hunched shoulders, cast-down head and her gaze, directed towards her knees. I asked whether she would like to try an experiment: what if she tried lengthening her spine? As she slowly began to do so, her upper-body rose and I observed a tense squirm in her shoulders; she raised her head, a little frown appeared, followed by a quizzical look and a faint smile. Hannah was sitting up straight. When I asked her to notice what that felt like, she replied: "I can see you now, I can see into your eyes, like I'm at eye level, like we're in this together."

Observing her change of posture and being mindful of how different it made her feel emotionally – more directly connected to me, level with me, and hence with less power differential – was the start of fruitful change. Hannah could see how, by embodying the hierarchical, horizontal boundary that existed between herself and her line-manager, she was effectively putting herself down. When she returned to work, she practised paying attention to her posture and lengthening her spine before going into meetings and in situations where she was feeling cowed, anxious, or not fully engaged , and was delighted with the result. She also realized that putting herself down and not standing up for herself had been a familiar pattern – with her siblings and some of her friends. This opened up the more existential questions about how she saw herself and what she wanted from her life. At the end of therapy, Hannah reminded me of the experiment we did in the first session and concluded: "we make a good team, you and me."

Spatial boundaries are fundamentally connected to all areas of our lives, most intimately in relation to our bodies, our sense of personal identity, self-worth and security, but also in relation to others. A better understanding of them can therefore help us to live (in) our bodies in a more integrated way and to relate to others in a more satisfying way.

Note

1   I am indebted to Sensorimotor Psychotherapy for this exercise and other body-focused experiments in this book. These have helped me to deepen my reflections on boundaries.

Chapter 2

Finding My Place

Spatial Boundaries

Boundaries and 'my place'

I was having breakfast with my brother in the garden, in the one bright patch that the early sun was warming, when he asked me about the gist of this book. I told him about my dream and, as I was talking about the additional light which the perspective of space and time was shedding for me, he spoke of one of his favourite concepts, a lens through which he likes to look at his life, the concept of 'place'. This in turn set me thinking: I saw how, with understanding and compassion, the concept of boundaries could help us to clarify, delineate and change our 'place' in relation to our bodies, within our families, in relation to friends and acquaintances, at work and in the world. And how it could help to reconsider the place we create for ourselves in space and in time, the place we give, the place that was taken away from us, the place we take, or don't dare take, in some spheres, or indeed anywhere....

My body and my place

Our world, starting with our bodies, is criss-crossed with boundaries. There is the line which divides us vertically into left and right, assigning contrasting moral values to each side. The word for left-handed in Latin is *sinister*. Are you of the generation when left-handed children were shamed for being so and taught to write with their right hand? "For right hand is right!" There is the horizontal boundary, often imbued with moral connotations, that divides the upper from the lower part of the body: an offensive remark is 'below the belt'; the 'private parts' are where shame hides (*pudenda [membra]*, literally organs to be ashamed of). Some experience a tightness around their throat – a boundary preventing feelings and thoughts from finding expression. Some feel it around their chest, constraining their breathing: having a voice of one's own can be difficult, breathing and speaking out not safe. Others around their heart, keeping love at bay, keeping it from seeping out.

And where, I wonder, is *your* place in relation to your body? Do you feel at ease in your skin, well grounded in your body? Are your head, heart and body

DOI: 10.4324/9781003364504-3

attuned to each other and able to converse and speak in unison? Do they have equal value? Does your head feel well integrated with the rest of your body or does it feel cut off from it?

I find it difficult to believe now that it wasn't until I started training as a therapist that I suddenly realized that, without ever having articulated it, I had always sort of experienced my body as being on the right side of 'me'! So where was 'me'? Well, in my first year of secondary school, I was taught Descartes' famous saying 'cogito ergo sum', 'I think therefore I am'. This made perfect felt sense to me: I grappled with thoughts and had many which felt my own and gave me a sense of identity, ergo I was. That was 'me'. My body didn't come into it; it was the thing I didn't much care for, but dressed and took basic care of. That was how I functioned in the world. Plato, one of the heroes of my adolescent years, confirmed that 'truth' for me: I latched onto 'soma sema', the body is a tomb for the soul – a view endorsed by the Catholic Church whose teachings imbued the supposedly secular country in which I lived. Interesting how philosophy and religion can help create an experience of splitting and dissociation in which the body is felt as separate, something to be despised and rejected, an object of shame even. At university, Sanskrit literature with its delight in the human body sowed the seeds of the thought that it need not necessarily be so. Yet, it is not until, on my therapy training, I read Merleau-Ponty's Phenomenology of Perception, an arduous, yet passionate and beautiful explication of our embodied nature, that the penny finally dropped: Descartes' 'I think therefore I am' did not express the reality of who I was. There was no disembodied me with a body on the side. Interestingly, this philosophical shift from Cartesian dualism to Existential-phenomenological non-dualism had immediate, observable repercussions: a dance teacher who had not seen me for a year, took me aside in the lunch break and remarked on my transformation. "Laura, instead of moving from your head, you now move from your solar plexus. What's happened?" As I write this, it feels strange to think that this mind–body split ever was my embodied experience: this dissociation feels as alien to me now as my present experience of embodiment would have felt to me then.

It is interesting how a philosophical paradigm shift can translate itself into a completely different way of feeling and experiencing oneself in one's body and in the world. Interesting too how these felt lines and boundaries that we draw in invisible ink on or around our bodies can be apparent to others. Clearly, my dancing teacher was able to tell that something quite significant had shifted in the way I lived (in) my body. For we send out 'vibes' (for want of a better word) about our felt sense of place in our bodies, about our feelings of bodily connection and disconnection, groundedness and ungroundedness, about the value we attach to our bodies, or the shame or disgust with which we invest parts that lie on the wrong side of these invisible, felt splits and boundaries. And these vibes may be picked up by others. In that way, a whole embodied, yet unspoken, conversation is constantly taking place: between the messages our invisible internal body boundaries and felt sense are sending out to the other person, their experience of their own body and ours, and our awareness of theirs. A conversation that impacts on our respective felt sense of place in our bodies and in the world.

Skin, the body's most visible boundary, is also its largest, measuring approximately 2 square metres. From its inner side, it holds us in and, on its outer side, it exposes us to the world, while keeping it at bay. Watertight and solid, it can be, metaphorically speaking, permeable, thin and ultra-sensitive. How much of the world shall I let in? What if it gets 'under my skin'? Will it 'bring me out in a rash'?

This boundary also comes in a whole spectrum of colours that expose it to the judgements, emotions and behaviours of others, and often of society as a whole. A colour boundary that may be used to justify power dynamics – from the strongest of all, the master and slave dynamic, by which one person denies the other their freedom and humanity and imposes themselves upon them with violence to bullying and the myriad of subtle and not-so-subtle forms of discrimination. Even where strong power dynamics and violence do not prevail, the skin's coloured boundary is intimately bound with a sense of identity, whether through self-identification and/or identification by others ... or through self-disidentification.

Nathalie was an engaging 44-year-old woman who came to see me following a serious accident. While most of our sessions concerned the life-changing consequences of her accident, a particular event led to a moving exploration of the place which the colour of her skin had had in her life. Nathalie had been one of the very few black children in her neighbourhood and had experienced this, she said, as a matter of total indifference to her. She had always had many friends and the colour of her skin had never been an issue, she felt, either to her or to her classmates, teachers and neighbours, nor later in life to boyfriends and her husband – all white. And now she was seeing me, a white therapist, which did not present any problem for her (nor for me personally, but I was aware, professionally, of potential issues). But the week preceding our session, she had gone to London and, at peak time, had found herself jostling for space on a train with a crowd of mainly black men and women. She was shocked to experience a sense of "total non-belonging". Or rather, as we explored her experience further, a strong sense of not belonging and of "yes I do belong ... but I'm not sure how much I want to". Suddenly, the world had felt out of kilter. Something disquieting had happened on the train, something that had jarred painfully, and she now found herself struggling with what felt like the clash of two realities: the factual reality of her ethnic background and what she had considered to be her experiential reality.

As Nathalie began to reflect upon this confusing, painful clash and the emotions it was bringing up, she realized that she maybe needed to question her experience of herself as a person whose life had been totally unaffected by the colour of her skin. Could there have been some chinks and cracks in that experience that she had rushed to paper over as soon as they had appeared? It began to dawn on Nathalie that, with the help of others, she may have created a "colourless bubble" for herself in which, for all these years, such reflections and emotions had had no place. But now that bubble had well and truly burst.

For Nathalie was a black woman and her African ancestry was more than some abstract ethnicity category: this was her history, those were her roots and, as such, part of her identity. She could not simply ignore these without a cost to herself and one day to her children. She needed to own her roots. Her "yes I do belong ... but I'm not sure how much I want to", replete with negative internalized identifications and painful emotions from disgust and shame to guilt and grief, needed to be unpacked and properly considered if she was to find her genuine place in her body, her life and her history. And that in turn would help her children find theirs.

The visible bone structure may also create a boundary that affects a person's place in the world: as the shape of the nose and the flatness of feet were deemed to signal Jewish ancestry and mark out those whose place 'belonged' in ghettos and extermination camps.

And what of the boundary that still divides humanity in two in a large number of cultures – the boundary that emanates from the body's sexual organs and characteristics? A boundary that, commonly still, seeks to confine a woman to her 'place' by closing the doors to education, possession of money, electoral rights and rights over her own body, let alone to equal opportunity and pay. Also intertwined around the body's sexual organs is the boundary of sexual orientation which brings its own historical baggage of legal and moral prejudices and human rights violations.

These boundaries are now themselves being differently challenged. Dissolving the rigid binary boundary that separated the sexes has created a new multifaceted complex of boundaries that each operate along a continuum according to criteria of sex, sexuality, gender, fluidity, rigidity, etc. It has created a new world in which a person may explore their place afresh with greater openness. Yet, despite the greater opportunities which these new boundaries have offered, they have not resolved related issues around safety, identity and place: from high-level sport competition to public toilets, finding one's place has become an identity and safety issue for trans- and cis- women and men alike.

It is worth noting how these new ways of looking at sex, sexuality and gender boundaries are challenging us to question the binary lens, a boundary that has been a part of our Western culture for over two millennia, as attested by pairings such as 'night and day', 'black and white', 'right and wrong' and by Aristotle's logical law of non-contradiction – things are either A or non-A, they cannot be both nor can they be neither. Unfortunately, besides this rich questioning of our traditional binary way of viewing the world, there has been a dangerous challenge to the boundary between fact and fantasy, drawing conspiracy theorists and their followers across an invisible boundary into a parallel world that could be termed 'fake reality'. This leads them to live across boundaries: one foot in a world from which they feel alienated, another in a parallel world with people who share their alternative 'reality' underpinned by fake news.

Boundaries, the family and society: Finding my voice and my place

Boundaries spoken and unspoken, subtle and not-so-subtle also dissect the family, conferring on each member a different sense of what 'my place' means. There is the cruel cut of estrangement – "we're in, you're out", that wreaks its damage on all concerned and often perpetuates itself through the generations. There is the camp boundary – "she's dad's favourite, I'm on mum's side"; there are the hierarchical horizontal boundaries that define the pecking order – who's on top and 'wears the trousers', who comes next … and who comes last; there is also the horizontal, above–below social boundary – one tinged with admiration (we're so proud of our Johnny) or discomfort/ embarrassment/jealousy, etc. "cause he's got this fancy education/car/job/ girlfriend, he thinks he's better than us". There are unspoken circular bound-aries that must not be breached – tiptoeing around a family member who is depressed, angry, "in a mood again", grieving, etc.; boundaries that ring-fence emotions and send messages about what emotions are simply not allowed – anger and grief being the most common taboos; or boundaries that ring-fence what can and cannot be said – "we no longer talk about Sue/ about the accident". Sometimes, these boundaries are voiced: "don't cry, it will upset your mum, you need to be strong for her", or even labelled: "don't cross Pat, you know he is mentally ill/bad/dangerous"; but, more often than not, they remain unspoken. Some boundaries are totally blurred: "where does mum end and I begin?" All these boundaries need navigating to find our place, and if the one we try to carve out for ourselves is not suitable to others, we may be 'put in our place'.

Stretching the concept of spatial boundary, there are the highs and lows, distance and closeness of the voice boundary. As family members seek to express their needs, wishes, opinions, emotions, whose voice carries regardless of the decibels? Whose whisper can be heard above another's screams and wailing, or above another's urgent calls for help? Whose voice carries and can be heard from afar?

And whose voice cannot be heard even when standing up close?

Jo's suicide attempt took the whole family by surprise. She would have died as quietly as she had lived, had her brother Ross not had yet another falling out with his boyfriend that night and tried to wake Jo up in the middle of the night for her advice. Ross knew Jo, she wouldn't mind, he could always depend on her – kind, dependable Jo. Except that clearly she wasn't as dependable as he had thought – she wasn't the equanimous older sister he had always taken her to be. Concern mingled with anger: How could he have not heard her distress, how could her despair have gone unnoticed by them all? How could she do that to him?

In Bren's family, it had been Paul's breakdown that had taken them all by surprise. She only now realizes that, beneath the constant joking and messing around, there was a debilitating lack of self-confidence that was crying out to be heard.

Some families have a boundary that allows a place for one person's desire(s) at the expense of another's: this boundary of entitlement delineates areas of collusion, betrayal and despair. Such is so often the context of childhood sexual abuse, where one person's place in the extended family is guaranteed impunity at the expense of another person's voice and rights that are silenced. The trauma of abuse is then compounded by that of betrayal, through disbelief, accusation, or punishment of the child at the hands of those who should have been its protectors. And beware the victim of abuse who wants to speak out, for the ranks may close, and the abused person risk exclusion from the family circle.

Lizzie's Nan had thought that putting a crucifix on her granddaughter's bed would do the trick, after all Derek was a God-fearing man. Only it didn't. And when Lizzie finally told her mother many years later, she was accused of being no better than her aunt Patsy – the one they never spoke about.

Silencing is not simply about the fear of public scandal: it can be about disturbing someone's accepted place within the family which may have long gone unchallenged – sometimes, over two generations, in the case of a grandfather, great-uncle, or close family friend. Silencing can be about not disturbing the unspoken rules that govern and protect the family.

Some boundaries encircle the whole family, even across continents, and give everyone within its circle a warm, protective sense of identity, mutual support and belonging. Others shut the world out, strangle the family and either suffocate its various members when they gasp for air or else expel them.

The boundaries that split and encircle our families can be found in other groups that define themselves as families, from educational institutions and religious communities to 'family businesses'. (I am no cynic, yet when members of an organization claim "We're all one happy family", this sends bells ringing loudly for me; I have witnessed too often how such claims can cover a myriad of ill feelings and hurt and, not infrequently, abuses of power.)

Families, however closed, can remain intimately connected to their community. This, tragically, can cut the victim off from their potential source of support – as when the abuser within the family is a respected member of the community. The child is then unlikely to either speak out or be believed. Quite commonly, it is a member of that community (religious, political, etc.) who is the perpetrator and parents who collude with its leaders to protect the perpetrator, while silencing or vilifying the child.

The big sex scandals of recent years in the UK highlight how the voice boundaries which enable collusion and betrayal within a family and a closed community can also operate within society at large. In France, the publication in 2020 of Vanessa Springora's Le Consentement laid bare the power dynamics underpinning whose voice is allowed to be heard. In this autobiographical account, Springora recounts her love affair – for that is how she saw it at 13 – with the 50-year-old author Gabriel Matzneff – and that is what he swore it was. The glory and lure of intellectualism in France had ring-fenced a place where Matzneff could sexually abuse children, and write about it, all with impunity. When in 1990 on a radio show a fellow participant (a female Canadian journalist) challenged him on air, she was rounded upon by a roll call of the French intellectual establishment who loudly acclaimed Mazneff's autobiographical, paedophilic novels. Springora's story illustrates how a woman can be harassed, publicly humiliated by the unauthorized publication of her childhood letters and photos, and her voice be silenced for decades when a powerful subsection of society has the voice that carries.

'My place' with friends and in the workplace

Some people have no friends and enjoy the place of self-sufficiency and safety which the boundary around themselves affords, while others experience that boundaried place as despairingly lonely. Friendship boundaries may be like tiny islands for two, in which each of the two inhabitants would never dream of going to explore an outlying island without the other. Other friendship boundaries can be viewed as concentric circles marking out different degrees of closeness, where each group of friends to which they belong is part of a larger group to which they all belong. Whereas others are more like overlapping Venn diagrams as in Max' case:

Max had many friends and acquaintances and while he seemed to have an accepted and valued place within each circle to which he belonged, still he lived in a constant fear of rejection. Invitations, especially multiple invitations for one same evening, filled him with deep anxiety.

M. *I know it's ridiculous, but if I choose to go out with one group of friends, I feel like I'm being excluded by the other group, as if they don't want me there. I know it's stupid, because it was my decision in the first place.*

L. *You know, Max, in my experience, when people say their behaviour is ridiculous and stupid, it's seldom as simple as that. This feeling of being excluded and not wanted by a group of people, is it familiar to you in any way or is it a recent thing?*

M. *Oh… Well it was always like that when we went on holiday with our cousins.*

L. *With your cousins?*

M. *Yes, I was the youngest. And they'd all decide to do something, some game or something, and they'd say for instance you have to be 7 to join in, and I'd be 6. And then when I was 7, they'd say 8 or whatever.*

L. *That sounds rather mean! …And very excluding for a little child.*

M. *Mmm. Mmm. Yeah, it was. This feeling with my friends now, it's nothing new is it! It's funny, it's so familiar, but I'd never made the connection.*

Max's insecure sense of place among his friends was, on the face of it, illogical, for he was clearly popular. Yet, it was understandable as it reflected his childhood experience of holidays with his cousins where he had so often felt excluded.

In society at large, an insecure sense of place often lies at the heart of bullying. A bully may view society's power-imbued, discriminatory boundaries, or their own fantasized ones, as factual lines in the sand marking out real superiority–inferiority or friend–foe distinctions, and hence, lines to be defended. Workplace bullying commonly involves exercising abusive power from a perceived, or *desired*, higher place within the organization: hard-earned hierarchical boundary lines and entry to the wished-for place are to be patrolled, and beware anyone perceived as threatening 'to overstep the line' and eye their place or the one they desire!

The following is not an example of bullying; it is a more subtle workplace interaction, yet it illustrates a context of boundaries and respective places, which are also mapped onto a power fault-line.

I remember one particular occasion at a hospital multidisciplinary meeting, when the lead consultant warned us that a young doctor would be joining us a little late, as it was the day new doctors were starting on their first NHS rotation. When he did join us, the consultant gave him a cursory greeting and was about to carry on with the meeting, when I suggested it might be a good idea if we all introduced ourselves. "But I know who he is" he said with surprise and some irritation. "Yes", I replied, "but he does not know who we are!"

The NHS, an organization that is there to care for sick and vulnerable people, is riddled with the horizontal lines which create the boundaries of hierarchy and can confine each within their delimited place: they govern grades and payment 'bands', but also, in the eyes of some, they create who counts and who does not; they may also, as in this example, annihilate all interest in the thoughts or feelings of someone more junior. The NHS, like many organizations, also has its vertical splits that may divide some areas into rival camps barely on speaking terms, each with their own top-down hierarchy of consultant, registrar and junior doctors. And what about the 'them and us' boundary of clinical and maintenance staff? Or indeed of patient and staff – the boundary between 'the sick' and 'the healthy'?

My friend Tricia had been a valued clinical supervisor to this particular team of cancer nurses for many years, but when she developed cancer herself, she felt, from their reactions, that she had crossed an implicit them/us line, and had challenged their sense of identity and security. She was not invited to return after her sick leave. To do so, it would seem, would have threatened the unspoken message which the group held: "cancer is what our patients get, not us."

During the pandemic, that boundary between sick patients and healthy carers was tested in a dramatic fashion. The uncertainty and insecurity this created was an added burden for exhausted staff.

I can only imagine that England's senior scientific and medical officers and her most senior politicians must have fantasized a similar boundary, when in the early days of the pandemic they sat together around a table discussing the coronavirus social distancing policy for the rest of the population. In Greek mythology, the goddess Nemesis used to strike down those deemed guilty of hubris; after that meeting, COVID did her job!

'My place' in the world at large

Casting our boundaries further out, there are the wider enclosing boundaries beyond which we do not like to venture. These spatial boundaries are not necessarily set to keep others out, they also delimit a place to which our identity is tied and within which we feel safe to move around and live – our district, our village, our town, our country…

Sholto was aware of using a strong aftershave on his daily commute to create a sense of personal space for himself – a smell boundary. I was reminded of how smell is a criterion in certain Andaman communities for defining tribal boundaries.

When I asked Jane, 43, whether she was from X born and bred, she replied, looking shocked and horrified: "oh no, I am from Y". You may think that Y was at the other end of the country, but no: there was a village sign at the entry to X, and on the back of that sign was the village sign for Y!

One of my Croydon clients had always wanted to go to the seaside (about 40 miles away), but he dreaded the thought of going beyond the boundary of the M25 which, he explained, defined his sense of safety and belonging as a Londoner.

G.W. Bush never had a passport before becoming President of the United States.

And Valery Panov recounts how, during the Cold War, as the Kirov Ballet were going on tour to the West, one of his fellow dancers, brainwashed by anti-capitalist propaganda, tragically jumped out of the train to her death just as it crossed the border, so terrified was she.

Spatial boundaries: Concluding remarks

Many clients who come to me are often painfully aware of some of the boundaries that impact their lives, leading variously to constricted lives, an inability to say no, a desire for fusion, difficulty managing family dynamics, etc. Indeed, that may be the very reason they have come for counselling. However, they may not realize how these same boundaries have also affected others around them. Some clients have no awareness of these invisible lines and their impact. In both such cases, I find the use of buttons surprisingly enlightening. I have my grandmother's box of buttons, to which I have added some interesting acquisitions over the years. There are buttons of all colours, shapes and sizes; some are flat and boring, others spherical and hence wobbly, others, though flat, are embossed, intricate, painted and beautiful. Some objects in my grandmother's box may resemble buttons at first sight, but are not. There is a bit of green, sea-rolled glass. "*Why did you choose that one,*

Joe?" *"Because I'm the big fat blob of the family."* There is a crystal drop from a chandelier – chosen by Victoria because she was, she felt, "all bling"; by Tommy, for his grandfather, because he felt that beneath his grandfather's rough exterior lay a diamond; by Lisa for her mother because it was a "tear-drop" for all the family she had lost. There is also a ferrous ammonite fossil that I found as a child and a piece of volcanic rock.

L. *What made you choose that one Bob?*
B. *Because dad's the rock of the family.*
L. *From what you have been saying, I'm not so sure. Maybe that's what he would like you to think; that's a small and rather misshapen rock, and volcanic to boot.*

This turned out to be far closer to the truth. For his dad was volatile and explosive and Bob came to realize that he and his wife were in different ways the rocks of the family.

If you have never used buttons in this way before, you may want to give it a try: first choose a button for yourself (why did you choose that one? At what age does it represent you?), put it on the table, then choose one for each of the significant members of your family and put each one in turn on the table. How have you laid them? If you have put them in what may sound like the obvious way – father, mother, children, in chronological order, all in a line, be assured that this is not 'obvious': I have seen very few clients do so. Such an alignment could represent a family where each member feels at ease within their rightful chronological place. In my counselling room, however, the few times clients have put buttons in a chronological line, it has represented a rigid, hierarchical family – rather like the von Trapps from Sound of Music (where each child had their own place and their own particular whistle roll call).

If you have not laid them in chronological order, all in one line, how have you placed them? Is everyone 'in the picture' or is one member 'out on a limb' – and how do you think that may feel to them? Who is next to your father, to your mother? Can each child be seen by each of your parents, or is one of you out of sight? Is one of you in the way?

Highlighting spatial boundaries can help us to understand where our place lies within the family and within the various intersecting or separate communities of which we are part. It can help us to acknowledge and better understand our own experiences and those of others around us and develop greater compassion where compassion is due.

Spatial boundaries delineate the place we create and take for ourselves, as well as the place we give to others. In a myriad of ways – chosen or imposed, protective or defensive, open or closed, rigid or flexible, violating or violated, these boundaries affect our relationships to family, friends, colleagues, fellow-townsmen, countrymen and inhabitants of this earth, and are in turn affected by theirs.

Chapter 3

Time

Understanding, Compassion, and Boundaries

Time

Yetunde

Yetunde has come to see me because she has had cancer. Her prognosis was good and her treatment is now over; she knows she should rejoice, but somehow she can't get on with anything. Before her diagnosis, she had been making plans to expand the nursing home she runs, but now, she says, "what's the point?"

I tell Yetunde that I would like to know something about her life: cancer doesn't come into a void, it comes into a person's life and more often than not, it (the diagnosis, treatment, and/or prognosis) turns that life upside down. She tells me of her childhood in Ghana where she grew up with her aunt, her older brother and a young niece for whom she was like a second mother from the age of 8; she recounts her arrival in the UK, alone, at the age of 14, to live with her mother whom she barely knew and her younger half-siblings whose existence she had ignored. She would take her younger brother and sister to school, and after her own school day and at weekends, do most of the household chores. When Yetunde was 18, her mother went back to Ghana, so Yetunde went to work to look after her younger siblings. (Interestingly, when we try and explore her childhood and adolescence, Yetunde has remarkably few memories: blurry, distant memories of Ghana, mainly of looking after her young niece.) In her early thirties, Yetunde studied to become a nurse; at 54, when she was diagnosed, she had her own well-rated nursing home, which she ran efficiently. But, she reiterates: "now, what's the point?"

I am struck by the way Yetunde tells her life story: despite the significant separations and losses she has had to endure, despite the relentlessness of the hard work she has had to do from her earliest years, it is almost entirely devoid of emotion. "This is how things were in those days" – and indeed, sadly, I have heard scores of similar stories. She also tells me that she is a very private person, that she keeps herself to herself, even at Church.

Yetunde and I worked together for a number of months from an existential perspective: we explored her losses, anxieties, choices, meaning and

DOI: 10.4324/9781003364504-4

purpose, etc. in the context of her diagnosis and good prognosis. But now, a decade or so later, as I try to understand her story through the specific lens of time boundaries, what strikes me is the unidirectionality of it – the sense she conveyed of relentlessly marching on, living in the present without ever looking back and never looking any further than the near future. It was as if time for her had been a straight tube with doors, which opened up sufficiently to let her move forward and closed behind her as she did so and, in the doors, small glass panes that allowed Yetunde to perceive recent memories and see a few steps ahead. There was no place, in the way she lived time, for either regret or gratitude for past events, nor for long-term life hopes and plans. That is how she led her life in a time-contained and self-contained sort of way that provided her with a sense of safety and control. But as the cancer diagnosis opened all the doors before her, suddenly, for the first time, she had become aware of death staring at her from the other end.

Yet, somehow, the "what's the point?", when she first articulated it, did not have the usual existential feel about it – it did not feel like a philosophical question applied to her whole life and/or to human life in general. It felt specific and concrete; it was only forward looking, and forward led inexorably to death, so what was the point of making plans about a nursing home?

Whereas it was the cancer diagnosis that had blown wide open the doors to the future, it was Yetunde herself who then, very cautiously, began to open the doors to her more distant past. As we explored the bare bones of the upheavals of her earlier years, she was gradually able to flesh them out with some nurturing memories, as she thought of her life in Ghana, her brother and her young niece. She could observe the choices she had made and talents she had developed along the way and integrate them into a story that was more than just a relentless march, one that now had more felt and articulated meanings to it. Yes, death was still awaiting her at the end, but the decision about expanding the nursing home was now to be taken within the context of her whole life, a life that had meaning; it was no longer a self-contained decision which the fact of death at the end of the line rendered pointless.

Changing the way we think about time can take place at a conceptual level, or, as with Yetunde, it can arise from the changed way we experience time. Either way, it can open the door to a different way of living.

Existential therapy makes an important distinction between 'linear' time and 'existential' time. Linear time is the conventional, objective framework through which we view the world and our lives within it. Time is like a river, we are told, it flows as present follows past and is in turn followed by the future so that, as Heraclitus once famously said, 'you can't step in the same river twice'. Linear time moves on, relentlessly and at a uniform speed, in one direction, and it can be measured scientifically as it does so. In linear time, a century always lasts one hundred years, a year 365 days and a day 24 hours or 1,440 minutes. This view of time is 'obvious', it is 'common sense'.

Yet this 'common sense', linear understanding of time is at odds with much of our *experience* of time, for our experience tells us that time can speed up, slow down, come to a standstill. Distress, boredom and pain slow time down, while enjoyment speeds it up. Even centuries can be concertinaed, as my own memories of my elderly relatives recounting their own early memories take me well into the 19th century: such as one grandfather's sighting of the first train in his part of Europe and one cousin's recounting of his work as a doctor during a plague epidemic in Odessa, only 13 years after Yersin's revolutionary discovery of the plague bacillus – which had seen the first significant change since the Middle Ages in the understanding of the aetiology and treatment of that deadly illness.

Sometimes time 'disappears', we 'don't know where it has gone!' We can also find ourselves *reliving* the past; we can even get *stuck* in it – whether stuck in the ever-repeating loop of a past traumatic incident; constantly dreaming back to a special time in our lives; or, like Peter Pan, remaining forever childlike. We can transport ourselves into the future and live there in a daydream, to the point of paralyzing ourselves for the present, or else creating a self-fulfilling prophecy for ourselves.

The world's recent coronavirus pandemic has highlighted the extraordinary ways we variously experience time: for many during lockdown, not surprisingly, time dragged painfully and intolerably, for some to the point of despair; for others, the peace of it felt blissful – there was now 'time to breathe'; for others still, even those who had no work and no children to look after, there still were not enough hours in the day for all the jobs on their list. Looking back, part-way through, at funny COVID-related videos that had circulated in the early days of the pandemic was like looking at another world. And two years into the pandemic, many had trouble placing events of the previous two years: there was the sense of a whole lost year.

'Existential' or 'lived' time is multidirectional and loops around itself: we all know the impact of the past on the present, but the way we see our future can also affect the present, as well as the way we view our past. Many are those who rewrite their past and change their way of speaking and dressing to fit in with their future ambitions. Similarly, changed priorities for the future, such as an ecological and sustainable lifestyle, can make a person view with guilt and horror the extravagant and wasteful lifestyle which they had once so prized. And while linear time is unidirectional – 'you can't turn the clock back' – existentially you can revisit the past and change your attitude to it. This is central to the therapeutic enterprise.

Some words that we use to quantify time such as 'little', 'long', 'short', or even 'in a minute' are ambiguous: they could apply to linear or existential time. This explains how two people may find themselves at loggerheads when one of them is speaking from a subjective, existential time frame of reference: 'I'll only be ten minutes' or 'I've been waiting for you for hours'. However, when we qualify time as being 'too little', 'too long', 'too short', as in 'It has been too long since we last met', 'life is too short for such quarrels', 'I have too little time left', etc., the lived aspect of time comes to the fore. All these expressions imbue time with value, purpose and meaning and highlight its *existential* dimension. Existential time involves our freedom to make choices and set priorities to shape our lives, with the responsibility and possibility for joy or regrets that those choices entail: the freedom to choose between wants, oughts and shoulds, between quality (i.e. living time in a fulfilling way) and quantity – filling time, cramming in as much as possible to leave no wasteful vacuum, no time for anxious reflection.

So, while linear time just *is*, existential time is personal, embodied, lived and characterized by meaning. Existential time has a *value* (to which we may become indifferent) – it can feel wasted or well spent. Existential time is 'time *for*': for studying, having fun, looking after family, for choosing between what I want to do or feel I ought to do... While linear time measures the lengths of time that frame our lives, existential time expresses the what and the how we live our lives.

Boundaries and ways we live time

Deprived of almost any childhood memories, with no hopes or dreams for her future (expanding the nursing home had not been a dream, just the next sensible step), Yetunde had felt disconnected from her own life.

We need to be able to travel to all areas of our life to gain a sense of both the ground beneath our feet and our finitude. It does not help to keep various areas out of bounds, but if we decide to close the door on some of them, we should not lock it, let alone throw away the key. Pretending some part of our life never existed or will never come to pass is one source of problems; not accepting that the past is past, or taking up residence elsewhere than in the present is also problematic.

Boundaries apply more obviously to space than to time, yet if we just pause to reflect, there are many ways in which we delimit and define time when we speak of it: there are the boundaries of our natural world – such as the geological ages of our planet and the seasons that divide our year; there are the timelines and boundaries through which we view history – such as 'ancient', 'medieval', 'renaissance', and which we impose on culture – e.g. 'baroque', 'classical', 'romantic' for musical eras. In everyday life too, we commonly set time limits: in injunctions such as "ten minutes until lights out", "only one hour of television-watching after dinner"; and also in our life plans "only two years of travelling before I settle down" or " I like to work hard and play hard".

Clocks and calendars offer some boundaries to our lives. However, we also impose boundaries on the way we live time as we do with any boundary-setting: to delimit and ring-fence safe areas and to defend and protect ourselves. Just as spatial boundaries separate us from the alien, the enemy, the unknown and the anxiety-provoking, so too, whether consciously or not, we set boundaries for ourselves that block off sections of time in an attempt to avoid a painful past, the anxiety of future change, or the intolerability of the present; we set time boundaries to try to protect our well-being.

Time boundaries can be rigid or flexible – the obvious example being our daily routines. Time boundaries can feel solid, or be fluid – as when we go with the flow or lose our sense of time; they can be see-through – offering us a view of our past and glimpses into a potential future, or else opaque. Time boundaries can be stretched – as so often happens with goodbyes, when we seek to push their finality away, or they can be tightly held. Both are common occurrences in the therapy room where clients may try to extend the therapy hour by a few minutes, or conversely drop a bombshell just as they are leaving the room – known as 'door-handling'.

We conceive and speak of time as divided into past, present and future, but how do we relate to these three dimensions in our everyday life? These questions have philosophical answers, yet also correspond to concrete, individual ways of setting implicit boundaries and living our lives.

What do we mean by 'present'?

'The present' is elusive and quasi-impossible to define. From the perspective of linear time, the present has elicited a search for ever greater precision, and still, it cannot be captured. From the sundial and hourglass to the modern chronometer, scientific instruments have sought to measure the passing of time and indicate the present moment. Such measurements of linear time impact upon lived time: so, for instance, in modern Olympic Games, it is according to hundredths of a second that races are won – a hundredth of a second which can lead outstanding athletes to view themselves/or be viewed as either 'winners' or 'losers'.

Time is being measured in ever smaller units, as the millisecond has given way to the zeptosecond (a trillionth of a billionth of a second!) Yet when I say 'my life at present', this can refer to how things have been this year, or even over the past few years, as opposed to the more distant past and what may lie ahead. While, as a result of encephalitis, Clive Wearing's experience of the present was reduced to a few seconds and 'it was as if every waking moment was the first waking moment'[1], and with every blink, "his eyelids parted to reveal a new scene". (id. 133)[2]

Thus, in our experience, 'the present' can refer to minutes, days, or years. It can even encompass a sense of timelessness: as I look out of the window and take in the view, the present may last a fraction of a second, a few minutes, yet time may also 'stand still' and offer me a context and growing awareness of myself in the world. In that instant in which I open my window and take in the beautiful view, I am aware of a deep intake of breath as my chest expands and I sense myself opening up to myself and the world. It feels like a gift of space and time in the present moment, without divorcing me from past and future. By connecting in this way to nature and its beauty, I feel I am also being connected to Time in all its dimensions as I look upon the age-old trees, mature shrubs, young plants, new buds, and the timelessness of beauty and the universe.

The future and living with it

Similarly, the future can be pictured linearly as stretching from the milli-second that follows the present millisecond all the way to infinity. But in our everyday lives, we experience the future as encompassing our whole embodied relationship to whatever has not yet been: our expectations, plans, anticipated hopes and anxieties, as well as the changes that will affect our bodies, our lives and our worlds. Our relationship to the future also encompasses our regrets for what cannot be, because of past decisions or for some reason outside our control. The future is that which is yet to be – but that is also the question: for me, will it be, or not be? And how do I live with the thought that maybe, for me, soon it may not be?

I had to walk past police protection for my bedside sessions with Patrick. Patrick was a tough guy, not used to deep thoughts, as he put it. I think that is partly what made his words to me that day even more poignant: "you know, before I thought the future was forever, now I realize it is tomorrow". Patrick's stay in intensive care had challenged his unquestioned sense of invulnerability. He had survived so many dangerous situations in his life, but this time the penny had dropped: one day he was going to die and it could even be some day soon. Suddenly, for Patrick, the boundary posts had changed. And by changing the boundary posts, he felt his relationship to his future changing. He might even have to rethink his lifestyle…

Terry, like Patrick, was not usually one for "deep thoughts", but I'll always remember his words, after he defied all medical opinion and recovered within a few months from a devastating accident: "I didn't fucking ask for this, it's not my fault… but I'm not fucking going to curl up in a corner and be a victim". Though Terry was unaware of it, he was expressing, in the vernacular, Heidegger's description, in Being and Time, of human existence, or 'Dasein', as 'thrown possibility through and through'. By saying he hadn't asked for this, Terry was expressing the 'thrownness' of human existence; by saying that he wasn't going to just curl up in a corner, he was expressing the freedom inherent in it. The raw emotion behind Terry's words certainly touched me in a different way to Heidegger's complex language! And, most impressively, he was applying his philosophy to his life. He was prepared to look ahead and see what sort of life he wanted for himself, what was important for him and what that required him to do about it now. Or in Heidegger's words, he was able to 'project himself upon the possibilities' before him; he was able to understand some of these possibilities as being still open to him, as paths to follow, as choices to make, while many others in his situation might have focused on the dead end roads or seen most of these paths as now being closed to them.

Patrick and Terry's situations were both extreme, yet each of us in our everyday life needs to decide how to engage with the future – in our most trivial decisions and our most potentially life-changing ones. And how we set the boundaries between present and future, and within the future itself (near, distant, infinity), is *vitally* important. There are so many ways of living with the future: for instance, we can make choices in full awareness of their likely far-reaching consequences, asking ourselves "three, five, ten years from now (if I live that long), what would I like to see, where and how would I like to be?", or we can refuse to look that far. We can daydream a little – for daydreams are the stuff that ambitions, hopes and wishes are made of, and daydreams of the future can open up possibilities. Or we can dwell in rosy daydreams of the future, out of touch with present reality, in 'cloud cuckoo land'. Similarly, while fantasies of catastrophes can help us in assessing present risk and forearm us for possible battles to come, foreseeing one doomsday scenario after another overwhelms and paralyzes the present. We may want to close off any thought of death and what might lie beyond. Yet this closing off usually comes at a price, such as a constant underlying death anxiety, a need for control, a loss of spontaneity and vitality.

The past and living with it

In linear time, the past stretches, from the millisecond that has just become superseded by the present, way back to infinity. Existentially, the past is my relationship to what has been, from before my birth to the present day. My past encompasses my roots, my *in utero* life, my memories, the choices I made, the obstacles I had to surmount, my regrets, the help I received on the way, my gratitude, all that contributed to the person I am today. Hence, traditionally, its central importance in therapy.

There are so many ways of living with the past: we can make brief incursions into it, revisit it at length, dwell there most of the time… We can give past events the power to determine our present life (e.g. blaming parents, a teacher, 'the accident' for the present situation); or we can acknowledge the contributions of our own freedom in shaping that past into the present that is now ours. We can also try to close the past off or deny it:

As Nathalie did by putting a thick boundary wall between herself and her own African roots. Yet, by trying to forget that aspect of her past, she was killing off a significant part of herself, leaving herself partly disconnected from the ground of her being.

Fortunately, however much we may try, we cannot completely cut off our past or we would have no acquired knowledge, no learnt resilience, no sense of continuity or identity. For who am 'I', if not that 'I' that has emerged and is evolving out of the way I have lived and am living time in relation to myself and the world?

Yetunde had imposed such rigid barriers to keep her childhood at bay that she had very scanty memories of it. Yet the way she conducted her life – her work ethos, her faith, her fierce self-reliance, her resilience, her very way of closing off the past and much of the future – all these traits that so coloured her life had emerged and evolved from that past and contributed to her sense of identity.

Even Clive Wearing, whose experience of time was reduced to a few seconds, had retained his musicianship and some pianistic ability.

Whether consciously or not, we all retain some embodied experience of the past; and our body, its senses and sensations are a bridge to it. Of all the senses, smell and taste have the strongest power to reconnect us with the past and evoke it for us in its immediacy – as Proust famously highlighted in his description of the small madeleine dunked in tea which brought with it the felt sense of the whole world of his childhood. Yet, other senses also have that power: it is not only the scent of lavender fields that can transport me back to the summer holidays of my childhood, so do their particular intense shade of blue, the particular yellow of provençal material and the sound of crickets on a summer's night.

It is because we can still almost feel the gentleness and warmth of the breeze, or the whipping of a winter wind on the beach when we remember holidays and walks, that we can use such sensations therapeutically – asking clients to think back to a special place or holiday, so that they may sense the resourcing impact it can still have on them now.

Revisiting the past plays a fundamental role in the therapeutic endeavour as we seek to gain new perspectives and better understand our situation. Revisiting a past decision-making process that now seems misguided and has brought about undesirable aspects to our present existence (the city we live in, our present job, our partner, etc.) can remind us of the criteria that were important to us at the time. Challenging the stories we have always told ourselves and offering ourselves and our parents deeper understanding and compassion may open new possibilities.

Some may feel that revisiting the past would be too unbearably terrifying or painful. Fortunately, recent developments in trauma therapy have shown that the route to healing need not involve reliving past traumatic episodes in their full horror: from out of the edges of these events, we can let the body speak and observe it as it learns to release the traumas it carries and gain a freer and more empowered stance in the world. And even in the hardest of lives, devoid of any pleasant memories, the past still has value as witness to a person's survival and resilience; it can provide encouragement in surmounting present challenges.

When the clock stops

At the other end of the continuum are those for whom the clock has stopped.

Every time I visited this German city, I would see her standing at a street corner, in all weathers, an anxious, expectant look on her face. I learnt that she had been doing this every evening since the end of the Second World War. Her long hair was now white, but she was still waiting for her fiancé who left for the front in 1942.

And there are those who have chosen to stop the clock so that the past perpetuates itself in the way they live the present and fantasize the future. The worlds of fiction and film offer us a number of powerful descriptions of this. Such is Norma Desmond in Sunset Boulevard, the silent movies film star, who cannot accept that those glory days are over. Charles Dickens' Miss Havisham, in *Great Expectations*, is another terrifying portrait of a woman for whom the clock stopped when her fiancé jilted her on her wedding day. Most terrifying in Dickens' portrait of Miss Havisham is the way she purposely lives present and future as a vengeful replay of her past and wittingly implicates others, with tragic impact on their lives.

Virginia's story

Everything about Virginia was dramatic: the way she first entered my room, the way she carried herself, the way she dressed – neither flamboyantly, nor expensively yet with dramatic flair, the way she sat down and looked at me. Virginia conveyed drama with, it felt to me, a touch of imperiousness; she might indeed have been rather intimidating were it not for a certain childishness about her. The events of her early life had also been dramatic. A history of a gilded childhood and youth, destined for an equally gilded adult life, had been followed by civil war, escape and survival, during which most of the family's assets had been lost. Virginia had been an able and educated young woman and could well have had a career in her country of adoption; she could have made friends, found a partner. However, it was as if the clock had stopped for her in the 1970s: the expectations of her youth had invaded her present and future and closed off any alternative possibilities. For Virginia, these expectations had not been mere hopes and dreams, they had carried a sense of entitlement: a gilded future was what her parents had destined for her, so that should be her destiny. Her dramatic way of being and imperiousness embodied that sense of entitlement; her childishness its present incongruence. Yet I admired the feistiness with which she maintained that stance. Thirty years out of sync with the world and her contemporaries, and somewhat contemptuous and distrustful of them, Virginia felt lonely and powerless beneath all the drama; my heart went out to her. Sadly, while she was able to trust me and take in some warmth, support and nurturing, she quickly shut down any gentle challenge to the status quo, any possible opening into a future that was alive. We were only able to work together for a few months and I sometimes wonder what would have happened if we had had longer: would she have entered the present and integrated it into a story with a different future?

Tragically like Norma Desmond and Miss Haversham, Virginia had deprived her present and future of any real vitality.

Living in the present – but too tightly anchored to the past, or totally cut off from it

Barry's story

Barry was one of my most memorable failures as a therapist.

Barry was stuck and he clearly was making it difficult for others to help him get unstuck: he had had a number of therapists over the last ten years, had asked to be referred to psychiatrists, yet had each time been discharged as not necessitating their services. So I certainly was not the only one who had failed him, but still, I have my own share of responsibility in what happened between us.

I met Barry on three occasions: once about 12 years ago, and twice a few years later.

We did not get off to a good start: first Barry tried to push the boundaries of the therapeutic frame, asking to see me outside hospital hours (which I refused), then he cancelled a couple of appointments for no apparent good reason. Barry finally entered the room huffing and puffing, sat himself down heavily in the armchair in front of me with what felt like a show of pathos and started moaning about the distance of my room from reception and the unhelpfulness of the volunteer who had given him directions. He then drew out a sheet of paper and handed it to me triumphantly. The contrast between this triumphant gesture and the preceding pathos was astonishing and awoke my curiosity as to what the paper contained. "Do you want to see my list of complaints and medications?" He leant forward eagerly and brusquely shoved the sheet of paper onto my lap. I noted that the list started in 1959 with his operation to have his tonsils out and recorded all his complaints and medications from the past 50 years. I acknowledged that he had quite a medical history and asked him what was so particularly distressing to him right now that had brought him to see me; he replied that it was his depression. In response to my request for clarification as to the form his 'depression' took, he triumphantly replied "well you clearly don't know anything about depression!" I think that what pushed my compassion's rapid ejection-button was his sense of victimhood, the strange mixture of pathos, triumphalism and glee with which he expressed it, together with the huge power which he clearly wielded over his family. For it emerged that what he had sought to do with me by trying to push my therapeutic boundaries, he did daily and tenfold with his family.

I usually enjoy working with grumpy, challenging and angry old men: there often is an energy in those moods to which I can respond and which facilitates the work. In their challenge to me, there is also a directness which I prefer to manipulative ways of relating to me. But sadly for Barry and our work together,

I found Barry's particular brand of power game – boundary-pushing, victimhood, abrogation of responsibility and triumphalism, particularly distasteful. I allowed myself to become ensnared by these into a 'vicious' triangle (see Glossary), without my realizing it until it was too late.

I remember how furious he became when I tried to point out his own resourcefulness (which he seemed to have in bundles) and to question his view of himself as an invalid (which he was not) and a victim. The first session was clearly too soon for such a challenge and he declined a further appointment. I was therefore very surprised when he contacted me a few years later. He insisted on his wife coming into the room with me as he said he was "in a constant state of nerves and shaking all over". Remembering the failure of our first meeting (and, who knows, maybe if he had returned to see me rather than ask for a different member of our team, it had not been a total failure after all), I thought I would be conciliatory and agree to see them together to assess the situation. I was shocked by the change I saw in Barry: he clearly was in a bad way. I acknowledged the anxiety he was suffering and decided to first focus on his body, helping him to ground himself in it, enabling him to relax and stop shaking – much to his wife's relief. He was then able to start describing his present situation: he felt powerless and unable now to do anything on his own, even though his physical health had not worsened. It felt as if his power games with his family had spiralled out of his control and were now controlling him. His tyrannical behaviour – expecting his wife and son to run around him and his supposed needs, always at his beck and call, had given way to what he perceived as his real need for them. He seemed genuinely panicked at the thought of being on his own, let alone of going out of the house alone. The only time he could bear his own company was at night when he watched soaps on iplayer. Gone, I felt, was the triumphalism. He certainly no longer pushed my buttons and I did feel compassion for him. We agreed that we would meet the following week and he would come into the room on his own, while his wife would wait for him outside. The following session, as he entered the room, his hyperventilating and shaking intensified; his wife started panicking and I told her calmly but firmly that I needed to see him on his own. He came in and, flailing and whining, threw what looked more like a child's paddy than a panic attack. Again, I helped him ground himself, and when his shaking and flailing had abated sufficiently to start talking, I pointed out to him how he had managed to do that and how he could learn to do that without me. He became absolutely furious with me: it's all very well my helping him relax, but he was fed up with the current situation of always depending on his wife and son and what was the point in learning to stop shaking. Before I could respond to this, he rang his wife on his mobile and walked out to join her. And that was the end of that.

As I now think of Barry's situation in the context of time boundaries, I feel I can best grasp it metaphorically. In rough seas, sailors sometimes need to cast down the anchor to stabilize the ship and then lift it up when they are ready to set sail again; so too, in the rough seas of life, we may need to cast down an anchor, or two or more, to ground ourselves. Sometimes we are aware of doing so, as we put help in place for ourselves – people we can lean on, routines that give us structure and offer us a sense of control over some areas of our life, when everything around us feels out of control. To be able to put such help in place for ourselves is a form of resourcefulness that helps to steady us, as the anchor steadies the ship. But we must not forget to lift the anchor(s) when the sea feels calmer and we are ready to set out again: for however long the rope, if it remains anchored in, we can at best only travel in a wide circle with the anchor at its centre. I suspect that for Barry, every time in the past that he had hit rough seas – and his life had certainly not been plain sailing, he had cast out anchors to steady his ship: he had, not unnaturally, leant on his wife and son, found safety in his own home and found areas of his life that he could control. During the few years between his visits to me, the seas had become less rough (he was no longer as ill), however these anchors hung at the end of short ropes with the result that they had kept his ship and those he had roped in (his wife and son) with little room to manoeuvre and nowhere to go, other than round in circles. Over time, the ropes had become more entangled and hence shorter; he now felt suffocated – one metaphorical way of viewing his hyperventilation and flailing around. Though not living in the past, he was tied to it in a way that led to a very constricted life in the present.

What strikes me now, beside the control and power which he had half-enjoyed wielding, is the fear and probably the shame and existential guilt that Barry must have experienced: he had effectively delegated all responsibility for himself, his life, the running of the household, the breadwinning and all family decisions onto his wife and son. In a sense, he was a shell of a husband and father. There are many parents who, for health or other reasons, have to delegate many of the above responsibilities to others, yet who in some ways are still able to 'be there', in a meaningful relationship, still retaining a valuable and precious partner or parenting role. This did not seem to be the case with Barry.

I also realize that I challenged Barry far too soon: even in our last session, when I had not intended to be challenging, showing him that he had the ability to calm himself down – which I thought would be an empowering and comforting thought for him, was in itself too big a challenge for Barry. Barry had abrogated all his personal resourcefulness and placed his resources in others, the very thought that he might be able to manage without outside help was too terrifying for him to contemplate. I should have paid greater attention to the probable presence of feelings of shame, rage, and guilt – both existential and moral.

Clients about whom I feel I could be doing/could have done better tend to take up a disproportionate amount of my reflections on my practice (and I am aware as I write this that 'could be doing better' is a baggage-laden judgement!). A few like Barry still haunt its shadows.

When the present is cut off from past and future: Yetunde's story

Yetunde, with whom this chapter began, had felt the need to live safely cocooned in a present that offered a very limited view of both past and future. One dream vividly encapsulated her experience: she was in one of the front carriages of a train, unaware of any of the carriages behind her, without any idea of either the destination or the stations that might lie ahead, other than the next one when it was announced. Living in a compartmented chamber had helped Yetunde to march on with determination, yet her lack of early childhood memories left her feeling as if she had no foundation for her life. And because she had not wanted to look into the distance, there had never been any vista before her, only the next immediate goal. But the cancer had announced the final destination and as Yetunde began to envisage the possibility of her death, she wondered how she might like to look back on her life and what a meaning-ful life story might signify for her. As we began to explore this together, to her surprise, suddenly and most movingly, a number of childhood memories began to emerge and, with them, a better awareness of the richness of her past and a stronger sense of her own resilience. These new perspectives enabled her to trust more in herself, make more spontaneous movements towards the world and even open up to the possi-bility of friendship.

Opening the doors to the more distant past and future had made Yetunde feel more alive, more connected to a life that felt more meaningful and more her own. It is only now, as I am thinking of her and focusing on time and bound-aries, that I am reminded that Yetunde gave me a clock as an ending present![3] It sits in my counselling room, and I treasure it, as I treasure the hourglass and the time-piece charm-bracelet that two other clients have given me. They remind me of them, of the preciousness of time and the preciousness of life.

Conclusion: Living contentedly with the three dimensions of time

Past, present and future constitute the three temporal dimensions of our lives and, though we may try to, we cannot avoid any of them. Each temporal dimension of our existence deserves, in itself and in its relationship to the other two, our acknowledgement, consideration and care. We have an existen-tial responsibility towards them and towards ourselves: for how we live these temporal dimensions of our lives constitutes our existence. We cannot bypass any of them, and, as the examples in this chapter have shown, the way we boundary our lives can affect our vital sense of meaning, purpose and enjoy-ment, and hence, the very essence and experience of our lives. Contentment and vitality in the present involve living in peace with the past and the future, for these offer the present its inescapable context.

We cannot live in peace with ourselves in the present if we are too tightly bound to our past – consumed with guilt, shame, or regret, or else dwelling in self-aggrandizing memories, or in victimhood. The past is the past and the present does not belong in it – it needs to emerge out of it. Living in the past destroys any possibility of an evolving and creative future; yet, to lock the door on the past is not helpful either, it does not make it disappear. Vitality and contentment involve the ability to look at our past – our history and ancestry, the life we lived, the choices we made, the person we were, and still partly are – and do so with compassionate understanding. The common injunction to 'just put it all behind you and move on' is unhelpful: loss, violence, accidents and life-threatening illness are some of life's major traumatic experiences that turn a life upside down. It is therefore important that we allow ourselves time to take stock and integrate such experiences and their impact into the story and experience of our lives before 'moving on'.

We cannot either live with vitality if our future is weighed down by fear. Some apprehension and anxiety are natural: these help us assess risks and enhance our sense of achievement when we have challenged ourselves successfully. Strong anxiety and fear, however, are paralyzing. Similarly, we cannot live with vitality if our future is dominated by unrealistic fantasies: these will disconnect the centre of gravity of our being from any grounding and lift us, untethered, high up into cloud cuckoo land. Yet, while planning ahead can be grounding and helpful, plans that are detailed and rigid, brooking no variation and taking no account of what life may throw at us, set us up for being derailed. For we cannot control Life and what it may bring us.

We can neither foresee nor change future events, just as we cannot change the past. However, we can change ourselves and the way we respond to the world that addresses us. Changing the tint of the glasses we wear will colour both our present world and our future differently: the choice is not restricted to the rose of optimism and grey of pessimism, there is a rainbow of colouring emotions and attitudes – from anger to zaniness. What is more, by changing our reactions in the present, we can transform our future. Such is the transformative power of, for instance, learning to say "yes" and "no" as we genuinely wish to and learning to open ourselves up to possibilities.

"You must live in the present" is another modern-day injunction of popular psychology. By all means, let us live in the present, but how? Seize it with both hands, or with the tip of our fingers; go with its flow or bang our heads and kick against it… the choice is ours. However, let us not forget that the present did not emerge out of a vacuum, it belongs in a life with a past history and it is pregnant with a future.

There may be times, however, when the present feels too painful to endure, the future looks truly bleak and only the past offers solace. There is then a way of returning to the past that enables us to rediscover a source of nourishment and strength, and helps us to take heart. I am reminded of elderly people I have met who would speak to me of their lives: the feeling they conveyed was that it had not been a bed of roses, there had been some very difficult times, and it may not have been an extraordinary life in its outward achievements, but it was their life and overall it had been a good life. And of course, it had been an extraordinary life because it was their life and theirs alone.

Notes

1 Wearing, D. (2005). *Forever Today, A Memoir of Love and Amnesia*, London: Doubleday p.127.
2 Ibid. 133.
3 Very occasionally, clients have offered me small parting gifts, and I have accepted them. I believe that to reject the gift could have been experienced as my rejecting them and our work together.

Chapter 4

My Place in Time

Introduction: My place in time

Even when we seek to live in the present with due consideration to both our past and our future, there are times when the past surreptitiously makes its way into the present, or else violently irrupts into it. This distorts a person's perspective and can create incongruence, confusion, mayhem even. It also creates a certain 'dis-placement' or dislocation in time.

It is not uncommon for outdated ways of being to slip through into the present unchallenged, creating a strange incongruence: for instance grown women who speak with little girl voices. Less common is the full panoply of childish mannerisms, behaviours and ways of thinking displayed by a man in a position of great power. As President of the United States, Donald Trump's childish pout and infantile vocabulary still expressed a child's world of 'I want that', 'it's not fair' and 'you're not my friend anymore', e.g. "you're going to be in big, big trouble" to the President of North Korea while attempting to de-escalate nuclear build up; or "she's nasty" of the PM of Denmark who told him Greenland wasn't for sale; firing and then insulting his once closest aides.

Unbeknown to us, beliefs may also slip across the boundaries of time and affect the present in significant ways. For beside our explicit beliefs, we each hold some implicit beliefs about ourselves and the world that were formed in our early years in relation to our parents or carers. These are fundamental beliefs about our safety, about how welcome we are in the world, what we need to do to be accepted and valued, whether we can trust and ever depend on anyone, etc. We tend to carry such beliefs through life, unless something or someone comes to challenge them effectively. Not infrequently our past perceptions may seep into the present, as when we evaluate traumatic past events through the eyes of the confused child that we then were, allowing past confusion to distort the adult's view:

When Peter was in his pre-teens, he would go to gymnastics competitions with his coach, who would ask him to come to his hotel room at 7.30pm for a psychological briefing before bedtime. On one occasion, as he opened the door, he saw his coach standing before him naked with a full erection, asking him to approach.

DOI: 10.4324/9781003364504-5

Peter stood there shocked and confused and then went back to his room. Peter's parents never understood why he suddenly gave up gymnastics. As he recounts the incident, he finds it difficult to acknowledge its seriousness, since 'nothing happened'. Yet, suddenly as he speaks, I feel I am looking at a 12-year-old boy before me. It is only when I ask him how he would feel if something similar were to happen to his nephew or niece that he regains his adult perspective.

The delay in reporting historical abuse is, as we know, partly due to paralyzing emotions – fear, shame, a sense of guilt or powerlessness, and to dissociation; but it also partly arises because it can take some adult survivors of childhood sexual abuse a long time to be able to part the child's veil of confusion and view what happened through adult eyes.

Trauma can lead to various 'out of sync' ways of living with time. To anyone who has witnessed the past suddenly irrupting into the present, it is clear that this is an experience that is quite different from that of the past seeping into the present.

Rodric used to get bullied at boarding school; this started with teasing around his food fads and his lunchtime rituals in the school dining-hall. He was now a serious and respected surgeon. Yet, at a dinner at which an old school acquaintance had also been invited, Rodric's partner was stunned to see him overreact quite spectacularly to a tease about whether he was going to cut his peas in half.

Here the eight-year-old Rodric had clearly been triggered and taken his place at the adults' dinner table.

Time boundaries criss-cross our bodies and all areas of our lives just as spatial boundaries do. They too express our sense of 'place' in life, and the confusing time dislocations we experience become etched on our bodies. Besides childish mannerisms, the most common temporal dislocations could be summarised as follows: 'That was then and now is now', 'Who is the adult here?', 'What values still guide my life?', and 'This does not belong to me'. These four sentences have a central place in trying to understand, and resolve, temporal incongruences within ourselves and in relation to others and help to heal the confusion and pain of dislocation. They can guide us in examining with compassion the life choices we have made, in exploring our place in our life, and giving them (our parents, our children) a place where they belong. And the first of these four sentences is also crucial to managing post-traumatic stress disorder. (*See Glossary PTSD*)

'That was then and now is now'

There are times when we realize that our reactions are disproportionate to the situation that gave rise to them, or else that they don't make sense – like being beyond ourselves with anger over nothing, feeling guilty for something that is blatantly not our fault, or cringing with deep shame for a very minor embarrassment. Why should such strong emotions arise without an obvious reason? Most likely because these reactions have deep roots that lie elsewhere.

I used to refer to this with clients as my 'briar theory': many of us have what I picture as a briar growing up inside ourselves, deep-rooted in a difficult feeling that goes way back – most commonly shame, anger, terror, or guilt. That deep-rooted briar of emotion will then attract the slightest emotion that feels at all familiar; this will get stuck onto the briar and be fed by it. We can however learn to uproot that briar, and when we have, these daily feelings of anger/guilt/shame no longer have anything deeper to connect to and simply wilt away like any other superficial feeling. Present needling situations become experienced for what they are, with their own emotional charge, small or great, and the emotional charge of the past remains where it belongs. Though aware of the past, we can then experience our place as belonging in the present without the burden of past emotions.

Many years later, when I learnt about the amygdala, default neural pathways and the window of tolerance (*see Glossary*), I was amused to recognize my 'briar theory' in scientific clothing.

Jonty describes a childhood home in which his father's mood would oscillate between sarcastic jollity and rage. Either way, Jonty found himself singled out among his siblings: the butt of all teases and jokes when his father was in a jocular mood, the object of his insults and beatings when he was in a rage. Jonty would try to tough it out, then retreat into submission; rage that dared not express itself, helplessness and shame were the emotional colours of his childhood. And still now, though he knows that he is well-liked by colleagues and close friends, the mildest embarrassing situation, the gentlest tease can suddenly occasion searing shame, a minor criticism hit him like a major blow, for the 'briars' of shame and rage have remained vigorous within him. At such times, Jonty is once again the family scapegoat, back at his childhood home; it is as if he had forgotten that he was now an adult living in a big adult body. Interestingly, this temporal incongruence shows itself in his physical build and posture which have evolved to parry any insults or beatings that might come his way – even if they no longer do. All the power resides in his large, macho torso with which he confronts the world, while a little collapse in his shoulders and upper chest hints at his deep-rooted shame.

As a therapist, there is an uncanny phenomenon that I observe quite frequently as the adult client before me suddenly becomes a child of a very specific age, say a 5, 9, 14 year old. It feels like looking at a hologram in which the figure of a child suddenly comes to the fore, while that of the adult recedes into the background.[1] It is more than a facial expression: there is something about their whole body and way of being that expresses that precise dislocation. It is uncanny to witness. For the client too, it is disconcerting: what is their place in time right now?

The experience of being both adult and child is commonly found in arguments, when suddenly one partner may feel like a child (told off, hurt, put down, etc.), or else notice that their partner is behaving like a child. Reactions will then come from a place familiar from childhood experience: for the 'child–adult', any hint of not being listened to may be read as another proof of their own unworthiness; any mildly critical remark could variously evoke ingrained beliefs and feelings of being bad, unlovable, about to be abandoned again, etc. Meanwhile, the other partner will be cast in the role of the dismissive, hypercritical, abandoning significant adult of their childhood. In couples where one partner's default place is that of the child, it is important to remember that it takes two to create such a situation: it requires one person to take that role, or give it, and the other to accept the situation; where there is no acceptance, such a default position does not occur.

And there are those who go through life like children in an adult world, feeling completely lost, with no proper sense of their place within it, little understanding of the rules of the games of adult life, like Josh Baskin in the film *Big* – a child who suddenly finds himself in a grown-up body. In real life, the dislocation this creates can be extremely painful and confusing.

The injunction to remember that 'this was then and now is now' is central to healing the scars of trauma. There are many whose lives are governed by a part of themselves that is still stuck in the traumatic past: for instance, they may live permanently on guard, despite knowing intellectually that the danger has passed. Yet, there is a part of them that won't believe it and remains hypervigilant – rather like that Japanese soldier who refused to surrender in 1945 and continued to carry arms and keep watch in the jungle in the Philippines for 29 years because he would not believe that the war had ended.

The flashbacks of PTSD are another form of living 'out of sync' with time as a result of trauma, when images, sensations and emotions from the past blast their way, unsolicited, into the present, overwhelming it. The person finds themselves not simply recollecting but *reliving* a past traumatic experience in its smallest details, thus challenging their sense of place in time.

Carmen could not walk down the road without being flooded with terror, just as on that day when the car lost control and, driving onto the pavement, knocked her down.

At the smell of a particular aftershave, Jen goes numb and blanks out completely.

Hugh freezes at the sound of any smoke or fire alarm.

For Ted, life is one long exhausting exercise in hypervigilance – for who knows what may suddenly happen. It weighs on his every action and on seemingly insignificant events with which life faces him, for these might bring down his world – as it did all those years ago.

When someone suffers from PTSD, they are, as it were, tricked by their bodies sounding a false alarm, not realizing that 'that was then and now is now'.

Who is the adult here?

Some children find themselves placed from a young age in the position of parent to their mother or father. This disruption to the natural parent–child order creates an incongruence that can persist through life.

Gideon is 45 and restless in his life. No degree, no responsible job is ever good enough for him, however high flying. He cannot take in any praise, for he feels he is a fraud, or in his words "I know I am a fraud to my very core".

L. *Wow, that's quite a statement! What do you mean by you're a fraud to your very core?*

G. *Well, I act like I am this hard-working, clever, efficient, cool-headed guy – I know that's how people see me, they've told me often enough….but deep down I'm shit scared because I know that when the chips are down, I don't deliver.*

L. *How do you know that when the chips are down, you don't deliver? Has that happened before?*

G. *'Plenty of times' is spat out contemptuously*

L. *Can you give me a recent example?*

G. *Well… I can't think of any recently*

L. *What about in your previous job?*

G. *Hmm, no not really*

L. *Or in your studies?*

Gideon looks up to the left and shakes his head.

L. *OK, so what springs to mind as a time you didn't deliver when the chips were down?*

Gideon frowns and hangs his head down; his lower lip curls up.

L. *What's happening for you right now, Gideon? You seem to have gone into a young place… a very painful place…*

It turns out that from the age of 12, Gideon had had to be the 'man of the house', getting his younger siblings ready in the morning, going to the corner shop after school and cooking dinner for them all. Being the man of the house had also involved always feeling protective of his mother, looking out for her, sometimes even trying to defend her against a violent boyfriend. As the young teenage 'man of the house', Gideon had felt proud of the responsibility, yet never quite up to the task, and in particular, helpless and powerless over his mother's depressed state. It is hardly surprising that the teenage Gideon should have felt inadequate and a fraud: indeed, at that age, he was a 'fraud' of a man. Yet, that feeling and conviction has remained with him to this day despite all evidence to the contrary.

Sadly, Gideon has been at odds with himself all his life, carrying into adulthood all his childhood hypervigilance and feeling of inadequacy.

Of course, there may come a time when parent–child role reversal has its appropriate place as parents become diminished or incapacitated with illness and/or age. However, if the parent can still be honoured as the patriarch or matriarch of the family, there is, as it were, a handing over of the reins without a total overturn of the natural parent–child order. It becomes more a renegotiation of roles than a role reversal. Such, however, was not the case for Mike:

Mike was an intelligent, witty, once very sporty man who had had a good job and a full social life centred around sport. The world he now depicted was quite other: it was, he said, "a crappy life". In saying so, he showed me that he had not lost his sense of humour, only that it had become a dark, gallows humour: he meant it quite literally, his life was indeed crappy, as he spent 18 hours a day in a room with his elderly, incontinent, deaf and mildly demented father. He described a life in which all boundaries of privacy customary in the West had been eroded or disappeared. All the senses felt offended, yet he spoke with an apparent lightness and humour that would have made for a dark sitcom, were it not for the rage, anxiety, despair and resignation that I sensed seeping out of every sentence. Yet, I also heard love and a deep loyalty. Mike wanted things to change; he wanted a little time and space for himself. However, the boundary issue with his father was not simply a spatial one, it was also a temporal one: Mike still felt he should defer to his father's wishes and decisions. Twenty years ago, in a crisis, Mike had returned to his father's home and it was as if, by doing so, he had felt obliged to remain forever the child of the house, even when he knew that he was the only compos mentis adult in it. This was an extreme mix of infantilization and reverse-parenting. Hence the rage, despair and guilt whose voice Mike was unable to silence in the counselling room, for all his strong filial deference and loyalty.

A certain degree of infantilization and being 'made a fuss of' when visiting or staying with parents doesn't do anyone any harm. It could even be argued that it is no bad thing to reaffirm the sense of the natural parent–child order from time to time. But the indefinite situation that Mike had lived out with his father represented a total confusion of his place in time in relation to himself, his life and his father.

What values still guide my life?

There is another very common type of incongruence which consists in living according to values that belong to 'another place in time'. Thus, ageing may bring dissonance to some as they struggle to adapt to technical progress and accept changes in social values. This unease may be compounded by what they experience as a lack of respect towards them, especially when, according to the values they hold, respect is due to them as elders of society.

We can also experience values and priorities shattering following some momentous event. Following the massive Indonesian tsunami of 2004, as in the aftermath of the 9/11 Twin Towers bombing, many counsellors and psychotherapists noticed a far greater demand for their services. These cataclysmic events shattered our basic sense of security, they challenged things that we took for granted: that the earth is firm under our feet, that the sea stays in the sea bed, that New York sky-scrapers stay upright, that the US secret services are capable of protecting the country against a handful of terrorists. Just as the early days of the coronavirus pandemic challenged our view of science as always objective and exact, and of pandemics like the plague or the Spanish flu (which, a 100 years earlier, killed more people than the First World War) as things of the past. Such challenges to our fundamental sense of security may render our old values and priorities obsolete. Similarly, a significant loss or a potentially life-threatening diagnosis may bring about a change of priorities and values which, if not acted upon, will create jarring and dissonance in life and challenge our sense of place within it.

Equally, if we live our lives according to the wishes of our (grand)parents, underpinned by values of a different era, it can be difficult to find our own satisfying place in life.

Until not so many decades ago, a good grasp of Latin and Greek language and culture was regarded by many as the benchmark of a serious education, and Classics at Oxford the pinnacle to be reached. I have had a number of clients whose parents had foisted this ambition upon them, with very unhappy consequences – as they were growing up and when they did not attain that parental goal. Or in the case of Alexandra, even when she did: getting into Oxford to read Classics had felt at first like a dream come true, it was what she had been working for all these years. Yet, despite all that Oxford had to offer her, she was feeling lonely, low and at times suicidal. It took a while for Alexandra to admit to herself that she had so wanted to gain her father's approval; but her dream – a dream that had no place in her family's culture and that she hardly dared express to herself – lay elsewhere. Art was her passion; she felt that, at her very heart, she was *an artist. She might not become a successful artist, but that was how she would find* her *place in* her *life.*

Of course, there often lies a great chasm between coming to understand the roots of our dissatisfaction and then being able to change direction in life: anxiety, shame, the desire to fulfil parental or societal expectations may keep us on the familiar and safe shore, unable to cross over, even if that leaves us feeling deeply unhappy. The devil we know often seems better than the uncertainty that lies on the other shore, let alone the risk of falling into what looks like deep waters before us. Yet, not surprisingly, 'my place' is most likely to feel right in a life that I have made truly my own, as opposed to one I am living to please others or according to now forsaken values.

'This is not mine'

'Yet He will by no means leave the guilty unpunished, visiting the iniquity of the fathers on the children and on the grandchildren to the third and fourth generations' Exodus 34.7

'What goes round comes around'. Proverb.

Punitive justice still has a deep and influential place in the Western psyche. Time and again, I have heard hospital patients ask me what they had done to deserve their diagnosis: "Why me? I'm not a bad person". But life is not fair, and some of the most wonderful people sometimes experience the most cruel illnesses and losses.

Interestingly, it is not uncommon for parents themselves, with greater or lesser awareness, to visit either their 'iniquities' or else their own traumatic experiences upon their children. As happened with some children born out of wedlock – in the days when it was a fate worse than death – who carried the burden of their mother's own 'sinfulness', shame, guilt and resentment. They carried what was not theirs to carry (*see Mothers Chapter 8*).

Handing down to the child what belongs to the parent can also manifest itself in various other ways, one of them being the choice of given name. I have known parents to name children after qualities they themselves lacked or the forgiveness they sought. I wonder for instance how many of the boys called Cain or Judas (in the United States: 233 'Cain' and 23 'Judas' in 2021)[2] were so named in full ignorance of their respective eponymous forebears, and how many reflected a parental betrayal. Meanwhile, some parents give names more likely to repeat their own experience of being bullied at school. It is as if they felt that their offspring could somehow carry responsibility for them and/or in some way redeem them.

Nor is it uncommon for parents to hand down their grief in the name of a lost beloved lover, sibling, or child. In *Memorial Candles, Children of the Holocaust*, Dina Wardi mentions the practice whereby many survivors of the Holocaust would sometimes give one particular son or daughter a whole string of names, the names of all their murdered relatives. While remembering and honouring murdered close ancestors is extremely important, what is a young child, or adult, supposed to do with this heavy legacy? Feel daily gratitude, or guilt, that they are alive when their ancestors have died in such unspeakably horrific ways? Live their lives for them? Eat for all these ancestors who starved to death, or starve in unison? These questions are not merely rhetorical: they express the often un-articulated, subconscious, dilemma that many face and may respond to in various ways – including bulimia, anorexia, overexertion, giving up, messianic zeal, unbearable guilt and suicide (*see 'David', Chapters 8 and 13*).

When we consider the broader picture, and look at families across three or four generations, we can sometimes observe the strange phenomenon of patterns repeating themselves: similar estrangements, medically unexplained pains and illnesses, deep distress among a number of young cousins, etc. Yet, far from taking a punitive perspective of this phenomenon, as in the biblical quote and proverb above, it is more helpful to consider it from the perspective of the family system as a whole which, when it is thrown out of balance, somehow seeks to right itself. Such is the first premise of Systemic Constellation work (*see Glossary and Chapter 13 Understanding*). It suggests that where someone has been in some way excluded from the family, or has excluded themselves from it; where there has been a premature or violent death; or else when a past family situation has been shrouded in secrets and lies, then, someone further down the generation(s) – a child, nephew/niece, great-grandchild – may become in some way 'entangled' with that person and their fate. Thus a person's life may become burdened with something that isn't theirs.

Many years ago, I was reading to elderly cousins some wartime letters from a great-aunt whom I had never known. "But Laura, my cousin asked, why are you identifying with this poor woman, you never even knew her!" It was not until she pointed this out that I noticed that she was quite right: even if I did not identify with her, I felt somehow emotionally involved with this great-aunt in a way that was difficult to explain, yet was somehow palpable to my elderly cousin. There seemed to be some strange and heavy bond between us. On further reflection, the source of that bond became obvious to me: I remembered as a child my grandmother comparing my looks to those of her "poor beloved" younger sister. (Though from the photographs I have seen of her, I cannot detect any likeness!). But that resemblance between us, even if only fantasized by my grandmother, had created a bond that had led to some form of 'entanglement' between us.

Yet strangely, entanglement can occur even where there are no obvious reasons for such a bond. Silence can carry with it just as much trauma and unbearable loss as daily outpourings of grief: the unspoken aborted foetus, dead child or war dead, the secret first wife can all weigh upon a family, heavy as a shroud. We may then see for instance one particular member becoming, as it were, the lightning rod for the whole family, the repository for their trauma; or we may see similar, non-hereditary symptoms mysteriously manifesting themselves among various family members.

Muriel suffered from debilitating pain and the doctors could not get to the bottom of it. Alarm bells started ringing for me when she mentioned that all her female line over three generations suffered from some form of debilitating pain. It could not be an inherited condition, for their pain was unconnected – or at least medically so. My systemic lens was highlighting the possibility that there might be a person in the family system whose pain they all variously carried. It was not until a few months later that Muriel evoked a hushed-up scandal involving her maternal grandmother who, as a young girl, had been raped by a priest. The baby had been taken away from her at birth, and she was later told that her baby girl had died, though she had never quite believed it.

While I know we did good existential work together, still Muriel's story remains with me as a possibly tragically missed opportunity. Our sessions ended very early in my training in Systemic Constellations. I still wonder whether, had I been more experienced in constellation work, I could have helped to effect greater change with her pain.

War is one of the greatest entanglers of fates. As a teenager on a trip around Israel, I met two young Germans in their late teens who were visiting the country before learning Hebrew with the aim of doing voluntary work: they were wanting to atone for their parents' and their country's sins. I remember being shocked and deeply saddened that they should feel so burdened by guilt and responsibility – a responsibility that was not theirs, but which they had made their own and was now governing the course of their life. This was almost 30 years after the end of the Second World War. Very recently, almost 65 years after the war, I have met people who are somehow still trying to atone for a grandparent who committed atrocities in that war. Over the years I have also encountered numerous adults whose lives became enmeshed with those of (great)grandparents who had suffered or been murdered in the war: whether somehow drawn to join them in death, living vicariously for them, or else replicating through anorexia the emaciation they suffered in concentration camp or Japanese prisoner of war camps.

History with its tragedies is the common context of our human lives: war, famine, slavery, displacement and genocide lie in the background of a significant proportion of the earth's population and create similar entanglements that affect a person's place in time.

Boundaries and my place in time: Conclusion

Questioning the place in which we find ourselves in our lives is more likely to occur when something feels out of kilter and we feel unsettled, lost, or unhappy. Yet, we can develop an awareness of "this place of mine in my life feels right" without relying on its opposite for comparison: for feeling 'right' in our lives is an embodied stance which has its own felt sense.

So, for instance, we are unlikely to feel contentedly right if we tend to stand hunched up or sitting with arms and legs knotted – for these positions neither *denote* nor *encourage* a sense of being at home in one's body, let alone in one's life. As we observe our lives from an embodied sense of "this feels right", we feel the ground firm beneath our feet, our chest feels open, yet not exposed, our shoulders and breathing relaxed. And with this comes a certain sense of belonging and, importantly, of a *right* to belong, to this ground beneath us, to the earth, but also to this town, to this group of people, to existence, to life, to now. This sense of belonging may take many hues – outward-facing, enthusiastic, quiet, meditative, grateful…

This embodied feeling of "yes, this place in my life feels right" might be a 'natural', lifelong experience for some, or one that was once there and then was destroyed or lost. For others, sadly, it will be totally unfamiliar. But what I do know, from personal and professional experience, is that such an embodied feeling about our place in our lives can be (re)gained and developed. Still, when the life we are leading, generally or at this moment in time, is not the one we would have chosen for ourselves and we cannot change its parameters (state of health, country, family, house, job, etc.), there is a way of carving out what feels like 'my place' within it. Carving 'my place' in such a life is saying: "OK, these are the givens of my situation, are there any that I can change in any way, any boundaries that I can push out a little? Are there a few hours in the week that I can make my own, a few moments in the day where

I can 'escape', where I can find time for what is now important to me, time to be some of the 'me' I would like to be?"

And if even that is not possible, how can I snatch brief moments that can be mine only – a pebble, a scent, a melody, a tiny spot on the wall, a specific time on the clock that I can invest with importance and no one can take away from me? Rather than resignation that closes avenues for change and may bring hopelessness and despair, this way of carving 'my place' is a form of active acceptance of the situation that allows an opening and, with it, some hope.[3]

This place-carving is an embodied feeling – that is to say you can get a physical and emotional felt sense of it. When clients come in highly stressed, describing the pressure that is sitting on their shoulders, the chaos and anxiety knotting their chest or stomach, I am always amazed to see how much better they feel as soon as they have given themselves a little time and space to breathe. You may want to give this a try right now: try lengthening your spine and then, with the fingertips of both hands touching, make the movement of very slowly pushing your pressures away. Sense yourself pushing your own boundaries out all around yourself, very slowly – above, pushing up from your shoulders and down to the sides, in front at chest level, to the sides and behind you. Do you notice any difference? Maybe your chest has expanded a little, your face muscles relaxed…Take a moment to notice and savour the space that exists within those expanded boundaries, breathe it in gently and out again. Often with clients, I can see almost immediately a deeper intake of breath and a less stressed expression on their faces. And how long has that taken? Two minutes. Two minutes for oneself can create a small space to breathe and be; two minutes can work mini miracles.

It is *vitally* important for us to remember and acknowledge that we each have a life that is finite, has value and deserves to be honoured. How? By reflecting upon it, nourishing it, making it our own, living it as best we can, according to values which we regularly reevaluate for ourselves, and finding a place within it that feels good … even if it takes our whole life to find this place. For, as I noticed in working with end-of-life patients, it is never too late to discover a new perspective which can transform the way we perceive our life story.

Notes

1   This phenomenon is very common and not to be confused with the multiple personalities of 'dissociative identity disorder'.
2   https://datayze.com/name-uniqueness-analyzer?name=cain
    https://datayze.com/name-uniqueness-analyzer?name=judas
3   While the strong existential position would be that the choice is ours, it would feel arrogant of me not to acknowledge the extreme difficulty of exercising that freedom in certain situations.

Chapter 5

What Gets in the Way of Compassion, Understanding and Boundaries

Introduction

The history of civilization has provided us with a treasury of writings to help us lead a 'good' or a more satisfying life; so what is it that prevents so many of us from discovering and enjoying such a life for ourselves? It is a question about the human condition which, over the last millennia, has exercised writers, philosophers, and theologians. Already 2,000 years ago, Ovid gave Medea these anguished words "*Video meliora, proboque, deteriora sequor*", 'I see the better [course of action] and approve it, yet I follow a worse one', one of the quotes I had posted on my bedroom wall in my own anguished teenage years. Aristotle called such a state 'akrasia', weakness of will; other thinkers have variously put it down to original sin, determinism, the power of the subconscious, etc.

The question of what prevents a person from creating a deeply satisfying life for themselves is one that I would have answered differently at different periods of my life. As a child, I was encouraged to see Vanity at play everywhere, the root cause of human problems; so it was Vanity, I was taught, that got in the way of the 'search for satisfaction' and the 'harmonization of desires'. Later, as an existential therapist, my answer would have been influenced by Sartre's idea that, as human beings, we have a fundamental life project that may hijack the explicit life choices that we make for ourselves.[1] Nowadays, I might suggest that while part of ourselves wants to follow one course of action, another part or parts will try to prevent us doing so, commonly out of a misguided attempt to protect us.[2] I believe there is some validity in all these views.

But now that I am following the train of thought set off by my dream and exploring compassion, understanding and boundaries as key elements of a satisfying and contented life, I ask myself what gets in the way of introducing these into our everyday lives. I believe the obstacles include ingrained beliefs, fear about what we might discover about ourselves and anxiety about the consequences of setting new boundaries and shame.

DOI: 10.4324/9781003364504-6

What gets in the way of offering myself compassion?

When I look upon myself with compassion, I see myself as I would see a dear friend or loved one suffering my fate. I do not look down on myself nor judge myself. I acknowledge at a deep, heart, mind and core level what I have gone through or done, and I offer myself understanding, love, support and care. This sounds so simple. So why does it prove so difficult, as client after client has shown me, as I myself experienced for years? What is it about offering ourselves understanding, love and care that can feel so particularly wrong? I am sure there are many answers to that question, but I shall venture only three here: firm beliefs, childhood experiences and the power of ingrained guilt and shame.

In the Western world, a distorted version of our Judeo-Christian heritage is the source of a common belief that gets in the way of showing care and love to ourselves: somehow, over the centuries, the second half of the biblical injunction 'love thy neighbour *as thyself*' has been discarded as selfish, self-indulgent, sinful even. Yet it is key. 'Love thyself' is at the heart of loving the other: for it is from a sense of genuine, loving self-centredness that love for others will flow. The French psychotherapist Paul Diel called it 'consequent egoism'. Without sufficient self-love, loving the other risks becoming in part an attempt at satisfying or quieting our own needs.

'Love thyself' does not mean showering ourselves with gifts, the latest gadgets or fashion accessories, it does not mean believing we are the best thing since sliced bread, God's gift to mankind. Loving ourselves is in many ways like loving a friend: it is valuing our qualities while accepting that we have faults; enjoying spending some time with ourselves – in serious reflection and in fun; helping ourselves and asking for help for ourselves in difficult times; trying to understand ourselves; and showing some loving care towards those sad, awkward, angry younger selves that we once were and sometimes still seem to be.

Some people only discover self-compassion after observing someone else going through an experience that reminds them of their own; and as they feel compassion for them, it lights up that possibility for themselves. Sometimes, the resonance is so strong (even when the someone, as with Yuval, is not a person but an animal) that it cuts through long held beliefs that have prevented any form of understanding and self-compassion.

Yuval was a remarkable young man whose life had been characterized by endurance, tolerance, perseverance, adventure, and success, yet little self-esteem. Whatever he set his mind to, in the most diverse of fields, he achieved. He put this down to his upbringing at the hands of a "rough" mother.

L. *You know, I'm really struck by how grateful and compassionate you are towards your mother who was so rough with you, and how you find it so difficult to acknowledge your own achievements and feel compassionate towards the young child that you were.*

Y. *I know mum pushed me quite hard, but that made me succeed. And she'd had it hard too. Without her pushing, I doubt I'd have done it all.*

L. *That may well be. But surely, it is your response to her pushing that got you where you are today; that was your choice. I mean, you could've chosen to remain in a helpless victim position, or you could've rebelled and turned to drugs for instance… Because your mother did more than just push you; from what you've said, she was at times very cruel towards you… and violent. Can you see that?*

Y. *Well, yes, sort of… but…*

L. *But what?*

Y. *But I owe her everything.*

L. *I am sure that there is much that you owe her, but you certainly don't owe it to her cruelty. And you definitely don't owe her everything. You owe so much to your own perseverance and your own qualities. I wonder what makes it so difficult for you to own that…*

Over the next few sessions, we explored some of the opportunities Yuval had seen and taken in his professional life, the choices he had made, yet still his self-denigration, together with his gratitude and compassion for his mother, coloured his life as a whole. Then one day Yuval arrived in a heightened emotional state.

Y. *Two nights ago, I was sitting on the sofa, I was just relaxing with an old film. Suddenly, I was sobbing uncontrollably. I didn't know what was going on. I was completely… I was in pieces. It was something about the way that young bear was being treated. It was so unbelievably painful.* Starts welling up. *It was so painful. And then it came to me, it was like a 'eureka!' moment, that bear… it wasn't only painful, it was familiar, it was so familiar, it was so, so familiar.*

For the first time, Yuval had seen the roughness he had endured as a child for what it really had been – cruelty. For the first time, he had felt a surge of compassion for his younger self, who had always tried so hard to protect those weaker than himself and do his best in all he undertook. This led Yuval to realize that the key to his successes in life had not been his mother's cruel and violent chastisement of the bad, wayward child she had accused him of being, but his own many qualities, including courage and determination. It was so hard for him to accept that the mother he loved, and who clearly had qualities of her own, also had some important failings and that she had at times done him serious harm. It had been easier to believe that her "roughness" was part of her plan for his success.

We tend to internalize and make our own many of the messages, spoken and unspoken, that we pick up from our caregivers. And if these tell us that we are 'bad', 'a useless waste of space' and 'unlovable', it can be difficult to love oneself or feel one deserves compassion. Tragically, such beliefs tend to be deeply rooted and they bear the poisonous fruit that is shame.

Another obstacle to showing care and love to ourselves are all the 'oughts' and 'shoulds' with which we admonish ourselves: "I should have known better", "should have stood up for myself", " ought not have been so weak", etc. Reflecting on the context without judgement releases self-compassion.

There is also the misapprehension and fear that to feel concern and care for oneself is to 'feel sorry for oneself' – the slippery slope to 'wallowing in self-pity', a state from which it may be difficult to extricate ourselves and which may lead us to 'sink into depression'. This fear rests on a complete misunderstanding, as compassion is almost the antithesis of pity. Where pity is commonly shaming, judgemental, often contemptuous, compassion is loving, caring and non-judgemental. Where self-pity draws us into a dynamic of victimhood and blame – of others, ourselves, the world – compassion frees us from the emotions that hold us in their grip. Self-pity shutters up windows, conceals doors, closes up opportunities for change – a state experienced as 'depression'; compassion opens up new perspectives on ourselves, others and the world, new possibilities.

What gets in the way of seeking greater understanding through therapy?

Stigma, fear of opening the floodgates to uncontrollable emotions, fear of dependency and fear of 'opening a can of worms' are the most common obstacles to accessing therapy which I encounter.

Stigma and fear of dependence on the therapist

Many see entering therapy as a sign of weakness; in truth, it requires courage. Partly because psychotherapy requires two giant leaps of faith: that by talking about things to a complete stranger, somehow it will make things better; and that the therapist will be trustworthy, ethical and competent, and they will neither judge, reject, nor hurt. There is no denying that therapy is in itself a potential minefield where pain and shame could potentially explode at any time, since one person is telling their most hidden secrets to another, whom they hardly know but are expected to trust. And yet, as I have seen time and again, it can bring the greatest relief and joy-ful transformation.

Anna had come to see me a few months ago after years of hesitation.

A. *I just can't believe how transformative these sessions have been. I just wish I had come to you sooner.*

L. *Hmm. What do you think made you so reluctant to seek out a therapist sooner? What were you most worried about?*

A. *I used to think: therapy is my last chance, and if that doesn't work, then what is left for me? Where do I go from there?*

L. *That sounds quite desperate.*

A. Nods
L. It must have been terrifying contacting me, it was quite a gamble.
A. Yes, but things had become really desperate. And now I think … why didn't I come so much sooner?
L. Yes. But you came when you did … and you were ready for transformative change. Just think, you could have waited another 25 years or even longer!

Not infrequently, in my cancer counsellor days, patients used to tell me at the end of therapy: "I can't say I am pleased that I got cancer, but in some ways, it is the best thing that ever happened to me". Each time, I was struck anew by the poignancy of that statement. For there is something shocking, yet deeply moving, in the thought that it sometimes takes a cancer diagnosis to access therapy and bring about long-desired change.

One of the most common concerns regarding therapy is becoming dependent on the therapist, which involves fears of losing control and/or suffering deep attachment followed by painful loss. Much ink has been spilt on the topic of client dependency. I would argue that this is indeed a real risk, either where the therapist's own psychological or financial interests are involved (the therapist who can't or won't let go), or where the client's own attachment issues are triggered. In the first case, there is an abuse of power that must be guarded against; in the second, if that is the client's problem and it is well addressed and explored, the therapy may indeed last a long time, but it could resolve a lifelong, painful way of relating to significant others.

If the need to depend on someone (or conversely the abhorrence of dependency, which can be the other side of the same coin) is not a familiar problem for the client, dependence on the therapist is unlikely to arise; if it does, this may be a time for the therapist to further question their own possible role in the process.

There are of course clients who come in need of support during a particular period of their lives, where there is no other adult who can fulfil that role; in a sense, they could be said to be dependent on the therapist. However, if there is neither excessive idealization of, nor infatuation with, the therapist or terror of losing them, I would suggest that they are temporarily dependent on the opportunity for offloading, exploration and support which therapy and the therapist provide, and there is nothing inherently problematic with that. For there are times in life when we need help, and it is good to feel we can ask for it. Knowing when and how to give, ask for and receive help are all valuable human qualities.

Whether or not dependence is a major presenting issue for the client, I believe it is important that the therapeutic situation is jointly revisited and questioned at regular intervals to double-check that it is still beneficial and meeting the clients' needs. This taking stock is important for the sake of transparency and honesty, but even more so for clients who have a tendency to be dependent, passive, to drift into situations, or avoid change: for they need to feel their own sense of agency and responsibility for the process and the timescale of their therapy.

Fear of what may be uncovered

We may also be put off therapy by a fear of having to dip into unknown or dimly perceived areas of the 'psyche' and discovering something shameful. For the influence of Freud and psychoanalysis on 20th-century films and culture generally has promulgated the idea that human beings have a cauldron of darker, chaotic thoughts and feelings boiling beneath conscious awareness which only a psychoanalyst can help them discover and understand. Yet seldom in my experience has any client discovered in themselves an unknown source of shame – none spring to mind. On the contrary, many who feared themselves to be mad, bad, or dangerous discovered a different, more compassionate and more accurate way of understanding themselves, their beliefs, their ways of being and behaving.

Another common fear relates to 'opening boxes that have been kept locked away at the back of the mind', lest painful thoughts and feelings come tumbling out uncontrollably. It is therefore of paramount importance for the client to feel able to negotiate with the therapist the parameters of the therapy: to say what, at this stage, is out of bounds for exploration. It's OK to say to the therapist "I just don't want to go there right now", or to signal what might require particular gentleness, care and lightness of touch. And a therapist should respect a client's request: while signposting areas that appear to be a valuable vein for future enquiry, edges can be gently tested without going in at the deepest point. Client and therapist alike also need to honour the client's defences and armour – for there are those who travel through life fully armoured – and treat them with respect: they will have developed for a good reason. Trying to destroy defences without first helping the client access other resources is counterproductive: they will most likely either seek to consolidate them, put up new ones or discontinue therapy, or they could possibly 'fall apart' in some way.

In my professional experience, even when painful thoughts and feelings do spill out, if the client feels metaphorically contained and held by the therapist, it is seldom as terrifying as they had expected and in itself brings some relief. Even the greatest grief runs its course: the loss is not forgotten, its pain is still felt, but the tears that were held back for fear they would never stop finally dry up. I like to think of the biblical expression 40 days and 40 nights: I quote it to convey both the relentlessness and long period over which we may cry, but also its limit. Though it may feel inconceivable, there will be an end to the tears.

Quite understandably, one area that many adults fear revisiting is their childhood sexual abuse and the impact it has had on their lives. They fear they will find themselves reliving the abuse and be reminded yet again of the overwhelming sense of shame, the pain of the double breach of trust – from the abuser and from the parents in whom the child did not dare confide, or did confide and was not believed. The protection of perpetrators among their ranks by religious, social care, sporting and other institutions represents a criminal third breach of trust – criminal not only in the legal sense, but morally so. In 2016, a number of footballers spoke out on UK television of their childhood sexual abuse at the hands of their coach, a youth scout for top professional clubs. By publicly showing their vulnerability, tears and brokenness, these men, some of them heroes to their fans, will have helped so many to understand the lifelong damage wreaked by childhood sexual abuse and, it is hoped, removed some of the stigma and fear of asking for help. And it is good to remember that there are now safe therapeutic ways of working with the trauma of abuse that do not necessarily require anyone to go into the details of what happened, let alone relive them.

We sometimes also want to protect ourselves from certain insights that lie at the edges of our awareness, from a new understanding that threatens our experience of inner stability, impacts our sense of identity, the dynamic balance within our family, or our very sense of entitlement to existence.

George couldn't understand why his mother had always singled him out for harsh treatment as a child, later often excluded him from family gatherings and behaved so viciously towards him on a number of occasions in his life. And even now, when she was gravely ill and all the family were gathering, she was refusing to see him.

We acknowledged how painful, confusing and shaming such mothering is for a child and how, to this day, it still affected him to his very core. He remembered, from the youngest age, always trying so hard to be a good boy so as not to get into any trouble. So why had he been forever punished and later excluded? I told him that this is a question to which he may never have the answer; it didn't mean that there was anything wrong with him. *There must have been something going on for his mother that he didn't know about.*

George sat still and stared at me wide-eyed. It was, he later said, like the proverbial scales falling from his eyes, all those clues from all those years – the whispers and snide comments about her, the various perplexing comments, his resemblance to his uncle Geoff in Australia…

G. Uncle Geoff is a weak man. Well that's what my mum and my aunts used to say. Uncle Geoff was quite quiet, but I thought he was all right. Wow! Strange or what? Uncle Geoff lived with us till I was three, I think; then he went to Australia, but he used to come and visit sometimes. I can't believe it… though that's the point, I really can, it makes complete sense. How crazy is that?!

My statement, that there must have been something going on for his mother that he didn't know about, rather than something intrinsically bad about him, had been quite innocent. I certainly had not been fishing for anything in particular. I had simply wanted to open up the alternative perspective that the source of the problem, whatever it might be, was probably not with him, if he had always tried so hard to be good, but with his mother. As a young child, George could not have known that *he* was not the 'bad' one, that he was the fruit of *her* 'sin'. Yet, at some level, he had known about his illegitimacy for most of his life, and he had also known that to confront his mother would have been dynamite. And so, all his life, he had defended himself against revealing that forbidden secret to himself and he had carried the blame and the shame – her shame. All his life he had kept on working at being a good son, hoping beyond hope for some sort of kindness, some sign of his mother's love for him. But now, there was no longer any point: forgiveness from his mother for whatever wrong he may have done would never be forthcoming, she would never tell him she loved him. Only now with the finality of her terminal illness and her total lack of any interest in him, could he allow in the thought of his illegitimacy. And, with the realization that she would never make peace with him (or rather with herself and hence with him) came the understanding that if he could not find some form of peace face to face with his mother, at least he was going to have to make peace with the situation and with himself. This new understanding was the beginning of a journey for which he was going to need gentleness, compassion and care from me.

Rare is the family that does not have its share of traumas and/or skeletons in the cupboard, such as affairs, abortions, babies out of wedlock – whether kept or given away for adoption, war invalids, violent deaths, 'black sheep' who emigrated, fraudsters, or other criminals. And few are the families that are transparent about this internally, let alone publicly. Family secrets abound, even where there is no social opprobrium attached: premature death for instance can be experienced with the force of a 'scandal' and kept secret as such; or simply kept under silence as there are no words to express the loss and pain. George's story highlights the impact of secrets and lies in the family.

Entering such painful territory is more than many are prepared to do. There may be a fear of recalling for instance their mother's pain, lack of availability or distance, or else an identification or comparison with the lost child – maybe feeling not as valued or loved as the dead child – experiencing the parent's "if only you had died instead of her". Then, there may be the survivor's guilt: "I do not deserve to live", "I need to live for two/work for two", "I must not enjoy my life, since he could not enjoy his". Hence, for some, the fear of exploring the past and the need to defend against it.

Like all animals, we have developed ways of defending ourselves against danger, our predators and enemies: we have learnt the value of vigilance, fight, flight, submission, feigned death and turning to others for support, as the situation requires. But one way in which we differ from other animals is in our highly developed ability to defend ourselves against ourselves – against those painful thoughts and feelings that come with the human privilege of self-reflection. Expressions such as 'to die of shame', 'be eaten up' with guilt or anger, 'destroyed by grief', 'crushed' by disappointment, and 'tortured' with hate show the destructive power that emotions can have over us. We could not function in our everyday lives without the capacity to protect ourselves at times from such emotions and from toxic thoughts about ourselves – such as "I'm unlovable", "bad", "stupid", "too much", "a fraud". From our youngest infancy, we humans learn how to defend ourselves against getting emotionally hurt, whether by shutting down or else by covering up in any number of ways – e.g. through self-deprecatory remarks, jokes, or going on the violent offensive. We may later learn to self-medicate painful thoughts and feelings with alcohol or drugs. This capacity of ours to protect ourselves deserves our admiration and awe. However, it comes to us at a cost. These defences may become so ingrained over the years that they prevent us from feeling spontaneity, equanimity and joy and from exploring the roots of our distress.

Danny was sitting upright before me. He now felt ready, he said, to think about making a start with talking about his childhood. It had taken many weeks for us to reach this fragile point of tentative determination. For much of the preceding few sessions, Danny had retreated to a corner of the armchair, his arms wound tightly around his ribs, his legs knotted up. The contrast between this child of a man – 66 going on 5 – and the Danny that he had once presented to me had been striking and heart-breaking. The Danny that I first met, the Danny that his colleagues and friends knew, was extrovert, blokey, jokey. He was a man they could, and did, depend upon: Danny would not think twice about driving across town or country to help friends in need with his excellent problem-solving and DIY skills. Nothing was too much for him. Or so it seemed. Yet, this whole act that had become his life was getting too much for Danny. His mask was cracking. And there was something else that was too much, something he hardly dared begin to think about. Something he had spent his life trying hard to forget, but now knew he could not keep hiding from. The price he was paying was too high. As he expressed it a few weeks into therapy:

D. *In my late twenties, I discovered that helping others made me feel wanted and stopped me thinking about things. Double bonus. So I was happy to do it, but forty years on, I still can't go to a friend's house without them asking me to do some job for them – well that's what it feels like.*

L. *You mean, it feels like you're being used?*

D. *Used? Yeah. But it's more than that… All these years, these helping-out outings have taken up all my free time, all my holidays. It's like… this whole charade has eaten up my life.*

L. *That's quite a statement!*

D. *Yeah. Sometimes now I come home and feel this huge rage… A few times recently I've even had outbursts of rage at friends' houses.*

L. *That must have been scary!*

D. *Yeah! It scares me stiff – what if I am falling apart? … And then after the rage, there's the shame.*

L. *Shame because your friends have seen your rage?*

D. *Well there's that too, because I'm always the cheerful, jokey one. But no. It's, I'm fast approaching my three-score-years-and ten, and... what's it all been about? It's like my life has been slipping through my fingers, while I've been looking for....*

L. *Looking for... what?*

D. *I don't know. Peace?*

L. *Peace?*

D. *Yeah. Peace. It's like all these years I've tried to forget. Like I thought... if I have no time to think, I can put the past behind me. Only it doesn't work that way.*

L. *No, it doesn't.*

D. *So, that last time I had an outburst – it was at Jim's, I got home and I thought, I'm just going to have to face up to it.*

L. *Mmm*

D. *That's when I decided to come and see you.* Looks straight at me and then down sideways.

L. *And I'm glad you did. And I know it will have taken a lot of courage.*

D. Looks up at me and holds my gaze.

L. *And we can tread very gently.*

As Danny's story shows, there comes a time when the defences and ways of being we have put in place to protect ourselves have undesirable side-effects and gradually stop working. Danny chose to seek help with confronting his past. He could instead have upped his level of defence, as one ups prescription drugs or self-medicating substances. But increasing either defences or self-medication without dealing with the original issue is likely to create a worsening, shame-ful spiral. For if something is troubling us enough to necessitate such strong defences, it is unlikely to simply go away, it will continue calling out to us for attention.

What gets in the way of setting boundaries

Setting boundaries and the fear of consequences

Setting a boundary requires taking a stance and asserting it; it involves taking action. And all actions, as we know, have consequences. One of the obstacles to setting boundaries is the fear of what might happen. It is true that there are situations in which saying "no" will have grave professional consequences or may even be life-threatening – these need seriously weighing up in relation to safety and its possible price. More generally, setting different boundaries will unsettle the *status quo* and bring change, which is anxiety-provoking. Yet, interestingly, I have regularly seen clients find themselves *better* respected and accepted by setting firmer boundaries with colleagues, friends and family – as happened with Maggie (in Chapter 1).

Louis, on the other hand, knew that he needed to relax his boundaries for his family's sake, but he was terrified of the impact it would have on himself. He had always been a "control freak", which had served him well in his work as it involved meticulous attention to detail, but it had invaded his home life and was becoming intolerable to his family. He felt caught between a rock and a hard place: his wife was threatening to leave him, but he felt that control was what held him and his life together.

Louis had been quite pernickety and rigid with me, but gradually he began to replace the barrier around himself, and around the dreaded secret that he had hinted at, with a more flexible boundary, one that allowed me in sufficiently to begin to explore his secret with him. And as he did so, he came to realize to his surprise that he no longer needed a rigid barrier of control in other areas of his life.

Sedimented beliefs as obstacles to setting satisfactory boundaries

Louis and Maggie's fear of the consequences of changing their boundary style was tied to a firm belief – for Louis that "without these rigid boundaries, I shall fall apart", for Maggie that "if I say 'no', I shall have no friends". Those were personal beliefs.

There are also those beliefs, whether clear edicts or unspoken rules, that are acquired from family, community, or society, yet ingrained in us: for instance, the belief that it is selfish and unkind to say no; that it is rude and wrong to refuse anything to a community elder/a superior; that it is perfectly all right for a man to put his hand on the small of a woman's back or her thigh, whereas the opposite shows forwardness/wantonness. Boundaries set in line with such beliefs will lead to unpleasantness, but they can also pave the way for sexual abuse and rape. Such societal beliefs can become sedimented, unquestioned for decades or centuries, hence, in part, the shock that greeted the #MeToo movement's loud and forceful challenge.

To feel unable to question or challenge the other's right to set boundaries we experience as invasive, boundaries that overstep our own, sets the scene for an abuse of power. To believe unquestionably that we have no personal right to boundaries and feel "I do not deserve firmer boundaries, I am not worth it" is a paradigmatic sign of shame. And shame deserves a chapter of its own.

Notes

1 For instance, an artist may want to change life-path to earn more money, or a highly successful, workaholic career woman may be determined to change her lifestyle, yet neither finds themselves able to do so. The Sartrean argument would be

that, more than a life choice, 'artist' and 'successful career woman' are for these two people a fundamental project, a way of *defining* their very selves. This, the argument goes, gives them an illusional sense of solidity – 'this is what I *am*', which they cannot risk losing.

2   So, with the above-mentioned artist or career woman, it may be that part of themselves fears that abandoning their present life path would be a sign of failure, and they fear the opprobrium and shame that would ensue, confirming their sense of worthlessness, etc.

Chapter 6

Shame

I have given much thought to shame in recent years, exploring it in my life and that of my clients, not in a judgemental or punishing manner but in a spirit of curiosity and interest. It is an umbrella term for so many different experiences: from fleeting to pervasive; from a superficial feeling to a deep existential sense and belief; from mild personal embarrassment to shocking public humiliation – one that can go 'viral' on social media. When ashamed, we cringe as we seek to conceal ourselves from the pointing finger, from all eyes, from an all-seeing Other – even if no one is looking at us. Shame makes us feel exposed, singled out for what we feel is our intrinsic, personal ignominy. In deep shame we whisper powerful insults to ourselves: "you are disgusting, a fraud, ugly, bad, unlovable"; we can feel shame tainting us to the core. The English language underlines the experience of shame with strong expressions as we speak of wishing 'the ground would swallow us up', we could 'sink through the floor', 'crawl into a hole'; we just want 'to go and lick our wounds', we feel 'mortified' – etymologically 'made dead', i.e. killed by shame. Clients variously describe shame as living in their gut, hiding in their genitals (the '*pudenda*' literally parts 'to be ashamed of'), as a smell enveloping or emanating from their whole body.

One great paradox of shame is that the object of our deepest shame (having been sexually abused[1]; sexual fantasies, or murderous ones; addictions or eating disorders; our perceived unlovabilility, etc.) far from being our own particular affliction is usually something we share with a multitude of others. The other great paradox is that we are even ashamed of shame, of feeling it, expressing it, discussing it; yet shame is an intrinsic part of the human condition.

The English word 'shame' conflates two different things: the experience of feeling ashamed and shame as a human emotion. The fact that 'shameless' and 'do you have no shame?!' are expressions of disapproval highlights the existence of a positive aspect to the emotion of 'shame' (and not only in English, French '*é-honté*' and German '*un-verschämt*' are similarly accusatory). The word 'modesty', now somewhat prim and dated, expresses the

DOI: 10.4324/9781003364504-7

healthy, moderating shame that curbs excess and prevents us from over-stepping various behavioural lines – such as ways of dressing and behaving deemed inappropriate, overeating, binge drinking, etc. This positive aspect of shame as a human emotion harks back to the Judeo-Graeco ground of our culture. Ancient Greek has both the word *aidos* to express the sense of shame and respect that are protective of our image and *aiskhune* which refers prin-cipally to the experience of shame. In Judaism, shame plays a significant role in the religious person's relationship with God. For shame is there to prevent shame-less, brazen behaviour in the eyes of God. And when Adam and Eve do not heed that shame and break their promise to God, they are a-shamed, in their exposure and nakedness before God.

The elusiveness of shame

Shame is a chameleon which frequently camouflages itself in the neighbour-hood of other, more acceptable emotions – more acceptable either to our-selves or to others. A person may admit to feeling 'a bit embarrassed', 'upset', or 'angry', when the dominant emotion is a shame that dare not speak its name. The interplay between shame and other emotions can be complex and lead to more shame.

Ginny, now 48, speaks of having lived with a deep sense of shame ever since she was sexually abused at the age of 13 by one of her parents' best friends. She knew she couldn't tell her parents, and she certainly couldn't tell her friends, let alone her pastor. So she developed a shell which she could put on whenever she felt the need for it and came to retreat into it ever more. Her parents must have assumed that Ginny's change from outward-going and open child to quiet, retiring and occasionally angry teenager was just a matter of hormones. At 16, they took Ginny to the GP who told them she was suffering from 'anxiety and depression' and, without even looking up at her, prescribed her Valium. Her shame now had another name, one that allowed her pain to be acknowledged by a doctor and her family and given a new, more acceptable name: she had 'anxiety and depression' and Valium was going to be the cure. For twenty years, Ginny collected her repeat prescription from the doctor's surgery without anyone questioning it. Even if she had long lost the hope that Valium was going to be the cure that would dissolve the 'anxiety and depression' and give her back her life, Valium and the pain of 'depression' were still preferable to shame and its pain.

Life did not treat Ginny kindly and, with every new family illness or loss, her sense of betrayal increased, as did her anxious and depressed state which, by the time I met her, had taken on a life of its own: it shrouded her daily life, her relations to others and her outlook on the future. The thought that she was letting her life fly past her filled her with shame and regret. Tragically, the source of her 'anxiety and depression', the sexual abuse and the original feelings of shame it aroused in her, had remained secret, and now a second layer of shame was arising from the existential guilt (the regret) of allowing life to fly past.

Ginny's sense of betrayal was mainly directed towards the illnesses and losses that she had suffered. But life does not have a duty of care towards us, it does not owe us anything. The real betrayal was committed by the abuser – a double betrayal, of Ginny herself and of her parents, his close friends. There was also a betrayal of duty of care by the GP and the GP practice that had allowed Valium to be offered in repeat prescriptions over 20 years before being reviewed. And there was a betrayal, most difficult of all to voice, by a family and church framework that did not foster sufficient trust and confidence for Ginny to mention the abuse. Feeling unable to express her anger about such betrayals attracted yet further shame.

Shame is often enmeshed with guilt, so much so that the two are often confused, yet they are fundamentally different: for whereas we mostly experience guilt in relation to something we have done or failed to do, when we feel shame, it is about our very being – 'I am ashamed *of myself'*. However, even when we feel guilty about what we have done, or failed to do, we may also feel ashamed of being capable of such an action or omission. Beneath the guilt, or entwined with it, may lie the question "How could *I* have been so stupid/ nasty/cruel? Is it that I am a stupid/nasty/cruel person after all?"

On the other hand, to feel guilt may feel preferable to feeling shame, for by feeling guilty, I am implying that I know better, that I have certain standards – standards of morality, politeness, etc. Indeed, shame can seek to hide behind guilt.

Mark, with whom this book began, excused himself profusely one day as he had missed the previous session and had forgotten to let me know that he had an appointment with the specialist that day. He felt really bad about it, this wasn't like him, he really didn't want to let me down.

When Mark's shame about his life and his very self was so great, there was some sort of comfort in feeling bad for breaching his high standards of punctuality and courtesy. For these high standards enabled him to salvage a minimum of self-respect.

Shame may also hide behind the expression of pride.

Ronnie frequently mentioned his artistic talents and his dreams of recognition. His sculpture held for him the hope of an escape from shame. Yet, as I pointed out, however talented he might be as a sculptor, the highly ambitious (not to say grandiose in the extreme) sculpture projects he had set himself were but the other side of the same shame coin. Rather than trying to big himself up by aiming for such dizzy artistic heights, far better to acknowledge that within him, the harming and the shame sat side by side with his genuine artistic gifts. They were all part of the rich tapestry that made him Ronnie, even if some of his actions had created very dark patches within it.

L. You mention your shame – and it takes guts to speak it as you do. You are already developing greater understanding about what led you to behave as you did. If you could look upon yourself with more compassion, accept that your life was such as it was, that since leaving prison you have successfully managed to walk a straight line for all these years, I think you might find that a more powerful antidote against shame.

R. *I don't know. It just doesn't feel enough.*

L. *Enough for what?*

R. *Enough to compensate.*

L. *Enough to compensate? For the harm done?*

R. Remains silent. Looks down.

L. *For how you see yourself?*

R. *Mmm*

L. *Mmm. That's hard. But I really don't think that aiming so high for yourself is the answer. You remember Icarus in Greek mythology? He's the one who tried to escape with wings made of feathers and wax. But he flew too close to the sun, so the wings melted and he drowned in the sea.*

R. Nods silently.

I thought that mentioning the myth of Icarus might be helpful to Ronnie as it does not condemn flights of creative imagination, only their degree – it cautions against aiming too high, against *hubris,* offending the Gods by arrogantly trying to overstep the boundaries they set to our mortal realm. The other myth that sprang to mind, but felt less therapeutically apposite, was that of Narcissus, in that there was a sense in which Ronnie was mesmerized by his artistic projects, like Narcissus by his reflection in the pond – except that the reflection which Ronnie saw was an idealized one of himself.

Shame and narcissism

Indeed narcissism[2] and shame often go hand in hand, as two opposite sides of the same coin. For instance, Liz and Jessie's narcissism was grounded in their sense of feeling 'a fraud' and their respective attempts to evince it.

For Liz, no amount of diplomas that she liked to parade could make up for the humiliation of having been treated as the family and junior school dunce, nor remove the doubt that maybe they were right. She was "just a fraud". At work, at which she excelled, she had been promoted to a position that commanded respect and admiration. Immensely knowledgeable about literature, art and the theatre, she liked to feel part of a group of brilliant people and shine among them – yet still she felt a fraud.

Whereas the stunning Jessie, once called the playground "fattie", surrounded herself with women whose looks could not deflect attention from her own. Like Liz, Jessie needed the admiring glance of friends to bolster her self-esteem, yet the very fact that their friends were thus selected was double-edged and added to their sense of fraud.

One could deduce from the above examples that the tendency of shame to go hand in hand with self-aggrandizing ways develops out of an original inferior position. However, that is not necessarily the case.

Take Giles, Old Etonian, scion of an ancient family, whose moments of shame would drive him to the edge of despair. His heritage, his family's history, his manners were central to his very being. A rare display of poor manners on his part, or the omission of whatever was due and proper in the circumstances, was a catastrophe that plunged him into a well of shame – as happened when he discovered that a serious etiquette offence of his had reached his cousin L.'s ears. That he had committed it was shameful enough, that it should reach his ears was unendurable. For Giles, failure in matters of etiquette was as bad as a moral failure: to him, the etiquette code had the value of a moral code. Indeed, he made little distinction between them. With his recent faux pas, he felt he had offended against the values inculcated in him from birth, against the family name; he feared he had disgraced himself. Hence his shame and despair.

Liz, Jessie and Giles all tried to counterbalance their sense of feeling deficient in some way by glorying in an aspect of themselves which they had invested with essential value. They felt the need to be on a pedestal or feel superior, yet could not shake off their belief that besides this admirable quality of theirs, there was nothing of worth, they were but empty, admireable shells. Sham is one letter short of shame.

Sylvan Tomkins coined the expression 'toxic shame' to describe the insidious sense of worthlessness, emptiness, self-doubt and self-loathing that can develop as a result of very poorly attuned, neglectful, or abusive parenting. A child is exquisitely attuned from birth to responding to its parents' facial expression. If constantly faced with a parent's scowling, weary, or dismissive look, they will come to sense itself as being in some way too much for them, a bad or unlovable child. Shame may then come to suffuse the child's sense of self as well as many of its emotions – because an emotion viewed as unacceptable by parents tends to be experienced by the child as shameful.

None of the above adults, as it happens, had been valued as children for who they were. Liz had been viewed by her academic parents as the family moron: how could a child of theirs let the side down so badly? The volatile relationship between Jessie's alcoholic parents had filled her with shame, anxiety, and often terror; and they had had little time for her. As to Giles' parents, they were of the school of thought that preconized that children were to be seen but not heard, and preferably not seen either. His nanny, who had arrived when his younger sister was born, had showed little interest in the serious and rather pompous little boy. The manners that Giles prized so highly had been the one way in which he had been able, as a child, to court his parents' approval.

Shame and the golden child

Shame commonly develops out of neglectful or abusive parenting, but it can also be found at the other end of the continuum in 'the golden child' of the family: the special child, apple of his father or mother's eye, who may seek to recreate for themselves in adulthood a world of which they are the centre, around which all turns, where no one can steal their thunder, while a self-castigating voice whispers in their ear.

Being the golden child is not always a bed of roses. Think for instance of the child on whom all the parents' hopes rest: "for he is destined for greatness". This may seem a wonderful vote of confidence in a child, yet it is founded on a parent's own dream for their progeny and is often a heavy burden to bear.

I have met a number of people who had been vested with quasi-messianic roles at birth, sometimes even told explicitly by their parents that they were born to save the fate of their community (whether religious, ethnic, or political), of the planet even, or else that they would become the first men and women of a new order. Two of these embraced their fate and did remarkable things, but needless to say they did not save the planet.

Faber, on the other hand, felt crushed by the role that had been foisted upon him. The youngest of five children by quite a few years, he was his parents' remaining hope for the survival of their community and the creation of a New World, which would be a better place for all. They had built a pioneering community in a small enclave in England in the 1930s and later joined up with two groups in Europe and America, but they needed someone of Faber's calibre, so they told him, to take it "to the next level and beyond".

F. *But the only beyond I could see was that it was all beyond me.*
L. *I'm not surprised!*
F. *I just wasn't cut out for it.*
L. *I didn't mean that you weren't cut out for it, but that it was a task that was beyond one human being!*
F. *I don't know. Father was amazing. He had such energy!*
L. *I can well believe it. He co-founded a small community and he was amazing at instilling commitment and hope, but even he could not create a New World.*
F. (Faber is silent) *It's good to hear you say these things. I realize that somehow I always sort of assumed that if only he'd had more time…*
L. *He would have changed the world?*
F. (Faber smiles, a sad smile, and shakes his head.)

Instead of seeing that his parents' expectations of him were totally unrealistic and could not be fulfilled, Faber had taken upon himself the responsibility, and the guilt, for not fulfilling them. So that by the time I met him, an old man, he had been feeling shame at his 'failure' and, tragically therefore, believed that his life had been wasted.

Whether embraced or taken on as a burden, the saviour birth-task is doomed to failure and the failed saviour to guilt and/or shame. Yet refusing to take up the role offered at birth is not easy. For it is more than a refusal to buy into a philosophy and a way of life: it is a refusal of the parents' (and the community's) Dream, viewed by them as the greatest act of disloyalty of all – and experienced as such by the child. In addition, the refusal of the saviour's role is an admission of vulnerability and ordinary human-ness. For a person to accept themselves as belonging to ordinary humanity when they were raised to believe they were so superior may become another source of shame... though mitigated by relief!

Born-to-be-saviours are quite extreme instances of parental wishes for their golden child. Far more common is the golden child vested with their father or mother's hope for a golden future or, more narcissistically, burdened with various roles and tasks – such as to honour them through reflected glory, to compensate for their failings, to redress an experienced imbalance within the family (e.g. between siblings or cousins), or avenge a slight. Indeed, it is not uncommon to see such dynamics and rivalries perpetuate themselves down the generations.

Existential guilt and toxic shame

While there was a strong focus on guilt in my existential psychotherapy training, I can't remember shame being discussed other than abstractly in relation to Sartre's famous passage in *Being and Nothingness*, in which a man peeping through a keyhole suddenly senses someone looking at him as he does so.

Existential therapy makes a valuable distinction between different forms of guilt – moral, neurotic and existential. Moral guilt is the feeling that results from taking responsibility for the wrong we have done or for our wrongs of omission. Neurotic guilt refers to the inappropriate experiencing of feelings of guilt – such as taking responsibility for what is not our responsibility or else feeling terribly guilty about something minor. Existential guilt is of a different order, it relates to our existence as a whole: it arises from the sense of failing ourselves in the way we lead our lives. It could be because we have tended to drift passively or reactively through life, rather than being in the driving seat, and feel no sense of ownership in the important moments of our lives; or because we feel we have not fulfilled our promise – we should/could have done better; or simply because we have followed one path that has prevented us from following another. Existential guilt can goad us into action. Yet it requires a degree of self-esteem, in that it reflects the sense of 'I owe it to myself'. For instance, we might feel we owe it to ourselves to let our voice be heard, to express our own needs and wishes, to stand up for ourselves and not allow others to treat us like doormats. And when we do not accord ourselves the rights, the place, or the choices that we feel we owe ourselves in life, deep regret ensues. Deep regret is an expression of existential guilt and can be a powerful catalyst for change.

Could there be a similar distinction to be made between moral, neurotic, and existential shame, I now asked myself. Corresponding to moral guilt – feeling guilty for a wrong we have committed, there is a manner of experiencing shame that could be called 'moral shame'. 'Moral' shame says: "this wrong that I did goes against the way I see myself and like to be – I have debased myself in my own eyes and in those of the people whose opinion I care about and I do not wish to do that again."

We could call 'neurotic shame', following the lines of neurotic guilt, a superficial embarrassment that we experience frequently and without much justification. That differs from 'toxic shame' which lodges itself in our core and attaches itself to the way we live our lives; in that sense, toxic shame could be said to be 'existential'. But, unlike the existential guilt that faces us with choices and possibilities – the guilt that asks "what do I want to do with my life now, so that I don't have deep regrets later?", toxic shame is so steeped in low self-worth, that it cannot ask that question. Instead it whispers: "you don't deserve anything better than this, you are not worth it". Toxic shame is judgemental in its essence; it prevents us from reflecting on our life situation dispassionately so as to make changes for the better. In that sense, while existential guilt opens up possibilities, toxic shame is more likely to close them off.

Toxic shame can be so pervasive and paralyzing that it requires a powerful force to counter it. So, how can we rid ourselves of it? Clearly, the self-aggrandizement of narcissism is not the answer. I would argue that rage is one such force, compassion another.

Countering shame: Rage

Rage is like a hurricane, it can burst dams and boundaries and overturn anything on its path. The danger is that rage can pull a person out of their paralyzing shame only to send them endlessly whirling into a vortex of equally painful and destructive emotions. Rage can turn against the perceived source of shame (the hypercritical parent or partner), or against the shamed self, and create havoc leading to violence, self-harm and even murder.

Who would have thought that Moritz, immensely successful and munificent, still suffered from shame and despair? Growing up in the shadow of his older sister, he was repeatedly told by his irascible and violent father that he was a good-for-nothing and would never amount to anything in life; he would be nothing but a "poor skivvy". And so Moritz set out to prove his father wrong. Rage he had in abundance, murderous rage at his violent father but also a rage for grabbing whatever he could (more or less legally) lay his hands on. He became a pugnacious businessman and, at 26, was already on the way to making a fortune. Every new acquisition felt like an act of revenge against his father. Yet his exultation at his one-upmanship over his father would quickly leave him feeling strangely empty and despairing. Not surprisingly: for no amount of success could bring him the recognition and love from his father that he had yearned for, and deserved, as a child. His success, as a rageful and vengeful response to his father's constant shaming, therefore still carried that shame at its very core.

Rage is not to be conflated with anger; rage is not simply a forceful acting out of anger. This is a serious misunderstanding. Rage is Janus-like, it faces in opposite directions: there is indeed the unrestrained venting of anger, as in so-called 'road rage' or at times in 'murderous rage'; and there is rage that has been channelled into a life force. The French speak of *la rage de vivre* (rage for life). Whereas *joie de vivre* describes a dynamic state, an upbeat attitude of acknowledgement, acceptance and contentment with life as it is, *rage de vivre* expresses a hunger for life – a forceful, forward-directed impulse. *A rage for life* implies an awareness of the precariousness of life. It is one aspect of what Peter Koestenbaum called 'the vitality of death', which I have witnessed time and again in my hospital work with people whose lives had been threatened. This rage and hunger for life can be channelled into a life force with the strength to surmount huge obstacles, but they may burst into a boundless, gluttonous craving for life. Therein lies their danger. In bursting their boundaries, rage and hunger for life lose their life-enhancing quality.

In Moritz' 'murderous rage', there was an element of wanting to act out his anger, yet his rage also contained a vigorous life force which he channelled into his work. It may well have blossomed in his personal life had it not been so intimately bound up with revenge.

The vicious cycle of humiliation/shame, boundless rage and despair is not only an individual person's experience, it can be shared with whole sections of society – such as ethnic, religious, or other minorities and the dispossessed – witness the rise of populist leaders in the Western world in recent years; and it can be observed at country level too – under dictatorships, colonial or wartime occupation for instance.

One of the most fascinating books I have read in recent years is a small monogram by James Gilligan[3] who, as a young forensic psychiatrist and junior lecturer at Harvard, began to question the astonishing and scandalous statistics of the prison population of the state of Massachusetts which was rife with homicides, suicides, riots, gang-rapes, cases of arson, and self-mutilation. He cites one high-security 600-strong prison which saw over 100 violent deaths in a decade. By the time he had been in charge of the state's prisons for ten years, the figure within the whole service had dropped to one homicide and two suicides, no riots or hostage taking. Gilligan developed a programme to counter what he saw as the root cause of violence: 'Shame as the pathogen that causes violence just as specifically as the tubercle bacillus causes tuberculosis'.[4] He highlights as the most common profile of violent prisoners a history of chronic shaming (by parents, peers, society) starting in childhood; this develops into a hypersensitivity to slights such that a minor perceived or imagined act of disrespect can trigger a very violent or even homicidal response. Indeed, the inmate's most common answer to "Why did you assault/kill x?" is "He dis'ed me" (i.e. disrespected me) (id. 29).

An act of humiliation is rather like the throwing of a gauntlet. There are a number of possible responses: one can go into a submissive stance; treat it with contempt; feel temporarily humiliated and outraged while retaining a sense of self-worth; or else pick up the gauntlet and rise to the challenge, either assertively or aggressively. Murderous rage is acted upon because, for the person who was 'dis'ed', it is as if nothing short of the other's death will allow them to survive. Violence becomes a way of maintaining face, proving manliness, but also of filling the emptiness within and erasing the shame, even if only temporarily.

Countering shame: Compassion and understanding

Rage is thus a double-edged sword in the fight against shame and humiliation: both sides have the power to cut through shame, yet only one side can channel itself into a life force, while the other may bring about a person's downfall.

There is another, surer way of freeing ourselves from the shackles of shame and humiliation, and that is to develop compassion for ourselves. The first step, however, is to uncover and articulate the shame-laden beliefs which hold us in their iron grip and impact our behaviour, and reflect on their possible source. There are so many possible sources of shame: a specific shaming event (at school, in the street, at work, etc.); the drip, drip, drip of small put-downs, dismissive remarks, insults and injustices, or of being called by an unpleasant nickname; discriminatory and shaming messages, whether explicitly voiced by society or transmitted in an implicit manner; the message read in a parent's eyes, from which the child develops a sense of being shame-ful, long before that word, and others like 'sinful', 'contemptible', or 'undeserving' enter their vocabulary. The young child simply reads it as "you are bad/there is something wrong with you". Not surprisingly, such forever-held beliefs are difficult to shift. Unlike the mild and potentially healthy shame that engages our freedom to aim for better behaviour next time, such pervasive shame has the paralyzing force of fatalism: "I have always been a good-for-nothing" or "I am sinful". For these are forms of self-definitions and self-definitions leave very little opening for change. Yet, change can begin to take place, as I have repeatedly witnessed, when the client understands how the belief and sense of being bad arose and can then show some compassion for their younger self.

Reality testing of the word 'always' in "I have always been a ..." is one way of discovering some crack through which a different perspective, and with it hope, may appear, as here with Noah.

L. *You say you've* always *been a wastrel?*
N. *Yeah.*
L. *I am curious about that. Do you remember a time when you did not feel a wastrel?*
N. *No.*
L. *Do you believe that babies can be born wastrels?*
N. *No!!*

L. *Do you think a three-year old can be a wastrel?*

N. *No!!*

L. *Or a five-year old?*

N. *No!! And yet, I can remember feeling like that, even then. I remember it well.*

L. *I can well believe that, but doesn't 'wastrel' strike you as a very adult word for a young child to use about himself??*

N. *I hadn't thought of that, but my mother always said I was a wastrel.*

L. *Mmm.* I notice Noah's sharp intake of breath and a little collapse.

N. *How sad is that?!* (Noah looks sad, and I can sense his heart going out to his younger self.)

L. *Yes, it is sad ...it's really sad for you ...and actually for your mother too, I mean, to feel her little boy was a wastrel... she missed out on so much...*

N. *Yeah. I can see myself now. I was timid, but I was a sweet kid.*

L. *I bet you were.*

For Noah, this opened the door to the possibility that his shamefulness was maybe not intrinsic to himself, as he had originally thought.

This sort of questioning also introduces a sense of curiosity: where do my beliefs stem from? If from messages I received from my parents, what led them to view me and treat me that way? What was going on for them? What was their relationship like when I was conceived, when I was born, when I was growing up? How were they viewed and treated by their own parents, or their community? What got in the way of them seeing me for who I was, rather than a mere object of contempt, dislike, shame, sin, unworthy of any gentleness and nurturing attention?

Yet understanding the beliefs that underpin our shame is not simply an intellectual process: for these beliefs are embodied and intermingled with memories and emotions.

Penny's relationship with her husband had hit crisis point and she was experiencing feelings that she couldn't understand and feared were about to boil over uncontrollably. After a lifetime of moving house to follow her husband in his career, she had been looking forward to a settled life in the UK. They had found a wonderful house with glorious views that she had made into a beautiful home for their retirement – and now he was saying that he could not tolerate the climate of the British Isles and wanted to move to southern France.

From the way Penny spoke, I got the impression that her husband was unaware, or dismissive, of the difficulties that such a nomadic life had involved and of his wife's role in these moves – creating a home for their family 14 times in 33 years. The word 'dismissive' pushed a button; her husband, she said, was generally dismissive of her viewpoint, frequently made fun of her and put her down. She told me that on a number of occasions he had even humiliated her at social events in front of his colleagues and their partners. At such times, she had felt boiling anger, only to be followed a few moments later with a sense of helplessness and despair.

When asked whether there was anything that felt familiar in that sequence of emotions, Penny mentioned that she recognized in her boiling anger at her husband the same murderous rage that she had experienced as a child. Penny related how she came from a naval family. Her memories of her father and his long absences were imbued with grief, longing, fun and terror: for the delight and merriment that greeted his return were soon followed by snide remarks and fierce 'punishments' that made no sense to her, for she had done no wrong. Distant-looking, eyes cast-down, she recounted how he would lock her in his study and, without a word, lift up her skirt and beat her. She didn't know what had felt most terrifying and shaming: his cold silence, the injustice of the 'punishments', or the violence of the beatings. There had been something deeply humiliating about having to bend down with her skirt lifted. And then her face flushed and tensed as she shook her head, "sometimes, I just wanted to kill him". And then, as the slightly narrowed eyes, the frown, the clenching of the jaw suddenly disappeared and the tension in her neck and shoulders gave way to collapse, for the second time in that session, I witnessed the heat of Penny's rage increase towards boiling point, before suddenly tipping into powerlessness and despair.

Our work with the cycle of shame, rage and despair was two-pronged: we focused on both developing an embodied sense of assertiveness and mastery (*see Chapter 13 Claudine*) and exploring this embodied, emotional cycle as a variant on the victim–persecutor–rescuer dynamic known as the drama triangle (*see Glossary*). For Penny kept the dynamics at play well concealed:

Penny's friends were totally unaware of both her murderous rage ('persecutor' point on triangle) and her humiliation and despair ('victim') for she was extremely loyal to her husband and supportive of him in his work and professional entertaining (rescuer) and spoke admiringly of her father.

Although Penny had experienced the sudden shift from rage to powerlessness and despair on numerous occasions with her husband, she found it helpful to see and understand how that cycle of shifting dynamics had already developed in childhood.

Another aspect of our work involved her acknowledging how confusing her father's behaviour would have been for her younger self and feeling compassion for her.

This was difficult, slow work for Penny, because, despite it all, she had idolized her father and she felt little warmth for the awkward, shamed child that she had been. At the same time, Penny found it helpful to wonder, with compassion, about her father's own upbringing and his experiences in the navy (and his father's before that) and speculate about what might have led him to behave as he had.

With a better understanding of the dynamics at play, a greater sense of embodied assertiveness and more compassion for herself, Penny could begin to clarify her boundaries for herself – what she was and was not prepared to accept. So that when her husband put her down, she began to pick up the gauntlet and rise to the challenge assertively. And by learning how to stand her ground and get her viewpoint across, she facilitated a different relationship with her husband in which her voice was being heard and shame, resentment and rage no longer played a dominant role.

Conclusion

Whether our shaming beliefs stem from our family or from the society in which, for whatever reason, we may have felt ostracized growing up, we need to articulate these for ourselves. We need to notice the extent to which we may have internalized them emotionally, cognitively, bodily and how they might be affecting our very life force. Only then can we successfully challenge them and develop a different embodied sense of ourselves. This process of understanding and challenging requires a spirit of compassionate enquiry. For shame, judgemental and obfuscating, attaches itself to every fibre of the body, yet if we allow ourselves to shine some understanding upon it, without judgement or blame, acknowledging our younger selves' pain, it will enable self-compassion to shine through the shame and dissolve its pervading darkness.

And if we are kinder to ourselves from this position of broader understanding, this in turn will leave room for self-worth to grow. For understanding, (self-) compassion and self-worth are intimately linked together, as is the setting of healthy boundaries. Suffused with low self-worth, we feel undeserving of firm, protective boundaries, we treat ourselves as proverbial 'doormats', and leave ourselves open to abuses of power, intrusion and violation.

Compassionate understanding is not a fixed goal or destination: rather, the quest for it is a voyage of discovery during which it gradually unfolds and develops and, with it, greater well-being. The journey can be an arduous one at times and, before setting out, it is wise to reconnect with all that sustains us: our qualities, but also those things that nourish and support us, be it some time to ourselves, friendship, music, nature, sport, etc. And because shame is commonly experienced in the look (whether actual or imagined) of another, this quest is also likely to benefit from the presence of a person whose look can be trusted to be warm and non-judgemental. A good and kind therapist can facilitate the emergence of different perspectives, offer a touchstone against which to test them, model good boundaries, and offer warmth and compassion.

This, I think, was what my dream about Mark was trying to tell me that night (the dream that led me to writing this book). However difficult the journey might be, understanding, compassion and boundaries were the best route to helping him try to begin to acknowledge those parts of himself which he loathed and tried to deny; accept that he had acted as he had and was going to have to live with that reality, but understand that these actions were not committed in a vacuum, that they took place in a life that was still worthy of compassion – mine and, more importantly, his.

Notes

1 It is a tragic paradox that the person who has suffered the abuse should also feel the shame.
2 I am using the word here in the lay sense of the term.
3 Gilligan, J. (2001). *Preventing Violence*, New York: Thames and Hudson.
4 Gilligan op.cit.:30.

Chapter 7

Mothers
Challenges of Motherhood and Mothering

Some preliminary notes

Whatever the reason for accessing therapy, a client will almost invariably bring their mother and their relationship to her into the therapeutic space – whether she be still alive or long dead. The mother–child relationship, like the father–child one, is therefore an ideal Petri dish in which to culture understanding, compassion and boundaries, and observe their impact. At the heart of this chapter is the importance of developing some understanding and compassion towards our mothers and ourselves, and of reevaluating the boundaries we have set in our mother–child relationships.

This chapter does not aim to offer research-based expertise, nor to be a guide for mothers. Rather, it seeks to describe some of the intrinsic aspects of motherhood that make mothering such a challenge. My intention has been to try to normalize, and hence destigmatize, some of the difficulties that mothers face. For it is from a heartful understanding of the difficulties inherent in mothering that compassion for our mothers, and ourselves, can emerge.

As this book reflects my practice, I have not written about any specific aspect of LGBQT+ mothering, since almost all my clients were brought up by cisgender[1] mothers, whether single or part of a heterosexual couple, and most of my female clients with children have themselves been cisgender women in either heterosexual relationships or single.

The nanny and the nanny–child relationship deserve far more attention and compassionate understanding than I can offer them here. More adults are now accessing therapeutic help in mourning the loss of their ayas and nannies, their main childhood carers who in many cases seemed to have left, or been left behind, suddenly, never to be talked about again. These nannies and ayas, some hated, but many deeply loved by the children, are often the Cinderellas of this world, whose feelings are not sufficiently considered. Many of these women give of themselves to children who are not their own, without thinking to protect themselves from the terrible loss they might suffer at separation.

DOI: 10.4324/9781003364504-8

This chapter begins by highlighting pre-birth and peri-natal issues intrinsic to motherhood and hence inherent in the mother–child relationship. It then considers that relationship from various perspectives: boundaries, attunement, love, the need for recognition and loyalty. Chapters 8 and 9 then offer a series of vignettes of typically difficult mother–child relationships that I commonly encounter in my counselling room. Most of these stories are seen from the perspective of the adult client speaking of something that feels, or felt, amiss in their relationship to their mother, or in the way they were mothered. My aim here is not to judge and blame these particular mothers, let alone mothers in general, but to highlight the impact on the child of these difficult relationships and of the additional baggage that many mothers bring into them, whether they realize it or not.

Before baby is ever born; baby's birth

Motherhood *as an issue* is a given for a woman and is present from the earliest age. The female infant is born with her full complement of egg cells and, from puberty until the menopause, menstruation brings a girl, and later a woman, a monthly reminder of her potential to be a mother. A woman also has a 'biological clock' that ticks. However, some women know from an early age, and others may discover later, that their body does not enable them to conceive or carry a baby – they have somehow been denied the biological aspect of motherhood that is commonly taken for granted as a given of nature. Yet, all women are born to societal and familial contexts that take positions on motherhood, sometimes conflicting ones. Motherhood is therefore always a question: for women are inevitably confronted from a very young age to physiological, psychological, familial and societal contexts to which they will have to respond. In that sense, it could be said that a woman has a relationship with her baby before she ever gets pregnant or adopts; and mothering always occurs within a context that is much wider than the mother–child relationship.

It is a fundamental paradox of human existence that we are not born for our own sakes. A baby is born to parents out of an act of love, indifference, lust or violence, planned or unplanned, wanted or unwanted. A baby may also be born for the sake of convention and belief – that married women must bear children, that foetuses should under no circumstances be aborted; for someone else's sake – the grandparents', the family line; to save the marriage; as a hoped-for clone of a dead father or sibling; to harvest their stem cells; or as a saviour for the community. Even children who are wished-for without any ulterior agenda are not born for themselves: they are born for one or more of their parents. This paradoxical existential given is therefore, from the very beginning, an element of the mother–child relationship and will colour it to various degrees. The degree to which it does will depend on how well the parents will be able to learn to see their child, love and value them for who they are and not for what they, or others, had wanted them to become.

It is easy to forget that even in high-income countries pregnancy and labour can still be a dangerous time for mother and child.

Dahlia was one of the first of my post-Intensive Care clients to confront me with that tragic reality. Dahlia went through pregnancy cut off from all of her support networks. During labour she suffered life-threatening complications and was admitted to ICU. When she came round, she had forgotten that she had given birth. This shock was followed by weeks on the unit, desolate and terrified, unable to be with her baby who herself lay in a special care neo-natal unit.

Babies may also be taken away from their mother, or given up by her, for fostering or adoption. How will that experience affect the mother and her relationship to her other children if she has any? And will that baby find a mother who is ready and able to acknowledge and manage the immensity of this primal loss?

Even where there is no such life-threatening or extreme trauma, a mother and child's experience of pregnancy and labour may impact on their relationship.

June's mother had suffered a minor injury and, for a few weeks after birth, carrying and feeding her baby had felt excruciatingly painful. When June developed into a clingy child, her mother had felt guilty assuming that it was due to a lack of early closeness. Whether or not her assumption was correct, it had given rise to a guilt which was colouring her relationship to her daughter.

While the context of a baby's conception and birth is likely to have some impact on the nature and quality of the mother's relationship to her baby, there is no doubt that many an unwanted pregnancy and baby will become a cherished, well cared-for child, as will babies born in seemingly less than favourable conditions. (Sadly the opposite is also true.)

The boundary dances of mother and child

Observation and micro-analysis of mothers and their infants, and recent research in the neurosciences, show the human baby as born to relate; and just as well, for the human baby is born totally dependent, with a need for a longer apprenticeship than any other mammal. The mother's path from physical fusion, total responsibility and care for her baby to her lack of any legal rights over her 18-year-old adult child is littered with obstacles, as is the child's path from fusion and total dependency to a sense of personal identity and independence. Both mother and child will therefore need to negotiate the changes of boundaries this journey requires. This process of gradual separation and individuation *for both mother and child*, even when sustained by love, acceptance, prizing, joy and fun, and satisfactorily managed, will be marked, on both sides, by varying degrees of anxiety, frustration, anger, sadness and grief.

Some biological, historical, psycho-socio-economic contexts will smooth that path, others, such as the lack of basic safety and necessities, the mother's 'baggage', political or domestic violence, substance misuse, severe 'mental health issues'[2] and trauma – whether the mother's or the child's – will make it far more arduous. Thus, a baby may be born to a mother who is deeply depressed, traumatized, or grieving, unable to take good care of herself and her child. Despite her wish to love and care for her child, she may be hampered by a pervading sense of disconnect and numbness, or by overwhelming strong and frightening emotions.

Early motherhood is a time for rhythms and patterns to emerge – between day and night, waking and sleeping, feeding and comfort sucking, stimulation and quiet – and for an intricate dance to form between mother and baby. There are so many different dances for the mother to learn, ever changing, with complex steps and choreographies specifically created for each mother and child couple.

There are the dances of love and needs – the mother and the child's; of chastisement and repair; the dances of emotions – some in which her joy, anxiety, frustration, or anger lead, others where it is the child's own heightened emotions that take the lead. There are the dances of closeness and distance, holding onto and letting go; the various dances around food; and let us not forget the cleanliness and potty-training dances. These mother–child dances are not created once and for all: the steps and rhythms frequently change and are different with each child; they may need to be relearnt yearly, monthly, or even weekly. The art of improvisation is also called upon.

Although this is not a dance competition, mothers often look to other mother–child's dances to see how theirs compare: the various stages of child development are treated as so many 'achievements' to tick and, as such, carry much unnecessary anxiety, shame, pride and frustration – for mother and child. Mothers tend to forget that, unless prevented by a disability or by some other major factor, all children end up walking, talking and being toilet trained and that none of these are regarded as noteworthy achievements later in life. Each child seems to develop according to their own clock or calendar: one of my children rolled onto their back at 2.5 months and walked at 13 months, another could not sit themselves up or roll over until 16 months and had their second birthday sitting down. By the time they were three, all such milestone differences had been ironed out.

Dances are also culture-bound and have their fashions: at times, more stilted and controlled, choreographed and learnt; at others, freer, with room for improvisation. Mothers are left with the tough task of finding their own way through old lore, assumptions and fashions about what is 'right', 'common sense', 'natural', 'expected' and 'desirable' and see how that fits with their own personal felt sense, needs and beliefs. In Normandy, for instance, it was once accepted practice – so 'right' and 'common sense' – to put Calvados in the bottles of sickly-looking babies to perk them up or else at bedtime, with equally disastrous consequences for their cognitive development. And the stakes can be similarly high today, as in the early days of COVID vaccinations when scientific advice was competing not only with misinformation and conspiracy theories but with other scientific advice.

However much wonder and joy motherhood may bring, first time motherhood is commonly very anxiety-provoking. Whose advice is the new mother to believe? Her peers may not be much more experienced than herself. Her own mother and mother-in-law's advice comes with family dynamics and baggage attached; that of experts is ever changing, sometimes from one decade to the next, or more frequently still. In addition, such advice so often takes on the character of an injunction to be disregarded at the baby's peril and the mother's shame. So the new mother is left having to juggle all these together with her own gut feelings and her sense of her young child.

Intricate, complex and emotionally charged dances *à deux* with swift changing rhythms are hard to learn. They require exquisite sensing, listening, tuning into, following, and turn-taking. A large dose of compassion may be needed to look back at how this was done: for we each have our own expectations and dreams of what having a loving, caring mother should be like, and we have strong feelings when our experience of being mothered (or of ourselves as mothers) has fallen well short.

Attunement

Mothering fashions – whether in feeding, dressing and transporting babies, or regarding discipline and educational priorities – vary across cultures and historically within a country. These fashions partly reflect the traits that each society prizes in its citizens. Thus, in the West today, autonomy, drive, teamworking and creativity are highly prized goals; greater independence for women is valued; 'mental health' is beginning to find a place on the agenda. And attunement to the child – allowing a sense of self and agency to develop – is regarded as a vital route in developing and attaining them. Yet these same qualities may be a luxury where the fight for survival is uppermost and they are counterproductive in societies where obedience, discipline, or devoutness are the variously desired goals.

It is interesting that 'attunement' does not merit an entry of its own in the dictionaries which I have consulted. It is only appended to the definition of 'attune' as a tuning or bringing into harmony. However it has taken a life of its own in psychology, where it defines a particular way of listening out for, being aware of the emotions of others and responding to them. With an older child, attunement necessarily involves sensitively and kindly navigating a compromise between what the child wants, what they need, the givens of the situation, and our own needs (for instance, our need for a little time for ourselves and for sleep). The particular qualities required – the ability to listen to and acknowledge the other and then respond appropriately – involve compassionate understanding, of the child and oneself, as well as a negotiation of boundaries. But with infants, how can we tell what constitutes good attunement? Take the everyday matter of baby feeding. Clearly, the rigid regime which was mine as a post-war baby – six four-hourly feeds, with weighing before and after each – paid no attention to a baby's individual wants and needs. Nor, arguably, was it conducive to developing a sense of agency – as when a baby cries and mother comes. But a child's wants were probably not high up on societal priorities at the time, and obedience was often prized over agency. Advice has now swung to the other extreme with feeding 'on demand', and I have seen mothers run ragged and drained, trying to attend night and day to their babies' every cry. A baby's needs and demands are complex and require interpreting: besides their need for food, a baby has a need for sucking, for drink (as opposed to food), for comfort, connection, and interaction. Responding with food to a baby's every need (other than a dirty nappy) cannot be fully attuned. Yet, paradoxically, both extremes come from a wish to do what is best for the child.

Aiming for perfection as a mother, *or hoping for perfection in a mother*, is unrealistic and unhelpful for both mother and child. To reach the perfect ten of mothering at all times is not within the realm of possibility: it requires the patience of a saint, the wisdom of sages, exquisite attunement, and many qualities beside. Better to remember that mothers each have their own strengths: some feel comfortable with the soothing and caring that an infant requires, some with facilitating their older child's tasks without getting into conflicts of will; some mothers are good at making things fun or at developing their child's taste for adventure; some are creative or good teachers. Aspects of motherhood that come naturally to some mothers may leave others feeling deskilled, anxious, depressed, out of control, helpless – and guilt-ridden. Each woman also brings personal traits to mothering: some are fighters, have depths of grit, resilience and perseverance, some softness, great patience, or acute psychological intuition. Yet it is important to remember that every mother has *something* to offer her child, in the very worst case scenario be it 'only' life and a historical line.

Each mother has her qualities, and each has her own trigger points: through her own personal history and baggage, a mother may be variously triggered by her child's emotions – for instance by her child's anxiety, frustration, or exuberance. She may be triggered by her child's actions such as rejection, proximity-seeking, talking back, staring, etc. Some mothers are triggered by their child's milestone events (starting school, puberty), by their failures, their successes, or by their very touch. Without an awareness of her triggers and an understanding of their origin, a mother's reactions may be confusing and scary for herself and her child, and they may bring with them guilt, shame and fear. So that awareness and understanding are the first step to (self)compassion.

Each mother has her qualities and trigger points, and she will also have her faults, including loving to a fault.

Many a mother would give her life for her child's, but when Connie, speaking of her now adult son, exclaimed "I loved him too much" she was expressing something else. She had come to realize that this 'too much' of love, this intensity and proximity that had existed between her and her son had not been helpful for him. For in this intensity, in this excess of love, was a weight that she had heaped on him: the weight of her own dreams for him and of her own anxieties. She knew he loved her, yet she could see that being with her was often too much for him, so that sometimes, for a year or longer, he felt the need to keep his distance from her.

'Too much' love is heavy for a child to bear, it can feel suffocating, too great a responsibility, alienating. In that sense, while 'too big' may be bigger than 'big', 'too much' love is never more than 'love'.

When clients want to start exploring their early relationship to their mother, or their relationship to their own child, I sometimes give them a cushion and ask them to hold it the way they sense they were held as babies and notice what happens in themselves as they do so. I have witnessed so many moving reactions as, for instance:

Billie holds the cushion with tense, outstretched arms, eyes wide open in terror.
Pam with her fingertips, a look of disgust on her face.
Arabella holds the cushion anxiously, awkwardly.
Emilia smiles beatically yet grips it tight enough to suffocate it.
Jo throws it across the room.
While Joanne, unable to hold it all, puts it on her lap and stares numbly before her.

And of course there will be clients who cradle the cushion gently while gazing lovingly at it. Observing the way the 'baby' cushion is held or placed can highlight the emotional colour, distance, feel and intensity of the relationship, and for the client, experiencing it can be revelatory. Maternal boundaries have a certain quality: they may be ultra-permeable, flexible, solid, rigid...; they can be thought through and reasonable; visceral, unpredictable and incomprehensible. While cushion work cannot easily show these characteristics, it can illustrate fusional and blurred boundaries, as well as show the (in)consistency and (un)predictability of the relationship as the mother holds the cushion suffocatingly close one moment only to cast it away two minutes later.

And then there were three: the mobile phone, as an extension of human verbal communication, of human *being* even, has become so ubiquitous that we are oblivious to the way it might be invading the boundary of mother–child intimacy. And that, despite our own frustration at a partner or teenage child constantly on their mobile in our company. The issue with mobiles in the mother–child relationship, as in any relationship, is one of boundaries in space and time: where is it taking us away from those with whom we are sitting, and for how long?

Love, the need for recognition, and loyalty

There are two aspects of love in the mother–child relationship that never cease to amaze me: the first is a mother's almost boundless *potential* for love. A mother's heart is so wide it can *potentially* hold love for any number of children: loving one child 'with all her heart' does not mean that she cannot equally love another. (Love is different from maternal feelings – a woman may not feel maternal yet love her child.). Sadly, this does not mean that all mothers love their children, nor that they treat them equally, far from it; but I believe it means that, where that love is or appears to be absent, or else is unfairly distributed, it is helpful to try to understand why that may be so.

And, mirroring a mother's almost boundless potential for love is a child's often lifelong desire and need for recognition and love. This may foster an equally boundless sense of loyalty to the mother, however cold, cruel, or abusive she may have been – though the loyalty is likely to conflict with feelings, more or less acknowledged, of resentment, anger, hurt, terror and hatred. Such is the child's tragedy and may become the adult's. "But she's my mother" is a phrase I have heard countless clients use to explain their loyalty to their mother, and their "forgiveness" for her neglectful, cruel, or abusive behaviour towards them. I put forgiveness in inverted commas, because, invariably, there are mixed emotions at play as the urge to forgive coexists with the urge to throw the whole weight of their hurt, shocked disbelief ("how could you do this to me?"), resentment and anger at her, to destroy her even.

I believe that just as a therapist should encourage the client to try to understand why a mother behaved as neglectfully or cruelly as she did, so too there are times when the therapist should help the client to question their closeness and loyalty to a parent. Especially when the parent has been neglectful or abusive and made no genuine attempt to repair. The aim is not to put an end to that closeness and loyalty but to ascertain whether the client is fully aware of the beliefs and emotions that might be underpinning it.

I am thinking of Bill for instance who hardly went out of the house, taking anxious care of his now elderly mother, although by now he knew that his mother's threats of suicide that had plagued his childhood and adult life were likely to be just empty threats. Yet, he could not give up now, for whether or not she did put her threats into action while he was out, either way it would make a nonsense of all these past years. Bill realized that his relationship to his mother reflected a loyalty which was costing him dearly, yet it felt better to him than giving up on it, as it risked making a non-sense of his very life.

Bronwen's loyalty to her mother, on the other hand, did not survive the challenge to which it was put. Bronwen had repeatedly expressed her reluctance to leave her young daughter with her parents overnight, without voicing any reasons other than her being "a bit young". For years, she had taken her mother's side in blaming Beth for "inventing" a story of sexual abuse at their father's hands. Beth's estrangement had been the price of Bronwen's loyalty to their mum. But the time had now come for Bronwen to address what at some level she knew to be true. She now realized that she had not wanted her mother to feel the guilt of collusion, let alone relive some of the darker secrets of her own childhood to which she had occasionally alluded. But she could no longer take her mother's side, she could not risk her daughter paying the heavy price Beth had paid.

As to Maria's story, it illustrates how a child's loyalty to the mother who abandoned them can anaesthetize the deepest pains of rejection.

Maria was 6 when her mother left her and her father to live with another man. Thirty five years on, and a mother herself, Maria found the total silence from her mother beyond comprehension. She still had memories of baking and doing craft with her, only happy memories, which made her sudden disappearance from her life so confusing. She set out to trace her, which proved surprisingly easy, and rang her up. When her mother picked up the phone, Maria told her "I'm Maria, your daughter"; they had a civil conversation but the mother said she had a new family and did not want to meet Maria. Maria replied "I quite understand".

Maria's loyalty coexisted with a hurt so great that it was there as a thread that ran through her whole life. Yet as she told me her story, it was hard to detect any sadness in her voice or demeanour, let alone anger – though the pain palpably seeped through her story into the room.

When it comes to the adopted child, divided loyalties between birth mother and adoptive mother, together with conflicting emotions towards each, can become an emotional battlefield where civil war rages. And it can become a civil war because the child's loyalty to their mother has been divided in two, because both mothers may share the one child's heart. Whereas one mother can potentially hold any number of children in her heart with equal love and without confusion, for a child to share love and loyalty between two mothers is at some level utterly confusing and guilt inducing: who is more deserving, the mother who gave me life but died/abandoned me/did not clean up her act sufficiently for me, or the mother who has accepted me, welcomed me into her family and taken care of me, yet did not give birth to me and to whom I am not genetically related? Every birthday can reignite the idealization of the birth mother together with the pain, anger, and incomprehension at having been given/taken away; every argument with the adoptive mother can lead to the glorification of, and yearning for, the idealized birth mother. And where an agreement is later reached with the birth family regarding contact, every letter from, or visit to, the birth family brings to the fore the confusion of belonging and not belonging to each family, and the sense of divided family loyalties.

Some adopted children and their families manage to negotiate the situation well, but it requires immense tact, patience, self-denial and compassionate understanding. 'Self-denial' in that each mother has to not only acknowledge the other mother but also honour her for her contribution to her child's life.

Johnston's story: Loyalty, and the need for recognition and love

What touched me most particularly about Johnston, beside the poignancy of his story and his willingness and honesty in delving into painful and difficult feelings, was his sense of having striven all of his adult life to be a good man and his disappointment with himself at not having made a better job of it. He felt that despite always trying to be reasonable, kind, generous and fair, he had not managed to develop close relationships with his family, who saw him as over-cautious and "wet"; in addition, this striving for carefully deliberated, fair and kind action had stunted all spontaneity in him.

Like so many of my clients of African-Caribbean origin, Johnston grew up with his grandmother in the Caribbean until, as a teenager, he was called by his mother to come and live in London with her and her other children – younger siblings about whose existence he had been totally unaware. Unbeknown to him, he had stepped into a vipers' nest of family dynamics, and he had had great trouble understanding the conflicting demands made on him by various family members. He had tried to do his best by his mother and each sibling and was still flummoxed by the incomprehensible anger with which they had responded to his efforts.

When his mother returned to Trinidad some years later, he rang her twice a week and supported her financially, though she showed scant interest in him and his children, even following his serious accident. He also regularly sent her generous gifts for which she never thanked him.

L. *Hmm. You mean your mother never thanks you when you send her a gift?*

J. *Well, that's what children should do, send gifts to their mum.*

L. *Oh OK. And if you were living in Trinidad and your eldest son sent you a gift?*

J. *Well, if any of my children sent me gifts, it would be precious to me.*

L. *Mmm... Your children's gifts would be precious to you.*

J. *Of course...Hmm...*Looks quizzical. *I suppose she is taking the barrels and money for granted. I've been doing it for so long... I suppose she's taking me for granted... Well, she's not interested in me, not even after my accident....I could've died.* Looks despondent and then rather perplexed. *Why am I ringing her like that all the time? She clearly isn't bothered with what I tell her.*

L. *Mmm, why are you ringing her?*

J. *Well, that's what a dutiful son does.*

L. *Mmm... OK... Is that the only reason?*

J. *Maybe I'm hoping that one day she'll tell me I did good.*

L. *That you did good?*

J. *That I'm a good son.*

L. *That you're a good son? Don't* you *think you've been a good son?*

J. *Yes, I have, but it would be good to hear her say it.*

L. *Yes, it would. It would also be good to hear her say she loved you and valued you. You could imagine it would be a simple thing for a mother to say to her son, her dutiful eldest son.*

J. *But she's never said that to me my whole life.*

L. *No, and that's sad; that's very sad.*

J. *You know all along I thought I was just being a dutiful son ... I hadn't realized how much I just wanted to hear her say: "Johnston, you're a good son".*

This exchange heralded for Johnston the beginning of an exploration of his boundaries with his mother. Johnston continued to be a dutiful son, which was of paramount importance to him: he rang his mother and sent her gifts; but he rang far less frequently and only sent gifts for specific occasions. A part of him still hoped beyond hope that she would give him the recognition he craved, that she could show him an ounce of love, but he was gradually coming to terms with the fact that this was unlikely to happen. His new boundaries allowed Johnston to focus less on gaining his mother's recognition and more on what he felt was missing most poignantly in his life: spontaneity and joy.

Notes

1 That is, women who identify as women and were assigned the female sex at birth.

2 *For my use of inverted commas, see Glossary 'mental health issues'.*

Chapter 8

Mothers

Some Mother–Child Stories of Narcissism, Absence, and Trauma

Mothers are the objects of myths, fantasies and legends. As goddesses of earth and creation throughout the myths of ancient cultures, as virginal Mother of God, as figures of selflessness and saintliness in children's litera- ture, in art and implicitly in many modern adverts. They are objects of myth- like beliefs such as the myth of the innate maternal instinct that all women except 'unnatural mothers' have. Meanwhile, the wicked stepmothers of fairy tales and children's literature carry all fantasized evil and fears about mothers. Shorn of fantasy, the reality of motherhood still spans the whole continuum from selflessness to source of horror and terror. While in moments of fury or despair many mothers might feel like throwing in the towel and walking out, in times of real crisis, these same mothers may sacrifice their health, their life even, for their child. However, a therapist's consulting room is also witness to the extremities of cruelty to which mothers may resort.

In some of the vignettes that follow, I may appear to be judgemental. There is some confusion, I believe, about the injunction for therapists to be 'non-judgemental'. It is not up to us, as therapists, to judge our clients, their parents and partners, as human beings; this does not mean that we must condone all behaviour however hurtful. To do so is potentially a form of collusion and would be mystifying for the client; it is a breach of therapeutic honesty and hence of trust. We can try to help clients to acknowledge what happened and what is, to understand, with compassion, the context and possible reasons that led to that behaviour (theirs or the significant others'), to facilitate the exploration of feelings surrounding it and to examine various possible ways of responding to it now. I do not see it as contradictory to say that I am occasionally angered, horrified or even revulsed by some of the behaviour of some of my clients, their partners or parents, yet do not judge them as human beings.

Narcissistic mothers

The narcissistic[1] mother could be viewed almost as a therapeutic cliché: widely depicted in films and novels, the butt of therapy jokes, and the subject of

DOI: 10.4324/9781003364504-9

countless psychological self-help books. However, though often a caricature of herself, the narcissistic mother is no joke. The narcissistic mother is a
familiar figure in the counselling room, though more commonly brought in
by the client, rather than as client herself. The crux of the matter is that the
narcissistic mother cannot step out of her self-centred world-view: she cannot
see beyond her own needs and emotions, her own interpretation of situations
and ways of doing things; nor can she accept to be challenged. She cannot
even conceive of a valid world-view other than her own. The narcissistic
mother's partner may choose to submit to all her whims, even enjoy the role
in which they are cast, or else find a suitable compromise such as putting up
with her self-centredness at home, while carving out a different life for themselves outside. If however her partner offers no alternative perspective to her
own in the home, the consequences for her children may be devastating: for a
very narcissistic mother cannot see her children as separate beings with qualities, interests, emotions and opinions of their own, to be valued for their
own sakes. She cannot conceive that their thoughts and feelings could hold
any interest for her. Challenge and disobedience on their part are *lèse-majesté*
and tantamount to betrayal: "And after all I went through for them!" The
narcissistic mother's children are, as it were, mere extensions of herself, to
be valued for any beneficial role they might have, as mother's 'little soldier',
fashion accessory, confidant, her 'cross to bear', as someone who might bring
her added glory or, in Helen's case, who would be her mirror:

*Helen would like a better relationship with her narcissistic mother. While on a
good day she can be charmed by her mother's charisma, glamour and exuberant
eccentricity, at other times spending a few hours with her mother can leave
Helen oscillating between shame, fury and revulsion. Often the very thought of
her touch makes her cringe.*

*I point out to Helen that she cannot change her mother, so if she wants a
better relationship with her mother, she will have to discover a way of relating to
her that feels more satisfying. She needs to set aside any goal of feeling seen and
heard as she would like to be. This does not mean that it is totally inconceivable
that her mother could change, only that it is pointless to aim to change her.*

*Thinking of her mother's own upbringing helps Helen to put her behaviour
in context and feel some compassion for her. But the dual focus of the work for
Helen is understanding for herself the impact at different levels of growing up
within her mother's orbit, as well as learning how to deal with her now.*

*Though Helen is 44, she still has trouble looking at herself through her own
eyes: every so often when she glances in the mirror, she catches sight of an
extremely attractive and engaging woman, and there is an uncanny, split second,
double-take as she realizes that this reflection is her own. But usually a film of
criticism and shame comes between herself and her reflection; she is still seeing
herself through her mother's eyes. Helen's mother had wanted a 'mini-me', a
little girl who reflected her beauty and glamour, whom she could take for a walk
and dress up, like wealthy ladies and their lap dogs.*

H. *Instead, she got me – a podgy, clumsy, sullen-looking child as she kept telling me. Tim, my brother, was fine, he was a boy and he loved his role as mother's little knight errant. And dad, poor dad, he revered mother and just went along with her.*

In her teenage years, Helen's mother started berating her for being "unfeminine" and "awkward".

H. *She threw scorn on any views I expressed. I felt she was ashamed to be seen with me. I retreated into my books, and became a "blue stocking" – my mother's worst insult for a young woman. And I came to feel comfortable in that thick, knitted blue-stocking skin of mine that obscured all my shapes. And then at college one day, a friend saw a photo of my parents at my age and said how I was my mum's spitting image. It was like… wow! I couldn't believe it! Why hadn't I seen it before?!*

Her friend's remark had turned Helen's world upside down: nothing made sense any more – why had her mother told her she was awkward and unfeminine if she had looked so much like her? And who was she if she wasn't that blue stocking?

Helen's mother had wanted a 'mini-me' who would add to her 'glamour', yet when the mirror did begin to reflect the picture of a young woman who resembled her younger self, she could not acknowledge the resemblance. Was it that she had wanted a mirror, but one that, like Snow-white's stepmother's, told her she was still the most beautiful of all? Or was there something in that reflection – a reminder of something maybe, which she did not want to see? Disastrously for Helen, by denying her any entitlement to her own personality, opinions, even body-shape and emotions, her mother had signalled that these were to be ashamed of. So Helen had experienced her shapely body, her "blue-socking" self, and the intellectual interests and pursuits that were intimately linked to that self, as shameful. She had felt a failure in her mother's eyes and shame-ful to her very core.

In therapy, as Helen revisits the past, she begins to feel wells of compassion for her young "sullen" self – she realizes how difficult and painful it would have been for a child to be treated like a misbehaving lap-dog. But thinking of her "awkward, unfeminine", young teenage self still fills her with disgust and shame.

L. *You know, Helen, I think the emotions of teenage years can be so intense, it's often really difficult to take a step back and look at our teenage selves without seeing ourselves as we did then. But your teenage self deserves as much compassionate understanding as your younger, "sullen" self. Do you have any photos of yourself at that age?*

H. *Yes. I always look unbearably self-conscious.*

L. *Is that any surprise?! I suggest you dig one or two out and try and look at them with softer, more compassionate eyes.*

At the following session:

H. *You remember you suggested I dig out some photos of me as a young teenager? I've brought one along. When I saw mum with her photo-face hogging the centre stage and me shrinking in the background... I just cried. I was only 4 years older than Rosie now (Helen's daughter), I was only a child, and I did look awkward, I was awkward, but I looked nice.*

L. *It's strange isn't it how we see different things when we look differently. I do think it is important for you to learn to see this young teenage Helen differently and to value her. Because I think that, still now, when you look in the mirror, it's that teenager full of shame that you are looking at and that is looking back at you.*

H. *Mmm... It's like I am always looking through one of those fairground distorting mirrors. And then sometimes, for a split second, the mirror becomes normal and I see a completely different me.*

L. *Yes, that does sound like what's happening.*

It is slow work as Helen tries to practise self-compassion and develop more satisfactory boundaries in her relations with her mother. At times Helen really feels the need to protect herself from being 'hooked in' by her, especially on her mother's hypercritical and high drama days. She does not yet feel able to let her know when she is being unacceptably hypercritical and hurtful, however she does get pleasure from acknowledging to her those times when she has enjoyed her company. For Helen, and maybe her mother too, it is work in progress.

The absent mother

The expression 'absent mother' tends to conjure up images of the hardworking mother – whether the mother who has to do two or more jobs to make ends meet, or the ambitious career woman. The experience of a mother who is not there when children get back from school, working late into the evening, unable to attend school events, too tired or distracted to be emotionally present commonly breeds resentment in her children; however that resentment is often mixed with some admiration for her hard work, and gratitude. On the other hand, the absent mother who is physically present, yet 'not there', who is but an empty shell of a mother, is a very confusing figure for her children. Even in adulthood they may have trouble articulating what was going on, how they felt, and how they now feel.

Susan

"Depressed" is as far as Susan has got in trying to make sense of her mother. Yet 'depressed' has become a blanket term which conveys neither the specificity of

her mother's experience nor Susan's felt sense of her. She describes her mother's wan smile and the tired look in her eyes that accompanied every greeting – first thing in the morning as she prepared breakfast, after school, at bedtime. Seldom raising her voice in anger, never expressing a sense of fun or joy, never marvelling at anything – a piece of artwork, high marks, sporting success, let alone her daughter's development into an intelligent and impressive young woman. Susan cannot remember her mother being actively unkind, but she cannot remember more than a couple of acts of kindness either. Her mother simply did not engage with her, other than by providing food, drink and clean clothes and politely asking after her school day at dinner time. She was somehow just not there. (Father was not there much, but at least he was somewhere *– he was at work.) Home felt like an abyss of emptiness: inside her mother, between her parents, between her mother and herself, and still now in Susan's heart and stomach as she thinks of her childhood and adolescence. And with that emptiness, a "fathomless sadness". Susan loves her mother and now believes her mother probably loves her, but with a sterile love that never blossoms and blooms. As she says this, a flicker of anger appears and quickly dies down. It is difficult to be angry at an empty shell.*

We acknowledge and explore how confusing absent mothering is for a child: for like so many children with absent mothers, Susan had deduced from her mother's lack of interest and loving care towards her, that she was not worthy of interest, care or love. At university her first relationship had "verged on the abusive" – it can be difficult to find someone who truly values you, when you do not value oneself. However, when Susan became deeply involved in political activism, not only did she discover a purpose that filled some of her emptiness, but for the first time she was able to feel genuinely valued. That is where she had met Nick. Again, her mother had greeted their engagement with polite congratulations and that same wan smile. And as Susan speaks, I notice once more an angry frown, followed by a look of great sadness.

We both agree that to be able to express hurt, annoyance and frustration at her absent mothering might be a helpful first step towards allowing the scarier emotions of grief and anger for the loving mother-daughter relationship that never was and was unlikely to ever be. Susan can just catch a sense of their edges, somewhere in the shadows of her being.

We decide that trying to understand with compassion her mother's absence and her father's disconnect might bring some life and colour into the blurred, grey picture.

Susan cannot gather many more facts directly from her parents. But as she puts together what she does know about her grandparents, about her parents' own upbringing and the difficulties they would have faced as children during the war, it allows a story to emerge that fleshes out her mother's emptiness and makes plausible sense of her absent parenting. Susan knows it isn't necessarily the truth of the matter, yet it contains sufficient truth to breathe life into a sterile situation. It helps her make sense of her experience and minimize the unworthiness that she still feels at times, without placing all the blame on her parents.

Susan decides that, instead of the perfunctory visit to her mother every few months, she would like to see whether she can instil any vitality or meaningfulness into their meetings. It is no longer the hope of a close mother-daughter relationship that guides her, but the desire to understand her now elderly mother a little better in the time they have left. And even if she doesn't, it might be good to spend some time with her, without her usual feelings of emptiness and unworthiness.

When trauma takes centre stage

Violent, tragic and very distressing events have the power to emotionally destroy a whole family. How well the family survives such events is not a matter of 'strength' and 'weakness'. These are unhelpful, judgement-laden concepts which I like to deconstruct with clients as they are commonly misunderstood and come with a baggage of misplaced pride, shame and guilt. More important are the ways in which the trauma is dealt with and spoken of at the time; the meaning and place given to it by the person(s) concerned and by the family as a whole; as well as family dynamics. In some families, one member will implicitly be left to carry the burden for the whole family: that person may suffer in silence and unnoticed; they may become central to the family as all tiptoe around them; or become demonized as 'mad' (with a psychiatric diagnosis), 'bad' or 'dangerous'. One family may react as if a bomb had hit it, with desolation centre stage and family members scattered on the periphery, wandering around staring at the hole at its centre; the trauma may also be the elephant in the room – invisible, unspoken.

Family secrets and lies are mystifying; they can be traumatic:

In Paul and Catherine's family, mealtimes were like being in a Carmelite monastery where all had taken a vow of silence; they never did find out what had made their mother always look so sad, a bleak presence in their midst.

As to Bernice's mother, she would cook for her children, then eat her own dinner locked in her room. Who knows what secret lay behind her unusual behaviour.

In other families, the trauma that takes centre stage is known. The three vignettes that follow illustrate three very different stories of traumatic loss and mother–child relationships.

Mary's story: Where Mourning reigns

Mary had avoided therapy for decades; it could hardly be described as a fear of raking up the past, for the past was omnipresent and held her whole family in its grip. Mary's double tragedy, and her family's, was the result of her parents' reaction to the loss of their eldest daughter. Alice had been Mary's adored sister, the golden girl of the family: kind, hard-working, fun, attractive, the ideal daughter whose qualities, it would seem, none of her three younger sisters could emulate, certainly not in their mother's eyes. She had made that quite clear to them. It was as if Alice's fatal accident had also brought about her mother's death, a living death, and from that moment on, centre stage within the family, there stood a huge statue of Alice with their mother, in tears at her feet. Her husband, Mary's father, had made it clear to his daughters that their priority was to avoid causing their mother any further distress – and first of all that meant recognizing that their own grief was as nothing compared to their mother's. Implicit, yet equally clear was that Mum's sanity and survival depended on this. Even Alice's young husband seemed to have picked up the message that his ever going out with another woman would be more than Mum could bear. So, life went on in this manner for the rest of Mary's childhood: they tip-toed around Mum who wailed behind closed doors, sometimes threatening suicide, with Mary fearful of falling asleep at night in case her mother were to act on her threats. Needless to say Christmas had ceased to exist, birthdays were cursory affairs.

Mary and her sisters found different ways of bearing this almost unendurable double burden. Mary married very young and left home. With courage, and the help of a very understanding and compassionate husband, she set out to create a new family in which her sister was not forgotten, but where Mum's Mourning did not rule. Yet, she knew that the box that held all her sorrow was still weighing heavily on her life.

It was a routine offer of counselling following her illness that brought Mary to see me. Mary had always been able to feel compassion for her mother – she understood her loss all too well. But as we explored her childhood, she now began to experience compassion for herself, for the 9 year old Mary who had lost in one fell swoop the older sister whom she worshipped and a loving mother capable of mothering. When asked to think of her own children when they were 9, the thought of how young they were at that age filled Mary with still greater self-compassion; but there was also anger towards her parents for their total disregard for her sisters' emotions and her own. This new compassion for her younger self encouraged Mary to speak to her sisters about the impact of their mother's uncontainable sorrow on them as they were growing up, and their father's role in sustaining it. Mary's therapy was opening new doors for her sisters as well, so that for the first time in over 30 years they were able to mark together *the anniversary of Alice's death.*

I felt awed by Mary's deep therapeutic work and the transformations she was able to effect in a matter of weeks; serendipitously, my offer of counselling must have arrived just as she herself felt ready to open herself to new perspectives and blossom. When, in our last session, I used the word 'mourn' to describe what she and her sisters were finally able to do together, Mary corrected me:

M. I don't want to mourn any longer, I associate mourning with what my mother did, what we all did, each in our own corner. Mourning is what destroyed our family. What my sisters and I were able to do together this year for the first time was express our grief.

And as Mary spoke, I pictured Mourning as a black hole in the centre of her family, sucking the life out of it, life that their joint expression of grief was now allowing to flow again.

For decades, Alice and Mum had remained at the centre of the family, ring-fenced with a boundary so rigid that none had been allowed to share in the sorrow, so solid that scant any love and care could emanate from Mum. And yet this boundary had been unable to contain the overwhelming sorrow and prevent it from seeping out at every point, pervading the air that the whole family breathed.

Lesley's story: Lost in mother's ambivalence

The reaction of Lesley's mother to the loss of her child bore little resemblance to that of Mary's mother, yet the impact on the family boundaries was equally dramatic.

As Lesley entered my counselling room for the first time, I felt that she must be carrying a very heavy weight: Lesley's morbid obesity spoke more of painful baggage, I sensed, than of illness or poor diet. During the first session, I was struck by Lesley's changing facial expressions and bearing from young child to serious adult. At times, she looked so confused, I even asked myself whether she had some significant learning difficulties, yet that did not seem to be the case.

It must have been the third or fourth session and I had been having the feeling that I was sitting opposite a very young child rather than a grown adult.

L. Lesley, may I ask you a strange question?
Lesley, pouting: Yes
L. How old are you feeling right now, as you are sitting here with me?
Lesley: 4? came the rather coy answer.
L. I asked you that strange question because that's exactly what it felt like to me. Is there something particular you remember about being 4?
Lesley: Well that's when Sam died.

I then learned that when she was 4, Lesley had been playing with her younger sister by a river, when her sister fell in and drowned. Lesley could still remember that sense of feeling completely lost – it still came over her sometimes. Her parents' marriage did not survive the tragedy and a few years later, her father left them.

Lesley: Since then it's always been just mum and me. Mum never speaks of Sam. Sometimes I used to think that I'd maybe invented the whole story. Then I'd feel the big hole in my tummy and I knew it was true. And now I am 38 and it's still just mum and me. I live on my own, but we ring each other a lot. Mum sometimes says: "you're not a little girl, you just have to learn to manage on your own." But when I manage and I have gone two whole days without ringing her and just getting on with things – I like to make Victorian-style collage cards- mum rings me, she says it's to check up on me, but she just tells me all her troubles with work and the man next door. Then, she asks me why I don't have a proper job instead of making silly Victorian cards.

But sometimes, it really gets too much for me on my own, so I go to mum's. She's got a really nice and cosy house. But then she's on my case the whole time: "why don't you have a job like normal people, why don't you get a boyfriend, you're 38 now. What are you waiting for?" Then she'll hug me and cover me with kisses and call me her baby girl.

I asked Lesley whether she would like us to explore her experience of her mother's way of relating to her with the use of cushions; Lesley was intrigued and willing to give it a try. She chose a cushion for herself, holding it so tight as to suffocate the life out of it, then cast it off and threw it across the room.

Lesley: It's like she's holding onto me, she doesn't want me to die, then she sees I'm not Sam and she throws me away in disgust.

L. Are you sure that's why your mother throws you away as she does?

Lesley: A few times, when mum was really angry, she said that Sam would never have been so much trouble. Sometimes I think she even blames me for what happened to Sam.

L. That sounds like a really harsh and painful thing to hear.

Lesley: shrugs her shoulders and does a childlike pout. I've tried talking to mum about Sam a few times, but she just gets angry and says it was a long time ago and anyway how can I possibly remember because I was only little.

L. Would you like to tell me about Sam?

Lesley recalls her memories of Sam.

L. Although you were only very little when Sam died, it seems that you really remember what it was like having a sister and you can still see some things really clearly.

Lesley: Yeah. I do. And when I make my Victorian cards, I always like to put a little girl there. And mum doesn't know it, but I know it's Sam.

L. You like to give your sister a place in your cards?

Lesley: Yeah

L. That sounds like a beautiful way of giving her a place in your life too,

Lesley: Yeah, Lesley's eyes are brimming.

L. That's important, isn't it?

Lesley: Yeah.

As time was limited, rather than explore the painful, heavy weight of Lesley's burden of loss, comparison and rejection, Lesley and I decided to focus on her relationship to her mother in her everyday life.

As part of our work on boundaries, Lesley played with the thought and sensation of an invisible boundary around herself. She could notice how different it felt and how it opened up some space to breathe and think for herself. She could feel a sense of centredness, could even sit up straight, instead of huddled and apologetic-looking (for her very existence? I sometimes wondered). So, I suggested that she stand up and from this point of centredness in herself, that she try placing cushions for herself and her mother at a distance that felt right for her, and which she felt her mother could tolerate. Then I asked her to get a cushion for Sam and find a place that felt right for it too: a place where she and her mother could both see Sam. Lesley put her mother's cushion and her own facing each other and Sam's to their side.

L. What's that like?
Lesley: It's like I can see mum and mum can see me, and we can both see Sam and when we both look at Sam, she isn't in the way between us.
L. So, when your mum looks at Sam she can still see you properly?

Despite the small number of sessions, it was remarkable to witness the change in Lesley's relationship to her mother: to her delight, she now felt able to manage more than two days without ringing her mother and what's more, she found ways of warding off her mother's calls when she wanted space for herself.

Human beings are not machines, and psychotherapy and psychology are not sciences: one can neither predict how people will react to tragedy, nor deduce from a behaviour what might have given rise to it. Mary's mother lived her life holding onto her dead daughter, keeping her centre stage – hallowed be her name. She had lost all interest in the living. Lesley's mother on the other hand did not explicitly allow her dead daughter a place in the family and alternated between holding onto her living daughter with all her might, and casting her off in disappointment and contempt. Unlike Mary and Lesley, David never knew the family he had lost. And so his mother and grandmother tried to walk the tightrope between keeping him connected to his past without handing down their own pain, terror and guilt.

David's story: Guilt

David's mother had fled Germany as a teenager with her mother, just before the War. In London after the war, his grandmother had created a semblance of pre-war German life for herself, meeting up regularly for coffee and cake with other Jewish refugees, yet without ever reminiscing about those who could not be with them, who had not survived. David's father had been largely absent from his life, wrapped up in his work; meanwhile David, wrapped up in cotton wool, had been the focus of his mother and grandmother's lives – he was all they had and they weren't going to lose him too. University had given David the opportunity to put some distance between himself and his mother and grandmother. He had chosen one far from home: he knew he needed to get away from all the molly-coddling;

he needed to be able to breathe. Yet, this had felt like a deep betrayal and still filled him with guilt.

D. *Mother never ever spoke of her childhood in Germany. My grandmother told me amusing stories of the good old days, but they were stories of a world she had lost. She hardly ever spoke of her mother whom she'd had to leave behind in the care of an old friend. She never ever mentioned our other murdered relatives.*

   She never explicitly spoke of the guilt that was crushing her, but it was there in her every word. It was years… years before I realized how much close family she'd lost … we'd lost. I can see now that it must have been as if all the horror and all the emotions were seeping out of her stories and I was soaking them all up like a sponge. It feels like I too've been carrying that guilt, her guilt, all these decades. I can see now that it was all too much.

It was slow, at times almost unbearably painful work for David. A turning point occured when he understood that by trying to distance himself from his family as he had done at 18, he had not so much been rebelling against their mollycoddling, as trying to say no to all the dead they were carrying, and to the pain and guilt that came with it.

David's mother and grandmother had tried to protect him, their only living descendant, from the horror of their indescribable loss. Yet, pain, fear and guilt had imbued all their love, all their efforts to protect him, and so David had absorbed them together with their love and their efforts. It was as if his mother and grandmother's skin had offered a boundary so porous that all their overwhelming emotions had seeped out through their skin and under his own.[2]

Despite and in their very divergence, Mary, Lesley and David's stories illustrate the long-lasting impact that trauma and the way it is handled in the family can have on mother–child relationships.

Notes

1   Taken in the everyday, rather than psychoanalytical sense of the term.
2   *See Chapter 13 for further work with David and his overwhelming guilt.*

Chapter 9

Mothers

Some Mother–Child Stories: Broken Bonds

Broken bonds

The bond that ties a mother to her child can take on a tone or a tension that adversely affects their relationship; it can also break. And what makes that all the more painful is that however absolute the estrangement, at some level a bond still holds mother and child. Tragically for many mothers and their children, while it takes only one person to break a bond, it needs both mother and child to mend it. The pain of estrangement can be numb, it can feel angry and violent, despairing and powerless, guilt- or shame-ridden. Sometimes the cause of the break remains significant: a parent who persists in not acknowledging their child's sexuality or identified gender; a refusal to accept a new step-parent or daughter/son-in-law; an insurmountable clash of values or beliefs (religious, political, etc.) Sometimes the cause is objectively trivial, though not experienced as such (e.g. a tactless remark about an "unbecoming" dress, or about the other's cooking, that touches a very sensitive spot), often it is unknown or long forgotten. For pride, resentment, hurt, guilt, shame and anger can get in the way of reconciliation, even where love is present, sadly even *in extremis*. And more often than not, beneath it all, lie the sense of not feeling recognized and the fear of rejection.

As I think of broken bonds, Linda and Mavis immediately spring to mind. Both rather gruff, fiercely independent and proud women, with a history of loss, abandonment and broken relationships. Both had been seriously ill and had refused to contact their children. I was immensely fond of both of them: I admired their resilience, enjoyed their directness and their sense of humour, I respected their pride and felt touched and privileged by the trust they placed in me. Linda's chaotic lifestyle had been the cause of the estrangement between herself and her children. It had been 15 years now, so how, she asked, could she contact them after all this time? Guilt, shame and pride vied within her with (self-) compassion and love for her children: guilt and shame at her desertion of them, shame at being seen in her diminished state, and compassion for all that she, and her children, had had to endure. Compassion and love won: for whatever other emotions were in the way, Linda felt she owed it to her children to give them the

DOI: 10.4324/9781003364504-10

opportunity to reconnect, as well as the opportunity to refuse to see her. And Linda felt as prepared as she ever would be for the possibility of their rejection. But fortunately for her, her children were more than willing to try to reconnect with her.

It might seem extraordinary that we should ever qualify a mother's bond to her biological child as 'broken', since genes, pregnancy and labour create an indestructible, physical and emotional bond – whatever the physical experience and emotions involved. And yet paradoxically, from birth, indeed already in the womb, this indestructible emotional bond can also be of the most tenuous kind. Maybe, like an invisible nylon thread, it can bind the fabric of two lives together, leaving barely a trace of a mother's love.

In contrast to Linda, Mavis' bond with her mother seems to have been very tenuous from the start: her early years only held memories of feeling cold and numb, amidst the rough tumult of the home. Like so many children faced with their mother's chronic lack of basic attunement, Mavis' aim had been to seek safety and keep out of harms' way, rather than seek connection. And still now, though she yearned for connection, the risk of being hurt and rejected was too terrifying, and the need for security therefore predominated.

I never found out what had led to Mavis' estrangement from her children, I am not certain she herself even remembered. They'd "had words" and that was that. Evacuated during the war, given away by her mother to a relative on her return, Mavis felt abandoned to her very core. She was terrified by the possibility of abandonment and rejection and saw clues to it even where there were none. In relationships, she made sure she was always the first to reject. So, when the fear of abandonment and rejection were so overwhelming, it is no surprise that nothing on earth was going to induce her to contact her children.

It is clear that Mavis' own history of abandonment impacted on her relationships and left a trail of severed bonds behind her. At the same time, Mavis' traumatic, personal experience of evacuation and abandonment (like David's experience of loss and guilt) can be seen to reflect on a microcosmic level the broader history of the 20th century and the impact of its man-made cataclysms.

The last few centuries have exemplified to an unparalleled degree the destructive power of humans – as well as their adaptive and creative potential. And the traumatic impact of wars, famines, slavery and genocide can be observed within families, cascading down the generations.

The ongoing psychological trauma of slavery and broken bonds

Nicole's story

It was Nicole who first voiced directly what I had felt for a while and was looking for the right time to suggest.

N.   You know, Laura, when I look at all the violence in my family, and all the
fathers that were never there, and all the broken mother-daughter bonds...
you're going to think it's weird, but I'm sure it all goes back to our past, to
slavery and what it did to our families.
L.   It doesn't sound weird to me at all, Nicole... actually it makes complete
sense to me.
N.   Really?
L.   Of course. It is such a heavy, heavy history.

The link between broken family bonds, domestic violence and slavery was
one that I had made on occasion to clients, but very tentatively and always to
clients I felt I knew sufficiently well – for fear of my clients experiencing my
interpretation, coming from a white psychotherapist, as reenacting a form
of white on black power dynamic. But Nicole had come to that thought herself and had felt able to share it with me, so that we could both acknowledge
together the weight of that past and its ramifications down the generations.

Nicole's relationship with her mother had been difficult long before that fateful
day when her older half-brother had raped her and her mother had accused her
of provoking him. Then Nicole's father had left. Her mother had never forgiven
her and they were now estranged. Nicole felt doubly, trebly betrayed.

Besides the occasional beating, Nicole's only memory of her mother touching
her as a child was when she would brush her hair on hair-washing day. That
weekly touch had felt functional, devoid of gentleness, empty of love. And in the
forty five years between that time and when I came to know her, Nicole's life
experience of touch had been barren of all emotion other than rage, lust and the
desire for power and possession.

Nicole had worked hard to reach her present position in the firm; she was
highly efficient, well-liked and respected by colleagues. She was also a devoted
mother: though her three daughters were all born in extremely challenging,
power-laden circumstances, she had brought them up with love and care. Yet,
she herself still had great trouble tolerating the basic level of physical intimacy
required by their daily activities of communal living. An exception however had
been brushing their hair when they were young which, unlike her mother, she had
done with pleasure and loving care.

As a black woman, Nicole had found herself repeatedly confronted with
lack of respect and abuse of power, so that all she had asked of her chil-
dren was due respect and consideration, which she saw as the most important
tokens of love. And when one of her teenage daughters had failed to show her
that respect and consideration, she had seen no alternative but to throw her
out of the house.

Her daughter's behaviour would have been viewed by many mothers as a rela-
tively mild misdemeanour in a teenager, but respect takes on a vital importance
where it has historically been denied in its most basic and fundamental form –
when historically, and often still now, black lives are seen not to matter.

Nicole felt torn between her love for her daughter and her deep hurt at having been disrespected. She felt conflicted between the need to punish a vital transgression – the crossing of the red line of disrespect, and the sense that she risked recreating between herself and her daughter the broken bond that existed between her mother and herself.

It was the realization that she was perpetuating something bigger than herself – a pattern of broken family relationships instituted and enforced by slavery, that spurred Nicole to reflect on what setting that red boundary line of respect had signified for her, and what crossing it might have meant to her daughter. She came to see that she had invested that boundary with the weight of all her past encounters with disrespect, violence and the absence of love, whereas for her daughter it had just been a boundary that she had wanted to test, as teenagers do.

Nicole had turned respect into the expression of love – it was the only love she had dared to expect, yet it had blinded her to the real love, admiration and respect that her daughter felt for her and which she was now beginning to recognize.

Nicole's story highlights the difficulty of trying to break the cycle of multiple generations of deficient parenting in families torn apart by the trauma of slavery. I am not using the term 'deficient' in a judgemental sense, but as pure description of a situation that is bound to arise when, down the generations, for 150 years or longer, families have been forcibly separated and subjected to extremes of power, including rape and murder. And as we know, dynamics of power, violence and separation not infrequently breed similar dynamics.[1]

The cruel mother

I still remember the shock, in Vienna's Belvedere Museum, of suddenly finding myself confronted with Giovanni Segantini's painting 'The Evil Mothers'. I stood transfixed by the chilling depiction of maternal iciness: in a bleak and barren landscape, two bare trees stand in a snowy plane, and entwined amongst their twisted branches, almost indistinguishable from them, two mothers, recoiling from the babies at their breast. Despite the romanticism of it, there was something only too realistic about the image: I was immediately reminded of Tonia and Emily whose respective mothers seemed to have taken pleasure in twisting the knife in their children's wounds. How icy cold must their mothers' milk have been!

Emily

Emily was terminally ill: her doctors had tentatively said August, we were now in June. Emily felt this was now "final chance time". For there was one thing she was hoping she might be able to sort out before she died, something that might put a different complexion on her whole life. She wanted to write to her mother and understand why she had had it in for her and had behaved quite so badly towards her throughout her life; she was also hoping for some sign of care from her, maybe even of love… It was not simply that her mother preferred her sisters to her, nor that she often put her down, was dismissive, verbally abusive or even hot-tempered towards her – such preferences and behaviours, though unfortunate and destructive were, she knew, commonplace. But violent beatings as a child, malicious accusations and this cold shutting her out? Surely that was not normal. And did it really make no difference to her mother that she was now dying, did she really not feel an ounce of love for her?

L. *Writing a letter to your mother may well be helpful for you – whether you send it or not. But you may need to prepare yourself for her not replying, … or for a very painful reply. After all she hasn't shown any interest in you so far, and you have been seriously ill now for over a year.*
    Emily sat for some time in silence. *That's a difficult thought; but I suppose I needed to hear that.*
    After a couple of minutes, she asked: *But how can she be such a pillar of her church and not show any forgiveness?*
L. *Forgiveness? Have you done anything serious that requires her forgiveness?*
E. *Well I was born!*
    As she flippantly uttered these words, it was as if something suddenly flipped in her. Clichéd though it may sound, I saw a shadow briefly sweep over her eyes.
L. *You were born?!…..And that might require forgiveness?!*
    The room fell very quiet.
E. *You know, it was something I always knew. Or rather something that was always there for me to know. It's like suddenly all these pieces are falling together into a picture – like a puzzle I didn't even know existed. People's looks, you know…And the disgust and. and… the hate in her eyes… But it wasn't my fault; I didn't do anything!*
L. *No, it wasn't your fault. You didn't do anything to deserve her disgust and hate. But from what you are saying, it sounds like she, or someone else, may have. But we don't know. We are only surmising. And you may never know.*
E. *Gosh, I feel like, like… I don't know… I'll have to sleep on that.*
    At the following session:
E. *Strange though it may sound, I feel a sense of relief. It's like a stone has lifted off my chest. Like I can breathe…before my chest was all squashed down. It's like it was something I always knew and never knew.*

Emily had come to see me partly in the hope that I could help her write to her mother so that she might better understand her mother's attitude to her, perhaps even detect some love in her manner of relating to her, which had always oscillated between total indifference and vicious hostility. Understanding, she felt, would help put a different complexion on her life. Although Emily died without ever receiving any sign of love or even concern from her mother, and although the understanding she came to was not based on firm facts and was not the denouement she had hoped for, still it had offered her a sense of relief and lifted a weight off her chest. It had offered a number of concrete possibilities, instead of intangible questions. She had no longer felt the need to write; she had reached the end of the road with her mother. Sometimes the most helpful answers are not the ones we would have hoped for and are responses to questions we did not directly ask.

As a daughter and mother myself, the thought of a mother carrying her vendetta to her child's grave feels unimaginably cruel to me. Yet, it is not unusual to witness acts of great favouritism to the point of cruelty perpetrated beyond the grave as parents unexpectedly drop a bombshell in their will, cutting off one of their children or else revealing a destructive secret. However unimaginable and cruel this may feel, it is not beyond comprehension, for who knows the life history, emotions, thoughts and delusions that have fuelled that cruelty? And yet in some cases I have encountered, I have found it difficult to feel compassion for the mothers who seem to have taken malicious satisfaction in committing a final act of vengeance in the face of death.

Note

1   Confer 22-23/3/2019, Post-Slavery Syndrome: Intergenerational PTSD in the Consulting Room Today.

Chapter 10

Mothers

Maternal Feelings in the Therapeutic Relationship; Conclusion

Maternal feelings in the therapeutic relationship

Clients elicit various feelings in their therapists, including often maternal feelings.

As I reflect on my own maternal response to clients, the following questions spring to mind: how can I tell it is happening? When is it likely to occur? When am I surprised by it? When am I surprised that there is no such feeling present? When does it feel as if it is coming from me and when do I feel strongly drawn in by the client and how? And of course, when am I in danger of crossing the boundary into rescuing the client/trying to replace the client's mother?

I am writing in the first person as I can only speak from personal experience.

I become aware of my maternal attitude by the sense of an inner smile, a warmth and a movement that goes out from around my solar plexus to my client. I may experience the sort of indulgent 'aww!' that I feel around a young child, or the admiration and delight that I can experience with an older child or a young adult. That feeling is familiar to me from being a mother and a grandmother, but the two do not necessarily go hand in hand: many mothers do not feel maternal, and many people who have not been mothers do.

I would have thought that I would be more likely to feel maternal towards my younger clients, and although I often do, it is certainly not age-dependent. When I started working in hospital and had to brace myself to enter the old-fashioned, long, 24 bed, foul-smelling, soul-destroying male geriatric wards, I would sometimes surprise myself with feeling very maternal towards an elderly patient – and I don't mean a patronizing, 'there, there, dear' feeling, I mean a heartfelt warm maternal feeling. I now think that my maternal attitude emerges principally in response to a yearning for maternal acknowledgement, validation and care that I experience from certain clients. There are those whose deep yearning does not dare express itself, or expresses itself most tentatively, and those where it is concealed behind a smoke-screen of self-reliance and toughness. And there are those clients whose yearning feels like a cry of angry desperation as their whole way of being towards me

DOI: 10.4324/9781003364504-11

screams: "Be my mummy please! Why won't you be my mummy?" This angry and desperate yearning requires a particularly delicate response and an even greater and gentler steadfastness of boundaries.

So, what might alert me to a fuzzy maternal boundary being in danger of developing? There would first be some tell-tale signs, such as out of character reactions in the presence of a particular client, or even at the very thought of seeing them, as here with Sandy:

My colleague called out to me: "Laura, do you have a ten o'clock appointment today?"

I looked at my diary and replied: "Oh, it's Sandy, I love that girl!", then I gasped. Where had that come from?! First Sandy was not a 'girl', she was in her mid-forties, and secondly, I had met Sandy only once, the previous week, and although I took an immediate liking to her, there was no way I could 'love' her at this stage of her therapy!

Now there are many who might be surprised or frown at the thought of my ever loving my clients, but to me (and many other therapists) it is the thought of never loving one's clients that seems extremely strange. When you get to know someone very well, when that person, despite and in all their vulnerability, has shown the courage to tell you their story and talk about their deepest pain, shame, hurt and fear, when together you have worked hard and gone through very difficult times, when you care deeply about what happens to that person, when you look forward to seeing them for their session, and you are sad, yet proud, to see them go and stand on their own two feet, is that not a form of love? What would be reprehensible would be to not allow myself to feel this natural feeling, to seek to push it away when it tried to make itself felt, or pretend it did not exist. For, therapists who defend themselves against any possibility of a strong emotional response to clients (from love to boredom, fear and anger) risk turning a blind eye to certain aspects of their own and their clients' experience. A therapist's strong emotional response is indicative of an issue, the important question is whether it is the therapist's or the client's![1]

The pleasure I felt at seeing Sandy's name down for my 10 o'clock slot was quite genuine, as was the care I felt for her, but 'love' was inappropriate at this stage and required my attention. Was it something about her that reminded me of someone I loved, a relative or a friend? Was it something in her, as yet unknown to me, that resonated deeply within me? That is, was it principally to do with me, or some issue of mine, or was I simply responding to an issue or yearning of hers? (I discovered, as I got to know her better, that both these dynamics were at play.) Could it be for instance that she had a particular way of attaching herself to women of my age, in a perpetual search for something, be it approval, reassurance, security, or indeed love? And if love, what sort of love was she seeking? But these were early days and, armed with my awareness, I could set my questions aside for a later date and look forward to our session with pleasure, but in a more contained way. In other words, I could make sure my boundaries were well set.

I am an enthusiastic and outgoing person and, in everyday life, tend to wear my heart on my sleeve. Had I disregarded the strong feelings Sandy had evoked in me, my pleasure at seeing her today might well have spilt out in a number of ways – maybe in a sort of childlike fun or excitement, or in a very maternal and possibly over-nurturing way. Neither of these would have been appropriate or therapeutic; yet, when acknowledged and boundaried, fun, playfulness, maternal and nurturing feelings all have a welcome place in the therapeutic relationship.

The therapist who experiences maternal feelings towards their client and, on reflection, believes that they are coming from the client and not from a personal trigger, is in a delicate position. They need to navigate the situation carefully and find a balance between giving the client some of the nurturing they presumably require, without however trying to replace their mother. The therapist can offer a form of good mothering: they can listen to the client, see and value them for who they are, they can offer them nurturing and care, help them turn their life around, they can love them even, but they cannot be or replace their mother. Between a therapist offering 'good mothering' and a mother, there lies a fundamental *de facto* boundary that a therapist cannot cross and should not seek to cross. It seems to me that a therapist who tries to *be* a mother to their client is acting out their own baggage, which will not help their own issues and may be very detrimental to their client. As they are putting themselves in a rescuing role, this is also likely to enmesh them and their client in the vicious 'drama triangle' of rescuer-persecutor-victim (*see Glossary*), and impact negatively on both the therapeutic relationship and the client's relationship with their mother (whether she be dead or still alive). When the therapist is thus invested in the client (rescuing position), a break in the therapeutic relationship risks leading to the therapist's disappointment, upset or anger at their client's ingratitude or 'lack of progress' (therapist in victim position). This may lead the therapist to take it out, even if subtly or indirectly, on their client (moving into persecutory position).

From the perspective of maternal feelings elicited by clients, trying to be a mother to one's client is not the only danger to the therapy. Another is paying insufficient attention to a specific aspect of the mothering which a client seems to be asking for.

Mavis

As I am writing this section, I am thinking once again of Mavis – the woman I mentioned earlier who felt abandoned and rejected to her very core and had rejected all the important relationships in her life, from her children to her various partners, for fear of being rejected by them. Despite Mavis being twenty five years older than me, I could tell that I was experiencing maternal feelings towards her and that I partly represented a maternal figure for her. Maybe if I had paid greater attention to these feelings, I could have prevented her later rejection of me. For sadly, despite the significant level of trust she had been able to put in me, this did not see her through my summer break. Mavis had asked me whether I would be going to the seaside and if so, whether I could bring back a shell for her. The request was doubly risky and must have taken trust and courage: I could have refused; I might forget. To refuse to answer her question about the seaside directly, or refuse to bring back a shell, something so small yet so important to her, was not, I felt, an option in the light of our work. So, I agreed. However, although I knew I was most unlikely to forget to bring a shell back, I should have explored in greater depth with Mavis the possibility of my forgetting to do so.

My intention had been to convey that I would keep her sufficiently in my thoughts during my absence to choose a shell for her. But there had been too many broken promises in her life and, I presume, Mavis could not risk coming to her session after my holidays to find that I had forgotten the shell – that I had not sufficiently cared. As a maternal figure for her, I would have repeated, in a minute yet painfully significant way, her mother's rejection of her when she returned from evacuation.

I kept the shell in my office for her until my retirement, in case she were one day to come back to therapy, but sadly she never did. I was very fond of Mavis and it still saddens me that by insufficiently exploring the possibility of my forgetting, I had probably allowed Mavis to repeat with me her lifelong experience of rejecting and feeling rejected.

There are of course many clients who do not elicit a maternal attitude from me. It may be that it is not what they need from me, or that they fear reigniting their deep grief at the caring and validating mother they no longer or never had. There are also those that yearn for maternal caring but cannot afford the slightest chink in their armour. When my heart does go out to them, it is fleetingly welcomed and then rebuffed, as they retreat into their armoured self. And there is the client who barely knows how to reach out for the button that would elicit a maternal response, or does not dare do so; they gave up wishing, let alone trying many, many years ago. Instead, they built a little bubble around themselves in which they can feel safe. If my maternal heart does go out to them, there is a guard at the bubble's door who passes on its message to the child still within; the child within can hear it, uncertain, bemused and keeps their door closed. One day, we both know, they will be able to open the door to tenderness, from me, from themselves and from others, and allow it in.

Conclusion: Joy's story

I have chosen to conclude these four chapters on mothers with Joy's story, which expresses better than I ever could the need for recognition and love from a mother, the healing power of understanding and compassion, the need to reevaluate boundaries and even, where necessary, to turn them into firm barriers. Joy's story illustrates the extent to which a person can feel torn between their loyalty to their mother and the need to protect themselves; it also shows that the cycle of bad mothering can be broken and demonstrates the potentially redeeming power of motherhood.

Joy's story

Despite the laboured way in which Joy walked into my counselling room and then sat down, there was something very solid about her, and a feistiness too. She looked to me like someone who had had to stand up for herself (or others?) in life and fight. I surmised that it must have taken her courage to come and see me, and to ask for help. I didn't have to wait long to have my first impressions confirmed.
We started with the usual intake form:

L. Address? … telephone number? … date of birth? … ethnicity?
J. Why is anyone asking me about my ethnicity, how are they to know what it means to me, and anyway what does it have to do with my illness and what business is it of theirs?

In almost twenty years of having to ask people about their ethnicity, this was only the second time that I had had a patient react quite so vigorously. And, apart from it being an NHS audit requirement, I totally agreed with her: ethnicity is far too important a question for anyone to expect a single word answer. I thought it looked like we might be in for an interesting time together: I didn't simply mean that I thought Joy might prove a 'tricky client' – though I was preparing myself for that too. Rather, I took an immediate liking to her, I admired her feistiness and wondered what lay behind it; and I do usually enjoy working with clients who are prepared to challenge me as well as be challenged. As we had spent so long going through the necessary questionnaires, it was not until the next session that I was to hear of her tragic childhood: uprooted, abandoned by her mother, left at a young age to look after her siblings and maltreated by her father. Joy spoke in short sentences; she delivered statements in a forceful manner, as if they were aphorisms. I felt that if she were to tell her story ten times, it would come out the same every time: she seemed to have needed to create a firm framework to make sense of her childhood and find something in it that was worth holding onto. In her telling of this story there were no bad people and she was no victim: "mum must have had it hard", "my dad is a good man, he could have put us in a home", "my husband was a good man, he was just the wrong man at the wrong time", "I managed, I am strong."
There was in the forceful, matter of fact way in which she uttered these statements, something stoic yet a little childish, in a 'good girl' sort of way.

Though she felt solid to me, I did not experience her as properly grounded and embodied.

Joy had developed a philosophical approach to life. She realized that life had not been easy for her mother and that her father could indeed have put his children in a home when she had left. In that sense Joy had developed a level of understanding and compassion sufficient to enable her to go forward. She occasionally did state: "my father was a brute." Clearly the past hurt and she carried some anger about it, but there was no grimace, nothing about her facial expression or bearing that conveyed much contempt, anger or rage. Yet, I did not experience this as a sign of her being in denial or dissociated. It was as another aphoristic statement of fact, unconnected to "my father was a good man"; the two statements seemed to live side by side, without any sense of paradox. She was acknowledging that, like most human beings, her father had been a complex person with some very different parts to him.

J.   *He was a brute: he expected me to look after all my brothers and my sister; and do the cleaning; and do the dinner while he went to the pub. And when he went to the pub, sometimes I could tell I was in for trouble – he'd come in banging and crashing and swearing. Then he'd tell me to get dressed and leave. I'd go outside and just stay there on the doorstep all night. I'd be really cold and scared. I could probably have shouted and woken the neighbours, but I was ashamed. I never even told my closest friends.*

For years Joy had not wanted to look at her parenting any closer, preferring to live in a sort of "fairy tale", as she later came to call it. While her siblings had cut off all contact with their dad, she had helped take care of him till his dying day.

When she finally managed to trace her mum to inform her of her husband's death, their mum walked back into their lives, criticizing them and making demands. And then suddenly, without notice, she left the country again and resumed her silence. Joy's siblings saw no reason to forgive her for twice deserting them. But Joy remained in touch with her, which took some difficulty, as her mum moved around, keeping under the radar. Her mother on the other hand contacted Joy when she needed something from her. Yet, Joy was prepared to put up with this unequal relationship, as she so yearned for her recognition, for a token of her love.

But now, after her cancer diagnosis, Joy's life had been turned upside down. Joy was still far from well and had to rely on her children more than she wanted; she began to yearn for her mother's help during her convalescence. She was considering asking her to come to the UK. So, we explored that option, looking at what it was she longed for, and what she hoped and feared might happen. Over a few weeks, Joy came to realize that she could not formulate boundaries in relation to her mother's visit that would protect her from getting hurt, and she decided to rescind the invitation. It took a lot of courage for her to stand up to her family's entreaties and mercenary pressures, and to the opprobrium that followed her final, categorical refusal to invite her mother over.

J. I now know that the mum I wanted to invite over was the mum of my fairy tale. The mum who would cook and look after me. But that mum doesn't exist. I know my mum would expect me to look after her and buy her lots of things to take home.

Then, by chance, Joy found out that her mother had never even told her friends of her existence. For Joy, hearing that her very existence had not been acknowledged was the last straw that broke the fairy tale. Our last session was deeply moving, for both of us:

*J. I wanted to say thank you. It's been a journey and now I feel safe. I feel free. I can be me. You know you once said to me: "how come you can feel compassion for your mother, but not for yourself?" Well I've thought long and hard about that – about compassion. It's a heavy word; it's a strong word. It can fight guilt, it can bring you freedom. It's like I have been carrying my mother's guilt all these years. Like if anything went wrong with the kids – with my brothers and sisters, I felt guilty, because it was my fault, because I was their mum. I was 11. I couldn't be a mum at 11. And I can see I am strong. I am amazing. I am a mum now. I am proud of my kids. I did a good job. They are my kids. My brothers and sister were not my kids. I can't carry the guilt for my mother because she left us. Now I can see me, live for me. (*Cries*). I am crying for happiness, because I am free, I can feel it in here.* Points to her heart. *And I am thanking you because I couldn't have done it without you. It was like this illness opened a door and I came to you. And I thought it was a terrible thing that had happened, but now I see good come out of bad. And I see my strength. I see the child I was and I feel compassion. What happened to this child should not have happened. What happened to me should not have happened. And I cast off that guilt, that is my mother's. I am a mother. I could never have done to my children what she did to us. And maybe she had her reasons then, but now she's had lots of chances. I've given her lots of chances and she just made more demands of me. The guilt belongs to her, not to me. I feel free and that is good. I can now stand up and be me.*

As I write down Joy's words, once again I have tears in my eyes. I am struck anew by their emotional force and by Joy's courage and wisdom. From understanding and compassion, freedom had emerged – freedom from guilt and freedom to be herself – and with that came a greater sense of her own agency, the ability to set better boundaries for herself and hence find safety. There was also a greater feeling of groundedness about Joy. She owned the strong statements she made: you could see that they came from the heart and the solar plexus, that she stood firm in them.

Joy came to me and I was able to help her, and of course that felt rewarding. We only had 12 sessions, many of them on the phone because of her ill health.

She called it a "journey" and I felt awed at how steadily and far she had been able to travel in that time. But my overwhelming feeling, I pictured it vividly, was that she had been like a tree with buds just waiting to open into exuberant, exotic blossom and bear fruit.

Joy's story: Postscript

It is always with some trepidation that I approach a former client for consent to publish some of their story: there is the anxiety of contacting someone out of the blue and reminding them of past painful times, and there is for me some anxiety around possible rejection of my request, or worse of our work together. For Joy, and me, this renewed contact nine years on was a moving experience: she was moved to hear that she had touched my life and I got to hear how important our work had remained in her life. Joy's mother had since died, and seeing my view of our work in writing had, she felt, brought her a greater sense of closure. Only one thing bothered her: in my effort to conceal her identity, I had changed some factual details and had called her Felicity. This simply wouldn't do: the facts had to be correct. And it was not any person's story, it certainly was not Felicity's story, it was *her* story. And so, Joy asked me to call it by its proper name: Joy's Story.

Note

1   This also applies to erotic feelings, which if experienced need reflecting upon, discussing with a clinical supervisor; however, they must never be acted upon. This is a red boundary line.

Chapter 11

Fathers

I had toyed with the idea of calling this whole chapter 'Adam's story': Adam, as first man, who by his own actions fell from a state of innocence, was banished from paradise and, as first father, handed down life and, with it, the baggage that comes of being human and living in the world. From Abraham and Isaac to God, Joseph and Jesus, via Lot and his daughters, the Bible and New Testament offer us a heritage of complex (step)father–child relationships!

In many families and cultures, the concept of paternal lineage still carries powerful weight: the child bears, in addition to their father's surname, a patronymic that testifies to the father's first name. The son may even bear his father's name followed by 'Jnr' or a number II, III. The message this name carries is a proud one: 'this is the child of my loins, the son who will carry my name and the name of our family'; it may be a heavy one too.

Whatever a person's background and whether or not they bear their father's name, they have a paternal lineage and heritage – even if they have never met their father and ignore his identity. Some things have been handed down to them: with life has come some of the paternal genes, maybe a certain know-how, talents, a particular relationship to the world. Heritage brings gifts, but it is also likely to bring burdens and sometimes those burdens may feel greater than the gifts. Every son has a relationship to his paternal lineage which he invests with particular feelings and meaning, and to which he reacts: whether attempting to carry on the tasks, take on the burdens, overcome obstacles that proved too great for his male ancestors, failing to 'live up' to them, maybe sensing a gulf between himself and them, or else turning his back on his male ancestral line through indifference or rejection. That is not to say that daughters are not aware of their paternal line; indeed, they may identify with it, or respond to it more strongly than their brothers. However, even where the father wishes to make no difference between his sons and daughters, different layers of meaning and different messages are likely to be at play.

And where there is an adoptive father in addition to the biological father, for the children's well-being, each father figure has to be given their due place.

DOI: 10.4324/9781003364504-12

The client's relationship to their father is a common theme in therapy, often a major one; its exploration may span the whole spectrum of emotions from love and sweet nostalgia to terror and hatred. Yet, whatever the emotions, an exploration is usually enlightening and potentially transformative. The danger arises when the exploration is one-dimensional: dogmatic and theory-bound, or else focused for instance on blame or exaltation alone, oblivious to broader family dynamics, etc. Above all, the exploration has to be honest and fair, underpinned by a genuine desire to understand, and by compassion – for both the client's father and the client themselves. Feeling compassion for one's father does not mean exonerating him from all responsibility and blame where blame is due, as in the case of sexual abuse, violence or neglect. It means trying to understand the context of his behaviour and feel for him in the harsh experiences of his life. Such an exploration may lead to a rethinking of bound-aries with him (even if he is long dead.) And for those clients who are them-selves fathers, exploring the way their father related to them in childhood can help them to reevaluate their own fathering – acknowledging the good and viewing the not-so-good with clearer understanding and self-compassion.[1]

This chapter is accordingly divided into two sections: the first looking at my clients' childhood experiences of their fathers; the second at my clients as fathers, in particular at those seeking to break the pattern of bad fathering.[2]

Father–child stories

It is strange to think that over a century separates the fathers of some of my clients from some of my younger male clients. These 100 years span different worlds, marked *inter alia* by two world wars, a reevaluation of power relations across all areas of life – in particular regarding the place of men and women in the home – and a technological revolution. Criteria of good fathering have also changed over that period of time. However, a client who excuses their father's cold, violent or abusive behaviour with the blanket statement "that was how it was back then" should nevertheless be challenged and their curi-osity engaged.

It is often still in the form of stereotypes, albeit personalized ones, that my clients' fathers appear in my counselling room today: there are the fathers of Victorian literature – the great provider, the rigid despot, the upholder of the faith, the 'good-for-nothing' who drank the household's every penny; there are the Peter Pans and overgrown teenagers; the absent fathers; and there are the fathers of legends and fairy tales – the hero, the king with his daughter the princess, the many headed-monster… Stereotypes have a bad name: they pre-sent a generalized, sedimented and hence distorted view of a more nuanced and complex reality. Yet, the stories below are individual stories with their own complexities and their own truths which, I suspect, will speak to many in some ways. The oversimplification would lie in seeing each as the paradig-matic example of their title.

My father the hero

One of my most touching memories of a 'hero' father goes back to my early days as a therapist.

Jack had recently lost his father and was disconsolate. His father was his 'hero', how could he live up to him? We had been working together for a number of weeks when he asked me whether I would like to see a photograph of his father. I said I would be happy to. Jack pulled a photo from out of his wallet and held it out to me with care. Standing next to Jack, a tall, burly rugby player, stood a little gentleman, half his size. Clearly heroes come in all shapes and sizes, but I had not been prepared for this one.

It is telling that when a person refers to their father as a 'hero', they are using a term that hails back to antiquity and the heroes of ancient Greece – the brave soldiers of the Iliad and the Odyssey, the demi-gods of Greek legends. The father as hero is 'put on a pedestal' and 'worshipped', whether he seeks it or not. The worshipping son has his own criteria. These may cluster around *vir*tues: qualities of warmth, generosity and kindness; and remarkable talents – or talents perceived to be such. Other criteria cluster around perceived '*vir*ility': courage, stamina, strength, etc. (*vir* being Latin for 'man'). For many a 'hero's' son, the task to emulate his father and win his approval may feel as filled with obstacles as the quest of heroes of ore. And the sense of falling short can fill sons with anxiety, guilt, or shame.

Pete worshipped his father. An actor, successful sportsman and businessman, playful and extravagant, Pete's father had enjoyed a 'work hard, play hard' life-style. I was struck by how much space Pete's father seemed to have taken in the family: larger than life, he made a lot of noise with outbursts of loud joviality or anger, especially when he had had "a drink or two". Pete's mother seemed to enjoy her larger-than-life man and put up with his drunken behaviour. I had the impression however that there was no space for any other male but father in the family – no space for Pete to find his own place in it, and in life. As his father before him, Pete had not done well at school, but nor had he later found particular success in any field. Instead, it was as if Pete had felt that the only way in which he could follow in his father's footsteps was through his fast and noisy lifestyle. Yet this filled him with shame: it was not his rather laddish behaviour as such that shamed him (it differed little from his father's), but the fact that there was nothing solid that he could show to counterbalance it. And he himself did not feel "solid", he felt but a "shell of a man".

Father-hero worship has its place in childhood: it belongs in the child's world of benevolent and malevolent magic powers and can offer a sense of security, and help forge a sense of identity and belonging. But as they grow up, children will need to gradually lose their magical outlook, see their fathers in all their human reality and frailty, learn to 'separate' and gain autonomy. Children need to gradually discover their own freedom of choice and personal responsibility: responsibility for their own interests, beliefs, life decisions, actions and for finding their own sources of emotional support. They need to learn to set a different boundary between themselves and their father, the hero. There is a scene in a 1990s French film which has stayed with me all these years: a teenager is with a bunch of friends and they are about to go surfing, his father appears and says "I thought *we* were going surfing together". This scene depicted exquisitely both the young boy's guilt at feeling torn between the father whom he still idolized and his peers, as well as the father's own need to be a father-hero-best-friend to his son. Learning to see the father-hero in his frailer human form may be painful at times, for father and child, but it is part of the healthy process of growing up and developing a healthy father–adult child relationship.

As Ed recounted his childhood, I felt I was watching an old black and white film: reality in Ed's home seemed to have mirrored fiction. Ed and his siblings grew up in the 1930s/1940s; their father was a stuntman and performed the stunts for some of the greatest film heroes of the day. He became the hero both on screen and at home when he returned laden with gifts for the family. At those times there was an abundance of food and the house was filled with fun and joy. Mother would berate him gently for his extravagance. And then there were the lean times when father had no work and there was little to eat, but still on the whole he kept his good humour and loving playfulness. In his early teens, Ed came to sense, lurking in the background, the unspoken fear that the time would come when father would be unable to continue as a stuntman… or worse. This helped him understand that, though father was still his 'hero', he was certainly not immortal. Nor was he a magician; indeed, despite his even spirits, father seemed ill-equipped for the harder times that probably lay ahead. Ed told me how it had felt important in his late teens to take responsibility for himself and his own life, while also keeping an eye out for his parents.

Like Pete's father, Ed's father had been larger than life and the centre of his family's admiration, yet it seemed to me that he did not take up all the space: there had been room for Ed and his siblings. Ed certainly had felt seen and loved by his parents and this probably helped him to separate and carve his own way in life. For where a son feels acknowledged for himself and validated by his father, paradoxically, separation is likely to be easier. Whereas if the child does not feel acknowledged and validated in a core aspect of their being, any attempt at separation risks carrying, in addition to the usual mixed feelings at that time, an unhelpful emotional charge – be it of resentment, anger, failure, guilt, shame, vindictiveness/grandiosity ('I'll show him!'), etc. or a mixture of those, as with Moritz below. This also frequently happens where the father-hero offers a normative view of masculinity which the son does not fit, or exalts a career path for which he does not feel suited. Similarly, if the father has a normative image of femininity by which his daughters are expected to abide, and fail to do so.

There are also the fallen heroes, where separation from father-heroes has come through one or more violent ruptures, or where the father has fallen off their pedestals. It may be that the child comes to gradually realize, as they get older, that their father's behaviour towards them, which as teenagers they had viewed as a mark of trust in their maturity, was in fact totally inappropriate, criminal even. I am thinking of those clients who, as children, had to listen to their fathers' sexual confidences, whose fathers introduced them in their early teens to parties with drink, drugs and sex, or behaved in an inappropriate, sexualized manner towards them.

In Jemma's case, the rupture came abruptly when her father met his new partner; yet it was a while before he fell off his pedestal. Her mother had died when she was young and Jemma had been daddy's "little princess". Later, she had hosted, at his side, the receptions he liked to give and became his young companion at various social outings. Suddenly with the arrival of the new partner, she found herself banished from his kingdom.

At the time, the loss of her special relationship with her father had left her feeling deeply hurt, lost and confused, and very understandably so. The pain was all the greater as, for Jemma, he still stood on a pedestal. She went off to university and he showed scant interest in either her studies or her post-university life until her first child was born. It was now many years on, and she was still bewildered by it all. She was furious with her father, whose pedestal she had kicked and kicked, until he had toppled off it – though the empty pedestal still stood as a reminder. And she was furious with herself for still needing him to be on it, and for still feeling hurt. As we looked back at the days that preceded her banishment, when she acted as his co-host at events, she saw how blurred the boundaries had been between them: although there had been no sexual impropriety of any kind, her position on her father's arm as his social companion had not felt that of a daughter. She sensed the pride he took in having this beautiful young woman on his arm, whom those not in the know might have taken to be his girlfriend. She remembers feeling uneasily flattered and realizes how confusing this would all have been for an adolescent. And how painful to have then been so summarily banished! This new understanding helped Jemma to begin to feel compassion for the young girl that she had been, and for the young woman that she now was.

The work ahead lay in taking the pedestal apart, painfully, brick by brick, and building a new, more appropriate place for her father in her life and that of her child(ren).

Despotic fathers

When clients speak of the relationship difficulties they still experience with their father (dead or alive), the boundary issues they most commonly describe are more obviously power-laced. Power comes in various guises and the despotic father story comes in innumerable familiar versions, e.g. the control freak, the manipulative charmer, the strict disciplinarian: the father who prescribes what is and is not permitted in *his* family, who asserts his power, authority, wishes and rules, by various means including physical force.[3]

Most of us can cite examples of strict disciplinarian fathers they have known, through personal experience or that of friends. Another version of the father-despot, is the father **upholder of the faith,** which abounds in Victorian fiction, and still today in many families, regardless of religious creeds. Claudia's story offers a less common variation on that theme, in that her father was deemed, at home and within their community, to be the holder of higher powers and an arbiter of the rigid belief system within which they lived.

C. *Father and a few of his friends sat at the feet of a guru for many years – that was a long time ago, when I was very little, and when the guru died, father became the community's Enlightened Father. Enlightened Father! I wish they could have seen him at home! It was like … I just didn't exist: it's not that he paid no attention to me or neglected me, but like I didn't exist as a person in my own right. It was like… I only existed as a reflection of him, a reflection of his Enlightened Self. It's so difficult to explain, but it's like he would often pry into how I was feeling and then turn it into something about himself as a healer. So, if I was feeling good, it was because of his EW (that's what we called Enlightened Wisdom) and if I was feeling low or bad in some way, he would tell me that it was because I had closed my channels to EW. So he'd insist we do some healing ritual together, and then, I found out, he would tell other Enlightened Disciples that I had confessed to closing my channels to EW but that with EH (Enlightened Healing) we had opened them together.*

   You know, Laura, even my body wasn't mine. It's not that I had to mind how I dressed and what I ate and had to keep my body pure and attend to my channels so that EW could enter. We all had to do that. But it felt like I was to be the mirror of his perfection that he could offer to the world.

   So I made sure I chose a university at the other end of the country. That was tough. Father was a powerful man, well it felt that way.

L. *That must have taken courage.*

C. *It did. It was really scary.*

Claudia's story may sound too unusual to have relevance as an example, yet if 'EW' and 'EH' are replaced with more conventional forms of religious instruction and worship, the picture becomes a far more familiar one.
In the intervening years, Claudia's mother had died and the community had drifted apart. Claudia's father had aged fast.

C. *He' s looking really old, and he wants me to move closer, and I just don't know what to do. In a sense I'd like to be closer to him.*

L. *Geographically closer or 'closer, closer'?*

C. *Not so much geographically, but maybe, I don't know. I'd really like to feel closer and I'd like to be able to talk to him about the past, not in anger. No way the big A! But I am scared.*

L. *What are you scared of?*

C. *I'm scared he'll just trash the life I've made for myself – because I've left EW behind, and I'm not married, and I don't have children… or he'll turn things round and say it was his channelling of EH that furthered my career, or that it brought me back to the fold.*

L. *That doesn't seem to leave much room for you to take credit for your life choices.*

C. *No… there was never room for me to really be myself. But you know, the craziest thing is… that there's still part of me that wonders: what if EW and EH really are The Way?*

L. *And that's a scary thought?*

C. *Yes. Yes, it is. And I am scared that if I move nearer to him, or visit him more often, it'll reawaken all my old questions and doubts.*

As we explored further the unusual world in which she grew up, Claudia saw how the rigid, belief-led boundaries that had ring-fenced her behaviour, had gone hand in hand with insufficient boundaries between her father and herself. By holding the dual roles of father and community's channel for a higher wisdom, it had distorted their relationship : for he had sought to turn his daughter into the reflection of his spiritual enlightenment and powers. This made Claudia feel angry. She realized that, in addition to her fears, she was going to have to deal with the anger, the forbidden 'big A', before she could ever make any decision about whether to visit more often, let alone move closer to her father's home. And then they were going to have to be able to talk honestly. This, Claudia decided, was going to be her red line : she was not prepared to be there more for her father if the elephant remained in the room.

The 'bastard'

A number of clients refer to their fathers as "the bastard". Where does the despot end and the 'bastard' begin? Where does the distinction between the two lie? The despotic father's intentions towards his children seem good to him: he wants the best, if not for them, at least for the family of which he has to retain control, for he is, and has to remain, its 'head'. Yet, there are those 'bastard' fathers who would argue the same, maybe even believe it. It would be simplistic to see physical violence as drawing the red boundary line between the two. Many of my clients have spoken of fathers who gave them "a good hiding" or "thrashing" but were "fair", and with hindsight they accepted this as their father's possibly misguided way (their doubt, not mine) of trying to instil discipline and good behaviour. However, there is a level and kind of control, abuse of power or violence that goes beyond trying to instil rules and discipline, one that seems to come from a dark place. A dark place in which a father's sadism, violence, icy coldness, extreme narcissism, terror, incestuous lust and other such demons live. The father who is prey to such emotions and ways of being can become 'a real bastard'.

My counselling room has seen many adults whose fathers were 'bastards'. These clients come wracked with emotions from anger, vengefulness and terror (hypervigilant or numb), to deep shame. These emotions feel overwhelming at times, yet even in their manageable form, on a daily basis, they may get in the way of mundane activities of daily living. Some of these adults come to therapy specifically to find a way out of these debilitating emotions to a more satisfying way of being, others come with another presenting issue but soon realize, as they explore it, that it is firmly rooted in their relationship to their bastard of a father. They begin to observe, often in amazement, how beliefs and emotions familiar from childhood are still deeply affecting their present lives, underpinning many of their choices and patterns of behaviour, carried in their bodies as areas of tension and/or collapse. In addition, if they were sexually abused, neglected, beaten or constantly castigated for being worthless and bad, they tend to carry an ingrained conviction of their own worthlessness and badness that is hard to shift. These clients need a compassionate witness to their childhood experiences, someone to acknowledge what happened and validate their complex emotions, before they themselves can experience compassion towards the child that they once were and find a way to live *with, yet beyond,* their past. For they need to gain a sense of their own agency, to learn to develop trust in their bodies, their resources and their qualities, to trust in themselves.

Trying to understand how their father may have become such a 'bastard' can also be helpful. It is not about seeking to explain – human beings are not things or processes governed by scientific laws; still, there can be some form of understanding. So, unless one believes that human beings are born 'bastards', the question should evoke some curiosity. Even if the transformation from victim of violence to persecutor may be hard to fathom and cannot be excused, it is usually helpful for a client to acknowledge that their neglectful, terrifying and/or violent father may well have experienced terror or violence himself. Their father's experience may well have been at the hands of someone in a position of trust – e.g. family member, fellow member of a religious community, boarding school housemaster. For a whole generation of men however, it will have been in war.

(Grand) fathers and the war

I recently met up with a few former classmates in memory of one of our teachers who had died the previous year. School reunions run counter-culture to the French education system: in my day, school did not even pay lip-service to any form of pastoral care and was impersonal in the extreme, but Madame R. had been an exception among our teachers. I decided to risk asking these few classmates about their parents' wartime experiences – something we had never talked about at the time; though I do remember, when I was 12, the mother of one of my friends showing me the concentration camp number branded on her arm. Listening to their stories, I realized how many of us must have had parents who had been traumatized by the war (the Second World War).

In France, the story is more complex than in the UK, for the French experience is one of occupation and humiliation, a polarization of collaboration versus resistance, of persecutors versus victims, and it remained buried away for decades. In the early 1970s, the Second World War had not even made it onto the history curriculum; yet, the war had indirectly touched most of our lives. Now, as women in our sixties, we exchanged tales of fathers who had returned broken men from forced labour in Germany, of fathers in the resistance hiding in the intercommunicating cellars under our Paris homes, escaping with British soldiers at Dunkirk, or smuggled as young boys under the border into children's homes in Switzerland. We were the 'post-war, baby boom generation', the expression has a ring of optimism and is now associated with good fortune and plenty. We were the generation born to the hope of a Europe that would never again tear itself apart with war. Yet, we were born to parents and grandparents who, in many cases, had suffered terror, violence and loss.

In the last few decades, there has been a growing awareness of the extreme post-traumatic trauma suffered by veterans of recent wars, often resulting in substance abuse, homelessness, violence and suicide. Yet, in the UK, unlike Germany for instance, there has been little questioning of the *psychological* impact of the Second World War on later generations. My generation in the UK, and that of my children, was conditioned by old black and white war films: tales of heroism, patriotism and cooperation within the community. This was part of the story and it gave us little impetus to reflect upon either the war's darker shadow on our country, or the impact of the war on our grandparents, parents and now on ourselves and our children. As a therapist in the UK, I am surprised how seldom, other than with second generation Jewish clients, the Second World War enters the therapeutic space – unless I specifically ask about it[4].

Yet, so many 'ordinary' men and women had to do such extra-ordinary things to survive – some of the more recent films, such as the 2017 *Dunkirk*, depict this powerfully. Think of all the soldiers who returned to their wives and girlfriends, but changed men, unable to speak of what they saw, did or feel. And what about the soldiers who left their pregnant wives and returned, strangers, to an unknown toddler or young child? Or else to a wife whose loyalty they could not be sure of – "Is this child truly mine, and if not, whose is it? Has she slept with a friend… or did she sleep with the enemy?" Meanwhile wives who had shown independence, immense hard work and courage had to return to a subservient role in the relationship.

Such traumas can cascade down the generations. So, when I listen to my clients speak of their fathers' extremes of physical or emotional behaviour,

I might wonder out loud about their wartime past, or that of their grandfathers. This can feel like opening up a Pandora's box. Some recall memories of their fathers' nightmares and screams that repeatedly tore through their childhood sleep and filled them with terror, testifying to that past. Others mention stories of wartime heroics, hardship, loss and deprivation.

Joel's father, a concentration camp survivor would berate his son if he threw away the slightest scrap of food. And woe betide him, if Joel caught a cold, for his father would "go out of his mind", oscillating between rage and despair. It was some years before Joel understood that, for his father, as in the camps, a bad cold was the beginning of the end.

Christian's sadistic father had been tortured in a Japanese prisoner of war camp.

Martine had mentioned, when I first met her, that from a young age she had felt guilt at taking 'another person's place in the sun'. Only later did I learn that her father had survived the war while his two brothers had perished. Is it really too great a stretch of the imagination to see a connection between the two?

There are so many wartime experiences that have not found the words to express them and so many versions of the traumatized father/grandfather that go unrecognized: for these are not simply the irascible, guilt-ridden or alcoholic men prone to violent rages, but the numb, shadowy figures in the background[5].

Eve recalled the silent, expressionless presence of her grandfather sent back shell-shocked from the trenches.

Ted his taciturn grandfather who had been a stretcher-bearer in WWI.

What did these silent grandfathers and fathers see, suffer and do in these hells on earth? Was it the horror, terror or guilt of it that had pervaded my clients' childhoods? We can only speculate. But just asking the question allows the client to consider that the problem may not lie with themselves but with something in their (grand)parent's lives. And this may open the door to greater compassion and more possibilities for themselves, as well as a degree of compassionate understanding for their fathers and grandfathers.

Feeling 'missed'

Much of the suffering at the hand of fathers that I witness as a therapist has not come from a father's violence, neglect or significant boundary issues. Many clients speak of fathers who, for whatever reason, were unable to meet their children's basic needs for acknowledgement, validation, acceptance and a sense of feeling loved – or were not even prepared to try and do so. The ways a father (or, of course, a mother) can 'miss' his children and their needs, so that they feel neither heard, seen or accepted as they are, let alone cherished, are too numerous to detail.

Absent fathering is one of the most common ways of missing one's child; it comes in a variety of guises.

Julian was sent away to boarding school from the age of 7, while his sisters went to the local day school. Julian had long felt himself singled out for exclusion, but he can now see that his parents were just following in the family tradition. He can now well believe that his father loves him "in his own way", but it has taken him over twenty years for him to realize that. Probably like Julian himself, his father had learnt from a young age to keep his feelings for his loved ones "under lock and key" – just as his father and grandfather had probably done before him.

As to Alex, he had grown up at home with his parents and siblings under one roof, but his father's only source of interest had been his work. Alex had once asked him to explain what he did, but was met with eyes rolled up and an irritated sigh, so he never tried again. Alex had taken his father's absent demeanour and irritable moods personally; he had felt himself a very boring person, unworthy of his father's interest. A feeling that he was still finding difficult to shake off.

Jen's father used to just sit there in a dejected mood. There seemed to be no place for her in his world.

Greg's father showed not even a semblance of caring for his son: as he saw it, his wife had conceived him behind his back. He hadn't wanted that child and didn't see why he had to show any interest in it.

As to Jessica, it wasn't until her teenage years that she realized that the man who used to sometimes visit at weekends was her father. He would bring her sweets and small gifts, though seldom ever played with her. There had also been that holiday in Norfolk. But she still remembers, as if it were yesterday, the time when she was with her mum in the street and she saw him with a mum and her little girl – he didn't even say hello to her or her mum, just walked on as if he had not seen them. She remembers the confusion of it – because she was sure he had seen her, but he didn't wave back. That was the last time she ever saw him.

Hypercritical, dismissive, and demeaning fathers are also frequent 'visitors' to my counselling room. They evoke dejection, sadness, shame or resignation, or else are blamed for so much and raged at. They too have 'missed' their child.

Ben's father had not been an absent father, yet he too had painfully 'missed' his son – painfully for both father and son. In fact, far from being absent, he was "always on my case", dragging Ben to fishing, to Sunday morning rugby practice and to watch banger racing. It seems that Ben's father had wanted nothing more than to "bond" with his son, but did not understand that a bond requires a bonding agent that works for both sides. Piqued by Ben's reluctance to join in these "boys together" activities, his father began to taunt him for preferring other interests. In time, these taunts grew sharper and became directed at everything he did: from the way he dressed and the foods he avoided to his choice of A level subjects. It was, Ben said, like everything about me was a personal offence to my dad – how could a son of his have turned out like I did! And yet, I can see now I was a great kid, I just didn't share my dad's interests.

Gary's father used to say that words failed him to express his disappointment and disgust at what his son had become. Words to express his disappointment maybe failed him, but homophobic swear words for Gary he had in plenty.

When a child feels missed in some way, they may consider themselves to be the reason for their fathers' behaviour. And even as adults, they may find it extremely difficult to shake off the sense of not being worthy of attention, prizing and love. It is therefore of crucial importance for these adults to try to understand, with compassion, the context of their childhood and its enduring impact. All the more so as a part of themselves may still be seeking to gain their fathers' attention and recognition. Yet, it is also *vitally* important for adults who have been 'missed' as children to develop a personal sense of their own presence, their own potential, agency and worth. *Vitally*, because it concerns their own life and all its possibilities.

Unbounded loyalty

I am always astounded to hear how much some adults are prepared to "put behind" them to have a relationship with their fathers, leaving the past unspoken.

When I first started work at hospital I encountered a recurring story, which for some reason I never came across in later years: the power dynamic around Bingo night. Maud and Bronwen were two of a number of my clients whose fathers beat their mothers on Bingo night – it seemed to be an almost necessary ritual. Maud remembers being terrified for her mother and not understanding why she would put herself through this ordeal for the sake of Bingo. Later, her father would also swear at Maud and call her names whenever, as a young woman, she had ventured to go out with a boy, and he would beat her if she returned after 10pm.

For Bronwen's father, any excuse was good enough to justify a good thrashing, and now in her seventies, she still remembers the bewilderment and shame of being beaten black and blue when her father found out that she had started menstruating; these emotions were exacerbated by the voyeuristic behaviour that followed.

Yet, both Maud and Bronwen later looked after their respective fathers in their cantankerous and hypercritical old age. "He's my dad" each would answer when I asked why they were still prepared to put up with the insults and constant denigration.

We each owe our life partly to our biological father's sperm, and in that sense we each owe a debt of gratitude to our biological fathers who gave us life – though there are those for whom life has felt an unwanted gift. On the other hand, I believe that 'dad(dy)' is a title to be earned by a father's modicum of interest in and kindness to his children, as are the loyalty and closeness attached to that title. Where that modicum of interest and kindness were absent in childhood *and remain so*, an adult has to ask themselves why they are still being so loyal and doing so much for their father. If it is, for instance, because filial duty as a higher principle is a person's core belief, then the choice is congruent – yet even then there is room for conditions and boundaries. But when loyalty to a father is tied to an unspoken hope that he might signal his approval and love, I believe that this loyalty, or the way it is lived, may need challenging.

It is interesting how some people ascribe all the good that has happened to them in life to the actions of others or simply to good fortune, while putting all the bad down to their own faults. Meanwhile there are those who see themselves as life's victims, blaming others and bad luck for all that has gone wrong in their lives, crediting themselves for the good.

Ross was a variation on the former: he felt "intensely loyal to the old bastard" as he was convinced that he "owed him everything". Beaten in a cold and vicious manner, constantly denigrated, Ross had convinced himself that without his father "cutting me down to size" and telling him he would never amount to anything, he would never have "made it big" as he had. While this might well be true, he was unwilling to acknowledge the extent of his childhood suffering, let alone the high cost he was still paying for this, years after his father's death: rage at the contemptuous and hypercritical voice that he carried within himself at all times and, in times of business crises, nights disturbed by nightmarish replays of his humiliating beatings. And yet he also still felt a deep yearning for his father's approval.

Trying to gain the respect and approval of a hypercritical, hyper-narcissistic or demeaning parent can be a lifelong struggle with little chance of success. To pursue this goal beyond the grave, as Ross was doing, is to engage in a fantastical battle with ghosts.

Although Ross strongly believed that children should not be denigrated or beaten, his ingrained belief that he owed his professional success to his father's 'cutting him down to size' made it difficult for him to view his father's behaviour and his own strengths and capacities with any kind of objectivity.

A chance witnessing of a father viciously bullying his son brought memories flooding back. After sitting in his hotel room shaking, Ross started sobbing uncontrollably. Only as the crying abated did he make the connection with his own experience... and suddenly he felt overwhelmed with compassion for his younger self. Gradually, through our work together, he was able to see and value the child he had been and develop a genuine appreciation of his own resilience and gifts, without feeling himself beholden to his father for them. As he gradually let go of the need to fantasize about his dead father's approval or his search for vindication, Ross was able to keep his father's hypercritical voice well out of earshot, which until then even death had failed to do.

It is good to remember that interpersonal boundaries are not set in stone; they can be revisited at different moments of our lives. We can even revisit them in the absence of the other, for interpersonal boundaries are more than physical distance, they are an embodied attitude involving all aspects of our being.

Breaking patterns

A client's relationship to their parents is one of the most common themes in therapy. However, another significant part of my therapeutic practice involves offering support to parents and help with exploring aspects of their parenting: anxieties about their children, things they find difficult or triggering, and the way their own personal upbringing and life story impact upon their relationship to their own children.

One common danger for parents who have had less than good enough parenting is the aim to do the opposite of what their parents did. The problem is that *aiming to do the opposite is but the other side of one same coin* and hence cannot be divorced from it. It carries on its back all the emotions still attached to that other side.

Don came to see me after his stay in intensive care, but it was clear from the start that he was seizing this opportunity to try to improve his relationship with his young children. His mother had died when he was young and his father had been an authoritarian and disparaging father, and Don as the eldest of three boys had borne the brunt of his beatings and vitriolic insults. Don often imagined what life would have been like had his mother not died. And now, with his own children, he was trying so hard to do the opposite of what his father would have done. Yet, he was distraught as he not infrequently caught himself behaving like him: sometimes flying into a rage and then licking his wounds in silence.

L. *Could you give me an example of this happening?*
D. *It's like when I start an activity with them and I can't do it properly any more – you know, since the accident- and it drives me mad and I fly off the handle. Then I think "what's the point?" And I give up. And I think... I'll just keep my distance and won't answer when my children ask me to play. But then my daughter gets really upset and it's like she's fired an arrow into my heart.*

Was it that last sentence that led me to suggest to Don that we explore his situation with buttons? I cannot remember, but it was one of the most powerful and transformative pieces of button work I have witnessed.

L. *Don, would you like to choose a button for yourself and then one for your father?*
   Don picked a small black button for himself and a larger black one, clearly from the same set, for his father and laid them on the coffee table.
D. *The last thing I ever wanted to be like is like my dad and look, that's how I've turned out, I'm a chip off the old block.*
L. *Let's see about that, Don, but first could you place some buttons to represent the sort of things he'd say to you.*
D. *He often wouldn't say anything, he'd just scowl.*

L. *OK, so buttons to represent how he would commonly have interacted with you.* Don chose three large black buttons and put them on the table next to his father's buttons.

D. *And now choose some buttons for your mother and what you feel she might have said, or how she might have been with you.*

As Don looked at the buttons and the way he had laid them out, it hit him "like a thunderbolt". On one side stood a group of three black buttons, while facing them were three of my shiniest buttons – one, silver with an intricate embossed design of painted flowers; a gold one with a shiny 'diamond' in the middle; and a mother-of-pearl button.

D. *It's like I have turned mum into an angel, all shining and beautiful. And my dad is all black.*

L. *Mmm. Yes, you've made your mum into a beautiful angel who could do everything right, and your dad all black, who did and said everything wrong.*

D. *Yeah, but that's not how life goes, is it?*

L. *No, it isn't… And how about you now choose two buttons for your children, first for your son and then your daughter.*
Don chooses a yellow button for his son.

L. *What made you choose this button for Alfie?*

D. *He's so full of life and energy and fun.*

L. *And isn't it wonderful that you have brought into the world a child who can be so full of life and energy and fun? Not one who has to cower as you did when you were his age.*

D. *Yeah. When you say that it makes me feel… emotional.* Don's eyes well up.

L. *Yep. But it's important to remember that….and now, can you choose a button for your daughter.*
I notice Don taking a sharp intake of breath.

D. *You know what button I am wanting to choose, don't you? It's crazy, isn't it?*

L. *You're wanting to choose a beautiful sparkly one like for your mother?*

D. *Yeah!*

Not only had Don starkly contrasted his parents, but he had given himself the double burden of: being the opposite of his demonized father and trying to walk in his angelic mother's footsteps. However, the angel's Path of Perfection is a narrow and treacherous footpath for human beings, bordered with a precipice on either side. So that however carefully Don tried to stay upon it, he found himself lacking either the competence or the patience to do so, and he would fall off the path into the precipice below. There he would find himself in his father's world, black like him. But what also suddenly hit him, as he was about to choose a button for his six-year-old daughter, was that he had been expecting her too to follow her angelic grandmother upon the Path of Perfection. The button work helped Don to realize that his dead, adored mother had been a human being, not an angel. She was not patience and perfection incarnate. She too would have found some aspects of parenting difficult. This revelation was followed by an equally sudden acceptance that the limitations which his own disability imposed on his activities with his children need not be a cause for self-blame, anger and guilt.

Don had to go into a physical rehabilitation hospital some distance away, so we did not meet again until three months later. I was amazed to find out how, following that session, Don had been able to reframe many aspects of his world-view for himself in a more compassionate way:

D.   *You know, Laura, away all these weeks, well, I've understood the power of words. People say I'm 'confined to a wheelchair' but now I say "I'm a good wheelchair user"; and instead of thinking of myself as "puny" like I did, I call myself "wiry". And it makes a real difference. And like we said, I try to remind myself to look to the future and what I can still do, rather than to the past and all I've lost.*

And you know, Laura, it's been great to just watch my children play and have fun together, rather than trying to do activities with them that are beyond me. I know my sporting days are over, but it's not like handicraft and cooking and homework were ever my things! So, actually, it's a relief, there isn't all that frustration and guilt and shame. And sometimes they squabble and I can tell myself it's normal, it's only human.

Don could now see that, neither angel nor demon, he could be a good enough, human father to his two human children.

Fatherhood places a man in that liminal space between his ancestors and his descendants. It is a good place for a man to take stock, to reflect, compassionately, upon the family's and his own dreams and regrets, upon obstacles overcome and succumbed to, upon the baggage still being carried and future projects.

It may open up questions about the sort of fathering a person wishes to offer, possibly involving a renegotiation of their place as father, within the home, the family and maybe within society as a whole.

Rethinking a father's place in the home and in society

James is a thoughtful and sensitive man. He is a stay-at-home husband and the main carer for his children. When I suggested to him that he might find the experience of joining a men's group fruitful, his immediate response was telling: "But I wouldn't belong!"

From a purely logical perspective, the reply was nonsensical and hence comical: how can a person who was born male, and has always lived and identified as such, not belong in a men's group? Yet, James was clearly expressing a conviction that reflected complex feelings and beliefs associated with masculinity today and his own place in relation to it. As an open-minded man and a strong advocate of feminist views, James was clearly worried that he might end up in a group with men who displayed a particular form of hegemonic masculinity and macho behaviour that was particularly distasteful to him. However, the response which the idea of a group elicited in James also reflected a more pervasive discomfort about his own place in his life, as well as in society today, both as a white middle class man and as a father.

The last 30 years have seen a rich, sometimes emotionally charged, cross-fertilization between grassroot attitude changes, socio-political movements and academic studies. Feminist, gay and latterly LGBTQ+ activism have challenged the ways gender is both conceptualized and lived. This has led to a multifaceted questioning of the society within which gender in general, and masculinity in particular, has long been embedded and embodied – and fatherhood within it. This questioning has highlighted the gendered nature of society, the potential for new practices at societal level, as well as new ways of being-in-the-world-as-a-man. (And I use Heideggerian hyphens here to show that it affects every aspect of a man's way of relating to himself, others and the world; *see Glossary* being-in-the-world.)

Yet, traditional world-views die hard in society and in the home. From what my clients report, even men who describe themselves as strong advocates of change for women still find themselves at times confronted with a dissonance between their beliefs, actions and emotions. Many, for instance, are torn between their belief in the importance of their female partner's professional ambitions on the one hand and their wish be the centre of their attention, or else to be the family's principal breadwinner, like their fathers before them. For 'breadwinner' still taps into age-old images of the man who has earned his bread by the sweat of his brow, his family's 'provider', 'rock' and 'protector'. (Yet, interestingly, the concept of the man as the breadwinner is relatively new, having only emerged at the beginning of the 19th century.).

The acknowledgement of plural 'masculinities' does not simply represent an important theoretical reevaluation. It is a reevaluation of lived experience, on a personal level, in relationships, within society and the family, and it has intergenerational repercussions. It affords fathers a context within which to revisit the line of men who came before them, to envision those who will follow, and to offer their sons, and their sons' sons, a different palette of possibilities.

Conclusion

Father–child: An evolving relationship

Our childhood past cannot be undone, but our glance on it can change and be transformative for the present. A difficult childhood is but a chapter in a life's story, albeit sometimes a dark, unbearably painful one. It will always remain an important chapter out of which the rest of the story will evolve; yet life circumstances and human freedom can allow for any number of possible twists in the storyline.

The father–child relationship will be one strand of a life story, whether the father be still alive, dead, or of whereabouts or identity unknown. And that strand can be fleshed out through questions, so as to evolve and grow: who is this man who begat me? What if anything, beside life, did he give me? What do I know of his own life experiences, of his relationship with his own father, and with the rest of his family? What burdens did he carry, what were his dreams and ambitions – for himself and for me? What was his place in our family as I was growing up, and what was mine? What place, if any, did my father want for himself in my life? What place am I giving him: Am I still seeking his recognition and approval? Am I still allowing him to hurt me? And if so, what shall I do about it?

The answers are ours to discover and act upon.

Notes

1　'Fathering' not in the traditional sense of 'begetting', but as corresponding to 'mothering'.
2　The last few decades have seen many new possibilities and opportunities for father-hood; however, this book reflects my practice and I have therefore chosen not to write about any specific, differentiating issues of fatherhood and fathering in LGBTQ+ relationships, nor of growing up with fathers who identified as such, as I do not have sufficient first-hand professional experience to do so.
3　I must emphasize that I am not claiming that fathers alone fall in this cat-egory: mothers also can wield their violent power, they too can be despotic, sad-istic, or cruel.
4　It is worth noting however that while the Second World War trauma seldom enters unbidden in the counselling room, in Systemic Constellations, which address the client's broader context, the Second World War and its traumas frequently emerge and claim their place (*see Chapter 13 Understanding and Glossary*).
5　And there are also of course the many (grand)parents traumatized by the war in some way, who have nonetheless managed to live rich lives and engage well emo-tionally with others.

Chapter 12

The Family Holy Book

Most families have their own set of spoken or unspoken values and beliefs, their 'Family Holy Book'. The Family Holy Book not only provides an overarching framework but governs the family, and in particular the children, through explicit and implicit rules, sometimes in the smallest details of their lives. Where there appear to be no rules or boundaries, the Family Book injunction might be: "thou shalt be governed by no rule, restricted by no boundaries". Even if many families expressly seek, in their Holy Book, to communicate basic moral values, the most important commandments may be written in invisible ink: "each one for themselves", "the world's a dangerous place, keep hidden", "the world is common, we are above it", "the world is scary and incomprehensible, we just muddle along", "hit out before the other gets you", "never show your feelings", "never leave your parents' home". Some Family Holy Books advise caution, others value risk-taking, some urge submission, others a show of force.

A Family Holy Book also governs the way family members address each other, on what tone of voice, what are acceptable emotions and behaviour. Anger is the fuel that some families run on; while, in other families, anger is taboo. I have seen many clients for whom the implicit message was "thou shalt never express, or even feel, anger". The problem is that anger is a human emotion so that when a person can neither express nor allow themselves to feel it when it is justified, two things necessarily happen: anger becomes viewed as shameful and guilty, and it tries to find an outlet that is more acceptable according to the Family Holy Book – such as low, dark moods or tears. (Whereas in other families, "crying is for sissies".) This becomes mystifying for all concerned as these are substitute emotions and therefore, incongruent and off the mark.

When it comes to the body, what guidelines did your Family Holy Book provide? Was the body to be valued, taken care of, praised, loved? Could it ever be shown off? Was it to be dismissed as unimportant compared to the mind or the soul, viewed as shameful, dirty or even sinful? And what size and weight was it allowed to be?

Some Family Holy Books allow comfort for the body – comfortable mattresses and soft towels, food that nourishes and also pleases the palate,

DOI: 10.4324/9781003364504-13

and even some pampering; while others aim to fortify the body with unheated rooms, basic food that aims to (barely) nourish rather than please, cold showers or regular arduous training. The Family Holy Book may govern a myriad of beliefs and rules about food: who gets the bigger and better portion, whether food can be left on the plate, dietary edicts about forbidden, "poisonous" foods (e.g. sausages, sugar) and "lethal" ways of cooking (microwave, frying). The Holy Book's chapter on food may hark back to the family's trauma history: "if your fridge is not chockablock full, you will starve", "how can you possibly throw away this green potato, this mouldy bread, this apple core?"

The Holy Book chapter that deals with sex, gender identity, sexual orientation and behaviour is often written in red ink with exclamation marks. It may well contain crossed out, censored words. It variously enjoins: "Sex is blissful", "Sex is dirty and sinful", "Holding hand and kissing in front of others is pervy", "Monogamous heterosexual relations alone are normal", "Sex and gender are non-binary and can be fluid".

Some Family Holy Books enshrine discrimination and unfairness "sons are more valued than daughters", or more specific messages: "your younger sister is special to us and you can't expect to get what she gets"; "unless proven innocent, and even then, you're in the wrong"; "those who take after granddad A. will be the clever ones, those who take after B. weird" and allocating children to each side simply according to parental preferences.

A Family Holy Book usually provides guidelines about expectations, possibilities, work ethic, the importance (or not) of studying and the comparative worth of particular jobs. It may also command what boys and girls can play with or do, which football team to support, what food to enjoy, and what to wear: "you must wear your Sunday best to church", "you shall wear clean underwear every day, in case you get run over and taken to hospital", "only sluts wear crop tops". And of course, many Family Holy Books codify acceptable political, ecological, philosophical or religious beliefs, and whether state information can at all be trusted.

The degree of permitted disregard for a Family Holy Book injunction will also vary from family to family and even, within families, between family members: "no one's allowed to get angry, except dad"; "sex before marriage is an excludable offence, but not for Tom and Sadie".

Teenage behaviours, such as answering back, dressing a little outrageously, dating and kissing, that are viewed as normal teenage behaviour in many families, are labelled "disrespectful" or "dishonourable" in others and punishable by banishment from the family home. For in Family Holy Books that equate modesty with honour, these behaviours offend against the fundamental tenets: "thou shalt honour thy father and mother" and/or "though shalt not bring dishonour upon your family".

Jonathan's mum had worked hard all her life, often holding two jobs to make ends meet when her children were young. At home, she kept a tight ship and discipline was strict. Not that Jonathan and his siblings would have dared, or even thought to put a foot wrong! For God spoke in mum's ear, and she would know if they had sinned – and the slightest misdemeanour, from not clearing the table, or tidying their toys away, or not wearing clean underwear was regarded as a sin. Sadly, it was 'sin' that had since torn their family apart, when mum disowned her second daughter and the other siblings took sides.

To this day, Jonathan still feels himself observed and judged as he undertakes everyday mundane tasks, though he knows it is absurd. He also feels fundamentally "sinful" and only part of him believes that it is "probably" not true.

Where all edicts of the Family Holy Book are sacrosanct and to be adhered to rigidly, there is often little gradation between rules. The child learns very early on to fear breaking any rule in case it led to total exclusion, even where, to most people, the effraction appears minor or the rules absurd: such as "black tights are for whores", "reading Harry Potter is sinful", "Swatch watches are Satan's watches", "you must always be way top of the class".

Where the Family Holy Book is intimately linked to the community's, expulsion from the home may result in expulsion from the community. And vice versa, in families where the Family Holy Book's authority is superseded by that of the Church, the Elders, the religious order or political leader who holds sway. Theirs, as representatives or replacement of a Higher Power on earth, is the final say.

Conclusion: The family holy book

A child needs boundaries for their basic physical safety, emotional security, moral compass, and general well-being. There is a broad continuum of healthy rules and boundaries capable of providing the child with these fundamental requisites, which most families' 'Holy Books' enshrine in spoken and unspoken forms.

Some Family Holy Books however fail to create a place of safety for the child to thrive physically and emotionally and develop a moral and spiritual core. It may be that they only endorse the extremes of the various boundary continua, advocating totally lax or chaotic boundaries that leave the child feeling unsafe and confused; or ultra-precise and rigid ones likely to make home a place of entrapment, submission and fear. Or they may favour one person while tolerating the abuse of others; they may foster a situation in which grief, unsafe behaviour, or violence rule.

Understanding the role played by the Family Holy Book in our childhood is an invaluable path to understanding some of the more constricted and constricting, or indeed chaotic areas of our adult lives. Understanding how difficult it may have been for us as children to live according to such rules and boundaries, and acknowledging how they still impact our lives, is a route to the self-compassion that lies at the very heart of healing.

Chapter 13

Understanding

You may want to read the following paragraph and then close your eyes for a brief moment: without dwelling upon them, notice the thoughts that you have just brought to starting this chapter: are they questions? Judgements about the book? About yourself? Or are they extraneous thoughts such as what you might be having for dinner? Are all these thoughts jostling for attention in your head or just drifting in and out? Now drop into your body, do you notice any sensations (rumblings, tinglings, etc.), areas of tension, impulses to move, does the pace or the content of your thoughts change? Notice too whether there are any emotions bubbling up. Without becoming entangled in them, just notice the quality of these emotions, is there a dominant emotion (boredom, excitement, frustration, sadness, etc.) or a mixture of them? And where in your body can you feel these emotions?

When you have sat there with your eyes closed for a few moments longer, bring your mindful attention to what is going on inside you and, as you feel your feet on the ground, try to imagine that there are roots reaching deep into the earth beneath you, branching out laterally, seeking and bringing nourishment and connection. Roots that connect you to the earth and to your ancestry.

And now solidly grounded on this earth, try to feel your branches reaching out towards the world and the heavens above you.

While this exercise could be used as a meditation, it can also illustrate different forms of awareness and understanding, going from our roots to our spirit/soul, emotion, body and mind, without any form of understanding being deemed 'higher' or better than the other.

We commonly ascribe greater validity to our mind's understanding over that of our emotions, spirit, or body, yet there are times when we have strong 'gut feelings', 'we just know it in our bones', 'we know it in our heart of hearts', or 'the spirit moves us', and this understanding cannot be dismissed. Language has its own inner wisdom and, from the way it expresses the different modes, qualities, levels and nuances of our understanding, it reminds us of our own multifaceted wisdom as the above metaphors show.

DOI: 10.4324/9781003364504-14

Take the following example: if I told you that I was going to view London from the top of a double-decker bus, you would immediately be able to visualize the bus and imagine the sort of experience it might give me. You would not consider separately the concepts 'bus', London Transport, red, double-decker to imagine how I might be travelling round the city and what it might feel like looking at the sights. If I were speaking to someone from a culture that did not have public transport or buses, let alone red double-decker ones, I would have to explain separately each inseparable aspect and its particular impact upon my experience, e.g. the sense of height, pace, relation to other passengers, etc. I would also have to explain how these different elements are intertwined as parts of an integral whole, e.g. with my childhood memories, with excitement, possible incidents, anxieties, etc. When it comes to our understanding of the world, we can similarly separate out each form of our understanding: for each form highlights a different aspect of the way we understand, yet separating it out is artificial and destroys the integrality and significance of the whole experience. Still, I shall have to do so in this chapter, as I cannot at one and the same time write about understanding as a whole and about each of its inseparable aspects. The first section on cognitive understanding is more conceptual and if this does not interest you, you can skip to understanding from the body, which is more concrete.

Understanding 'from the mind'

When it comes to the mind's understanding, language is prolific in its vocabulary of nuances, as it distinguishes between the different ways in which the mind develops its understanding – reflecting, reasoning, conceiving, seeing, gaining insight, grasping and weighing things up, etc.; language also distinguishes between questions, judgements, assumptions, etc. In understanding one can be sure of oneself, categorical or more tentative. 'Belief', interestingly, is ambiguous: it can express either doubt in opposition to certainty, or else express the certainty of Faith – be it political, scientific, or the Credo (lit. 'I believe') of religious faith. The mind's understanding can be theoretical, intuitive, metaphorical, it can be abstract or concrete, blinkered or out of the box, superficial or deep, have rigidity and various 'shapes' – broad, narrow, circular, linear, etc. It can occur at different levels of consciousness: explicit, implicit, subconscious – as in the understanding dreams offer us. The mind's understanding can also have various qualities: logical, clinical, nonsensical but also cold, heartless or compassionate … And its field of interest is vast, ranging as it does from the infinitesimally small to the infinite vastness of the universe, from the human cell to whole societies and cultures, etc. But we need to remember that some forms of cognitive understanding, however rigorous, cannot be used appropriately across these various fields: for instance, while we can have a scientific understanding of parts of the body, from a cell to the brain, in all their respective complexities, and about the body's various systems including the neurological system, we cannot, *pace* some psychologists and doctors, seek to be scientific about human beings.

I shall always remember the words of one of my post-Intensive Care patients, whose name I do not recall but who, I trust, would have allowed me to use these words of hers:

My consultant was doing his rounds with all his ducklings [her brilliantly evocative name for his medical students]. He stood at the foot of my bed and said to them: "this leg will never walk again" and he started walking towards his next patient's bed. I said "Sir!" and he came back and asked "Yes madam?" (The condescension in her voice was chilling) *and I said to my doctor and all his ducklings: "This leg, Sir, belongs to me".*

It takes a great deal of courage to call a senior doctor back and speak to him publicly in this way, and a lot of courage to defy the odds. But clearly this woman had courage in buckets, for some months later she was able to walk, unaided, into my counselling room. The doctor had spoken from the height of his scientific, medical expertise on anatomy and physiology, but he had failed to take the whole person before him into account. I hope he understood his patient's wise remark.

From the perspective of cognitive understanding, this book is clearly the result of my mind's understanding, grounded in my own personal dialogue with the questions and reflections of others before me: from the early Greek philosophers and Soviet dissidents of my teenage years, to the home I later came to make for myself in Existential philosophy and therapy. And while Sensorimotor Psychotherapy and Systemic Constellations have added new dimensions to my conceptual understanding and my therapeutic practice, these remain embedded within an overarching Existential perspective. Before summarizing my personal take on Existential theory and practice, I would like to offer my reflections on compassion, for it has been woven, both explicitly and implicitly within the pages of this book, yet still not defined.

Compassion

'Compassion' and 'sympathy' both mean, etymologically, a *suffering or feeling with'*; yet these two words evoke subtly different emotions in us, as do 'feeling sorry for', 'feeling pity', 'empathizing'. These expressions all describe similar ways of being drawn to feel for someone. To use these interchangeably, however, is to confuse significantly different experiences: how many times have I heard clients say "I don't want people to feel sorry for me", when what they meant was that they didn't want others to pity them.

The predominant difference, as I see it, between feeling compassion, feeling pity and feeling sorry is that, in compassion, we feel ourselves somehow 'in the same boat' as the other, even if this be only the vast boat of shared humanity – we *'feel with'* them.

'Feeling pity', I would argue, is offered from either a position of felt superiority or at the very least a sense of being removed from the other's fate; pity implies 'it couldn't happen to me!' 'Feeling pity' for someone may veer towards contempt – conjuring up images of a person looking down their nose at a person begging. To feel pity may involve a judgement, which is why it is shaming and not welcome. (While to 'take pity upon someone' is closer to pity's original meaning of the emotion and act of 'piety' and mercy.)

Whereas when we feel genuinely sorry for someone, we feel for that person without such shaming judgement; we are seeking to convey heartfelt warmth and comfort. Yet, with feeling sorry, as with pity, there is still a sense of separation, of distance, between the other's world and ours. But, whereas in 'feeling sorry', we are aware of our different worlds and acknowledge that the other is somehow less fortunate (e.g. "they've had a hard time of it/fewer opportunities"), pity commonly passes judgement on that difference of fortune – the other is "not as strong-willed, talented, graced by God, hard-working, well-born, etc. as me". Even when feeling genuinely sorry, there may be a part of us that also thanks our lucky stars that we are not sitting in the same boat as that other right now.

It is presumably because 'sympathy', as a way of feeling *with*, has developed such a wide variety of meanings, from 'friendly feelings', 'support' and 'affinity' to an expression of 'condolences', that 'empathy' has gained popularity in recent years and replaced 'sympathy' in the therapeutic world. 'Empathy', etymologically 'feeling *in*', expresses that valuable attitude of trying to see things from the other person's perspective. However, "I know just how you feel" demonstrates the danger of trying to 'step into someone's shoes': for seldom can we know, in any significant way, just how the other feels.

The following example may seem quite extreme, but I hope it can illustrate those distinctions. Part of my work used to involve working as a psychotherapist with end-of-life patients. I would sit at their bedside and we would talk, or sometimes just sit in silence together. As my friend Hilary, the hospital chaplain, once put it, this is not a time for professional distance but for "professional closeness". I certainly felt no inclination to look down upon my end-of-life clients, I did not feel pity, but how could I not feel sorry? Most were having to leave family, pets, friends, a whole life that they did not want to leave; some were totally alone; some were desperate and wanted to die quickly, others were terrified of what might lie beyond; for others just being in hospital was torture. Most patients had a personal reason for me to feel sorry for them, and I was conscious of how privileged I was to be alive and well, mixing with family and friends in the outside world. Yet, I was also able to feel compassion: for as two human beings in the boat in which all human mortals journey, I was, as they were, personally aware of my own mortality, and my own dying – theirs imminent, the timing of mine unknown – aware of what it brought up for both of us. I too wondered, for instance, how one day I would pass from literally 'having a life' and being able to have human contact and/

or a conversation, as we both were now, to being dead. And I could 'feel with' them, even as they were being cast off in their solitary lifeboat onto the sea below with no chance of survival – only a matter of time. But theirs was a boat for one, another cannot step into it and know how they feel in the face of their ownmost, extreme, existential situation, another cannot truly 'empathize'.

Self-compassion

Just as we can feel sorry, pity and compassion for others, so too we can direct those emotions towards ourselves; yet of the three, self-compassion holds the most powerful key to personal healing.

For self-pity tends to involve a judgement: I may look upon myself as a 'miserable wretch', bemoan my weakness, lack of talent, unlovability, ugliness, etc. I may 'beat myself up', or else curse others or the world for my fate. By making such absolute judgements about myself or the world, I entangle myself in a persecutor-victim dynamic that may lead me to 'wallow in self-pity' or else to heap shame, contempt, hatred upon myself or the world. Self-pity is therefore seldom, if ever, helpful: the victim and shamed positions are more likely to close up opportunities for healing and change.

'Feeling sorry for myself' is less persecutory and victimizing than self-pity and differs from it in a number of ways: it is more measured than self-pity, and can often be justified, as when I am ill or hurt or else all kinds of catastrophes have befallen me. Feeling 'sorry' for myself is not necessarily unhelpful: it can help me to acknowledge that things are difficult and really not what I needed right now, while still encouraging me to hold out hope for the possibility of change and better times ahead.

In self-compassion however, I see myself as I would see a dear friend or loved one suffering my fate (Chapter 5). I do not look down on myself or judge myself – and where there is no feeling judged, there is no risk of feeling shamed. I do not just feel sorry for myself, I acknowledge at a deep, heart, mind and core level what I have gone through or done, and I offer myself understanding, love, support and care. Sadly, this may not come easily; it is certainly not something we are taught to do at school. The understanding we are seeking is neither coldly clinical and theoretical, nor is it judgemental; it is an understanding that listens to mind, spirit and body and merges the insights these bring with heart – a compassionate understanding.

Compassion is not collusion that exonerates oneself, or others, of all wrong or responsibility. It is an understanding that seeks to discover reasons (not 'causes', we are not machines) for our way of being and to make sense, with mind-heart-body-spirit, of the beliefs, experiences, choices, meaning, personal history, etc. that may have influenced our present behaviour. Compassion says "you/they acted like this, but let's try to understand the context to your/their acting in this way". Compassion does not seek to excuse actions, it seeks some understanding of the broader picture. Compassion and understanding are intimately linked: compassion is a disposition and a movement towards ourselves and others that comes from a wise and understanding heart.

When we have done something which we deem shameful or inexcusable, if we can acknowledge this and genuinely try to understand, with compassion, the reason or trigger behind our behaviour – and do so without abrogating responsibility – our compassionate understanding of ourselves will help us live better with the consequences of our actions. Similarly, if we catch ourselves holding prejudices and opinions of which we feel ashamed, compassionate reflection can help us understand their source. It can allow us to explore without shame, but responsibly, what this might mean to us and against what we might possibly be defending ourselves.

From the above personal reflections on compassion, I now want to turn to the major theoretical underpinning of this book, the Existential approach.

Existential therapy

Despite my various trainings, I still describe myself as an Existential therapist, for the philosophy in which it is grounded offers me a helpful and personally congruent way of conceiving of the world and human existence. In addition, this conceptual system and its therapeutic practice have been sufficiently broad and flexible to integrate what I have learnt from other modalities, in particular trauma therapies and Systemic Constellations, in order to make sense of my own life and the lives of many of my clients.

I like the way Existential therapy seeks to minimize the power dynamic that necessarily exists when one person comes to another for help. As I see it, Existential therapy is a joint exploration by client and therapist of the present situation, usually a painful one, which brought the client to therapy, of what this situation means to that particular client, and of the life and wider context within which it is embedded. I explore this alongside the client, as two human beings grappling with the often very difficult enterprise that is human existence. For I do not presume to know better about my client as a person, though I may have an expertise on some aspect of their situation (for example the vivid dreams of Intensive Care) and I am trained to consider different perspectives.

The most fundamental of all Existential concepts for me, in life and in therapy, is Heidegger's characterization of human existence as 'being-in-the-world'. This rich concept highlights the intrinsically embodied, relational and meaningful aspects of human existence, its openness to itself, to others and to the world, as well as its capacity to disclose these. 'Being-in-the-world' is a hyphenated word in which every term, including the hyphens, contributes to the richness of its meaning. The hyphens highlight the fact that all the elements of the expression belong together and cannot be understood in isolation. With the verbal form 'being', Heidegger highlights the dynamic, always transforming quality of 'existence' (*Dasein* lit. 'to be there'). The preposition -in- does not denote containment, nor does 'world' just denote a place – we are not in the world like sardines in a tin, or even fish in a fishbowl. Rather - in-the world refers to the fact that we dwell within a web of interconnected meanings, rather like when we say we feel 'in' limbo – that particular way of being-in-the-world in which all is uncertain, in transition, whether frozen or in flux.

Human existence as being-in-the-world is always 'being-with', being-in-relation: even a recluse is so in relation to others. Being-in-the-world is always in a shared world, in a world of shared meanings – of the particular era, country, culture, family, etc. in which we are born, with all its traditions, values, beliefs and practices, whether we follow or reject them. But at the same time, it is always a private world: it represents my own network of meanings, within which I myself relate and exist, it is my world, an aspect of my existence and it matters to me. Thus, for instance, 'hammer' has a shared meaning – if you ask someone to get you a hammer, you expect them to understand what you are asking for; and yet it also has personal meanings, for instance for me it is what I principally use for hanging up pictures, to my client Maud's father, it is what he would put by his pillow every night before going to sleep.

Heidegger describes being-in-the-world as being 'thrown' and as being-unto-death: that is, we have no control over the era, country, culture, family, etc. into which we are born ('thrown'), and from the moment of our birth we are inexorably living towards our death. Besides, in our everyday life we are also constantly 'already thrown' into situations over which we have had no say or responsibility. This realization of our thrownness and mortality is likely to be anxiety-provoking. Yet, in that time between our thrown birth and our death, we have the freedom to choose how we want to live our life within the givens of our existence – though these may severely restrict our possibilities. Existential philosophy has the reputation of being gloomy and anxiety-ridden, yet this view of freedom of choice is for me a very empowering, hope-ful thought.

However, our choices, made according to our priorities and what is meaningful to us, come with a responsibility to ourselves, to others and the world. In addition, choice is likely to involve some form of 'existential guilt': for choosing one path is likely to close some other path, down which we could have gone and which would have taken our life down a different direction. German uses the same word for 'debt' and 'guilt'; in a similar vein, English uses the verb 'owe' to refer both to a debt and to something we owe ourselves. If we owe it to ourselves to develop one of our interests, talents, etc. and we do not, then existential guilt may ensue. While existential guilt may overlap with moral guilt – guilt about something that we have done or omitted to do, existential guilt is very much about ourselves and our life, rather than specific actions. The everyday expression which best corresponds to existential guilt is 'deep regret' – a word that often figures prominently in the counselling room.

Existential therapy sees human existence as fundamentally 'embodied', as an inseparable body-mind-emotion-spirit being, itself inseparable from the world. And every element of our being is *equally* worthy of our respect, esteem and compassion; every element of our being deserves to be listened to and heard *equally*. (However, this does not mean that we should necessarily follow what it has to say: every element of our being's understanding is open to misinterpretation, error and undue influence from other elements!)

Existential therapy is informed by Merleau-Ponty's distinction between the body that we *have* and the body that we *are*. The distinction is one of attitude. When we observe, evaluate, pass judgement on our body, we relate to the body as something we *have* – as doctors do when they examine it. When, however, we open ourselves to something of beauty, when we experience disgust, when we are deeply involved in what we do – from eating to listening to music or being with friends, when we experience a sense of connection or groundedness, we *are* our body. We can also see how we *are* our body in all the automated gestures of our everyday lives.

German still has two words for 'body', that could be said to reflect that distinction: the more usual *Körper* (from Latin *corpus* 'body' and related to English 'corpse') and also '*Leib*', related to English 'life'. The body-we-are has a life force, it *is* a life force. And, just as two hands touching can simultaneously feel and be felt, the body-we-are touches and is touched by the world. The body-we-are is an integral part of what Merleau-Ponty called 'the flesh of the world'. When, however, we focus on the body we 'have', we objectify it, we view it as an object deprived of life force. There are times when we need to do that (e.g. for medical reasons or else to check it for something). There are also times when we choose to treat it as an object, whether admiring it, finding fault with it, comparing it with that of others or with norms. Objectifying our body only becomes a problem when it is our default attitude towards it, for we then create a split within ourselves. We cannot deprive our body of its intrinsic life force, but we can create a split within our life force. And this will cut us off from the possibility of a truly satisfying experience of our embodied living, of our embodied being-in-the-world.

Trauma shatters our relation to the body-we-are in a variety of ways: it can lead us to distance ourselves from our body and its experience, to turn it into a carapace and retreat into it, to remove ourselves from the present allowing it to hibernate, to split the body by creating boundary lines within it... These various splits – within the body, or between the body and its world, emotions and thoughts – prevent us from making and experiencing our existence as satisfyingly whole and integrated.

Human existence as being-in-the-world is embodied, relational, emotional, meaning-ful – that is an incontrovertible given. We are part and parcel of the world and respond as a whole to how it addresses us. However sometimes something happens to us, or to the world as we know it, to 'our' world that disrupts our whole being-in-the-world – our sense of embodiment, our relationships, our beliefs, all aspects of our existence. It may be just a temporary disruption, or it may lead to a conscious or unconscious rethinking and re-sensing (spiritually-physically-emotionally) of our whole being-in-the-world. When the French poet Lamartine, after the death of his beloved, cried out to the world '*Un seul être vous manque et tout est dépeuplé*' and '*il n'est rien de commun entre la terre et moi*', his lament was typical of Romantic era sensibility. ('One being is missing, and everything feels deserted' and 'There is nothing in common between this earth and me). Yet, it also bears a universal resonance: it is an expression of the world-shattering quality of deep loss, which leaves a person feeling no longer 'at home' in-the-world, alone, lost without the relationships and meanings that connected them to the world.

The COVID pandemic has been a Tale of Loss for our times shattering our basic sense of safety (or, for some, further emphasizing unsafeness). It deprived us of much that gave meaning to our lives: from meeting family and friends, to going to work, to the pub, the cinema.... Many were unable to go out of the front door: the world had become terrifyingly unsafe. For others, COVID challenged their already precarious sense of belonging in the world. For others still, it added fuel to their frustrations, their anger, sense of alienation and antagonism to authority. The pandemic experience was life-changing for all, but it was not 'traumatic' for all, and not equally so. Not surprisingly, there was a stark divide between those who enjoyed privileged living and working conditions, and those who did not; between those who were alone and those who had the support of family and/or friends; between those who had money and those who did not; let alone between those who fell seriously ill or else lost loved ones and those who did not. But many other factors, such as life history, values and beliefs, meaning and purpose played a part in whether or not the pandemic was experienced as traumatic, and if so to what degree. So, for instance, personally, I enjoyed lockdown – I loved being at home with time for myself. Yes, I was privileged on material and logistical fronts, but, importantly, my family, friends, work, nature, music, and this book, which I was revising, fulfilled my needs for close connection, beauty, meaning and purpose. And importantly too, I was philosophical about the possibility of my death. So, lockdown was not traumatic for me in any way.

Trauma is a Greek word meaning 'wound', 'hurt' and, in the psychotherapy field, it describes the experience of being wounded and the scar which it leaves. Some wounds heal and leave no scar; some leave scars that gradually disappear with time; or scars that heal over, yet retain a lasting tenderness or fragility. Some people scar worse than others, or scar unpredictably. Although they may leave no visible scarring, deep wounds (such as ligament damage, surgery, betrayal, loss) upset the balance of our being, they deprive it of its familiar bearings and distort its habitual ways of responding to the world. At the time of wounding, we learn ways of adapting and compensating as required by the situation. However, the ways of being we develop to manage these wounds may become ingrained, counterproductive even. This is poignantly the case with the deep wounding of chronic childhood neglect and abuse which created the belief in a world that is unsafe – and ways of managing it, which decades later still die hard.

Trauma as a disruption of a person's whole being-in-the-world articulates an Existential view of trauma which, I believe, has great therapeutic value. It can shine light on the changes which trauma creates within a client's existence. It can help them to understand the unfamiliar world in which they may find themselves: their sense of confusion and loss, the changes in the meaningfulness of things, in the possibilities that lie before them, in their priorities, their freedom to make some choices and the responsibility that accompanies it, etc. However, this Existential view of trauma has been unable to help me understand certain aspects of my own and my clients' experience; nor has it proved particularly suited for working with clients who were frequently reliving the traumatic event, overwhelmed with images and sensations of that time.

I therefore decided to turn to two other therapeutic approaches that have revolutionized the way I understand myself and work with my clients: Systemic Constellations and Sensorimotor Psychotherapy.[1] The former has provided me with a broader and more historical lens (*see below*); and Sensorimotor Psychotherapy has offered me a greater focus on the body, together with two additional, valuable, conceptual perspectives, underpinned as it is by neuroscientific research and attachment theory. 'Perspective' is the operative word: a perspective is not the Whole Truth of the matter, it is just one way of looking at it. And in an age where Science is viewed as the touchstone of reliability and validity, where 'scientific' stamps a seal of veracity, let us remember that while philosophical perspectives on human existence have tended to retain their value over the centuries and millennia, so many scientific theories have not. (Just think of 'the earth is flat' and 'smell is the plague's vector of transmission', to name but two major scientific theories).

Although the Systemic Constellations, Sensorimotor and Existential approaches belong within very different traditions, they are all three non-deterministic, non-pathologizing perspectives and all emphasize the embodied aspect of our existence. In addition, they can all be practised within the same phenomenological paradigm that is one that involves precise observation, non-interpretative description and a focus on personal meaning.

Cognitive understanding: Conclusion

All the above concepts, despite belonging to different modalities, have dialogued and evolved in me and I have evolved personally and professionally through them. However, I believe it is important that conceptual, theoretical understanding be held very lightly in therapy. In particular, there is a grave danger in attempting to use the fascinating results of recent neuroscientific research to turn therapies into pseudo-sciences, forgetting that therapy is, at heart, an art of human relating, not a science[2].

I also believe that philosophical and scientific concepts have greatest thera-peutic value when they are not simply reflected upon, but filtered through the therapist's embodied, emotional experience of them – as with Merleau-Ponty's Phenomenology of Perception that helped me learn to dance from my solar plexus instead of my head (*see Chapter 2*). Besides, only then can they become congruent with the therapist's way of being-in-the-world. It would not be congruent for me, for instance, to be a 'blank screen' or have extremely rigid boundaries as some theories predicate, or very lax ones as others allow. This would involve either shedding much that is fundamental to the way I am in life, and like to be, or else artificially barricading it away.

It can be scary of course to relax our firm hold on theory and on the belief that it detains Certain Truth about human existence and our clients. It can leave us feeling deskilled, naked and unsure before our client – before the mystery of the other. This is where we need to rely on the genuineness of our presence, the wisdom of our body and heart to create a meaningful relation-ship within which the client may feel able to open themselves to themselves and to us. There were days in hospital when the thought of going into wards to have a number of bedside sessions with patients I had never met before filled me with mild anxiety and/or weariness (especially in some of the rather grim wards). Yet, as soon as I remembered to ask myself: "Who am I going to encounter today?", I immediately felt a shift in myself. I felt my heart lift and my body lighten. I felt myself ready to engage with another human being and listen to what they were prepared to say to the complete stranger that I was to them.

Listening to the body's understanding

It is often said that 'you need to listen to your body'. But what does that mean? It usually refers to the need to listen to the signs the body gives us to let us know that it is getting overtired or overstressed and that it, that we, risk 'breaking down' in some way. Through areas of tension, heaviness and pain, through 'butterflies' and a sense of fizziness, or of numbness creeping over, our body is trying to communicate the special understanding to which it is privy. However, many of us have developed a relationship to our body akin to that of master and slave, prison guard, or else parent and child – whether to a lazy, wayward child that needs disciplining, or a spoiled child that can have what it wishes. We may therefore be so out of touch with our body's understanding, so contemptuous of what it has to say, or so caught up in another aspect of our lives that we carry on regardless, until we collapse with exhaustion – be it physical, mental, emotional, spiritual. The body under-stood the situation all along, it had warned us, but we had not learnt to value its wisdom, pay attention to it and understand its language… or we had been too terrified to do so.

Interestingly, the body's language can be surprisingly precise. It is not unusual for me to ask a client: *"have you noticed the movement you were making right now as you were speaking of x?"* And if the client has not noticed, I might imitate it, e.g. cupped hands moving out into a bowl shape, and then suggest they repeat what they were saying about x while making that movement. I might ask: *"If your hands could speak, what would they be saying to you right now?"* And the client might answer for instance: *"what really feels different"* or *"what I really would like for myself right now is this sense of feeling contained"*, thus naming a felt sense or a deep desire that they had not yet explicitly articulated for themselves.

At other times, the body confirms that it has truly understood a reflection or an interpretation.

Janine had been coming to me for quite a while. We had worked in some depth with her past history and her present ways of being, so when she came in saying that she had suddenly realized something very important this last week, I was intrigued to hear what this might be. To my surprise, she told me something that we had explored repeatedly – the impact of her controlling and hypercritical mother still now in the minutiae of her everyday life. The difference was that this time "the penny had dropped" and she had a felt sense of this thought, a sense of 'aha! Now I really get it.'

Janine had always had a tendency to live "safely cut off" from her body and the penny metaphor accurately represented that novel and valuable experience of 'dropping' from her thoughts into her body. And as she did so, her body offered her a different quality and anchoring of understanding. Her understanding now felt to her more embodied without it feeling threatening in any way; in fact, it felt surprisingly empowering. Over time Janine gradually became able to leave the safe refuge of her head to listen to her body.

In the last 25 years, trauma therapy has highlighted not only the body's wisdom, but also its memory. Trauma theory has demonstrated how the 'body remembers' and 'keeps the score' to quote from the titles of two seminal books in the field: how it remembers past dangerous and life-threatening situations, is quick to sound the alarm when it senses a familiar danger (sometimes too quick – a false alarm), and sets in motion the autonomic nervous and hormonal survival systems. The body can also hold the memory of experiences otherwise long forgotten. And by listening attentively to our body and its language, we[3] can not only learn to understand the emotional charge and the associated beliefs which it is holding, but facilitate their expression. We can also learn to communicate with our body.

Claudine came to see me as she had been experiencing strange physical symptoms – uncontrollable, emotionally charged movements that would often wake her up at night and leave her feeling overwhelmed with terror. Occasionally she felt a blinding rage. This followed a recent situation of bullying by her line-manager where she had felt profoundly hurt and betrayed.

L. Hurt and betrayed? Are those familiar feelings for you?

In response to my question, Claudine began to rock and gradually, whimpering, curl into a ball in the armchair, trembling, her tight-fisted arms rising together above her head. I gathered from Claudine's reaction that these feelings of hurt and betrayal were familiar to her, probably from way back, yet were still terribly raw.

As I mindfully observed Claudine whimpering and curling up before me, the tense jaw, the tense, trembling movement of her fists above her head were offering me an image that did not appear to be the quiet, resigned hurt and betrayal of neglect. She did not look like a child curled up in a corner unnoticed, abandoned; rather she seemed to be cowering, her whole body appearing to scream terror.

I explained to Claudine how the body can hold memories and feelings, and how these can lay dormant for decades until some event suddenly reawakens them – as seemed to have happened with the bullying at work. I also explained that just as animals instinctively shake themselves off once the danger has passed, so too human beings can allow their bodies to discharge pent-up states. Or sometimes, I added, the body tensions can be precursors to defensive movements that wanted to happen, but couldn't at the time. So I suggested we study in some detail the movements her body was making right now, and just follow them and see where, if anywhere, they might take us.

And then Claudine's arms started shaking uncontrollably for a number of minutes, before going completely limp as her whole body seemed to relax. The relief was short lived as this was soon followed by her head violently shaking from side to side. After a few minutes and a few yawns, Claudine seemed to melt into the armchair.

The 'sequencing' cycles of shaking and relaxation carried on during the following weeks. Claudine was able to take them in her stride and let the movements happen in the background, as she spoke. In fact, she welcomed the yawning and relaxation that followed, and at night, as she lay in bed, she began to allow her body to shake off its tensions, which helped her relax into sleep.

During sessions, Claudine occasionally had episodes of sitting, very tense and still, eyes tightly closed, grimacing, her right arm closed in a fist, half-covering her eyes, and then collapsing; she would feel rage and then a sense of powerlessness would come over her. The word she was wanting to utter was "no", with variations of intensity and feelings, from rage and terror to humiliated pleading. Yet, there were no proper recollections other than a sense of her grandmother's presence looming over her, and extreme terror and pain. Her body however seemed to remember precisely that her grandmother stood on her left, with her arm raised and something in her hand – something hazy which she could not distinguish but sent shivers of terror down her.

As I sit with clients, I find it astonishing to witness the detail in which the body may remember a traumatic event. And it is equally astonishing to see how such detailed body memory and such strong emotions can be so cut off from any conscious recollection.

While Claudine's symptoms might be viewed as due to purely physiological processes orchestrated by her brain and central nervous system and triggered by the bullying at work, from an Existential perspective of being-in-the-world nothing about a human being can be 'purely' physical. The body can no more be 'dis-enminded' than the mind be disembodied; nor can a human being be separated from a world of meanings and connections. We react as a whole, yet there are times when body, emotion, cognition and spirit lose awareness of one another, or of the world; they become 'dissociated'. Listening to one aspect attentively and understanding what it has to say can help us hear the voices of those other aspects of our being-in-the-world. Here, Claudine's emotions of hurt and betrayal at work, together with her colleague's abuse of power, had evoked powerful body memories, cut off from conscious thought and articulated memory. They had taken her out of her proper time and place in her world, back into childhood, to that time and place of terror, powerlessness, rage and despair.

Fortunately, as we learn to communicate with our body, besides facilitating the discharge of pent-up states of stress, we can learn to develop embodied resources, as well as a new sense of mastery.

After a few weeks, Claudine's shaking became less violent and body-wracking. Claudine was awed by her body's way of expressing and releasing its memories and feelings. It was time, we both felt, to try something new: what about if she were to try to focus on her right fist, when she was in her still and grimacing position, and see what happened next? As Claudine did so, the tension in her fist and arm began to rise. I asked her to focus on that tension until it became unbearable and then to allow her fist to follow any movement it wanted to make, but to slow it right down – really, really, really slow it down. The tension rose to such a peak that it started moving from its position by her eyes into a more actively defensive movement, accompanied by a guttural battle cry. The tears that followed that slow movement of fighting rage, had a very different feel, as did the way her body softened and relaxed. This was the exhaustion that follows the expending of vast fighting energy.

The following week, Claudine reported having felt a different sense of calm. I suggested we work on integrating that emerging sense of mastery. We both repeated the defensive movement and practised different ways of saying "no!" and "stop!" with it. Claudine discovered the tone and volume that felt right – even as she pictured her stout grandmother before her. She spoke of it feeling almost like an exorcism as her grandmother's image fizzled away!

Practising "no!" in this way reminded Claudine that this had all happened a long time ago – that she was no longer this small cowering child, and that she was now an adult capable of standing up for herself.

While Claudine and I could see that her body seemed to be reacting to a specific act of violence, we had been concerned all along about not speculating about her experience. It wasn't until she went back to France that summer to the village where she had spent all her childhood holidays, that she remembered the

old haberdasher's shop. She told me how, when she was a very young girl, her
grandmother had sent her there on a number of occasions to buy a new whip.
All haziness had now evaporated from the image of her grandmother standing
above her.

But where, she now wondered, had her grandfather been? And, worse still, had
her mother not known what her own mother was like? Therein, she felt, lay the
greatest betrayal.

Every body tells its own story, harking back to childhood. Some bodies,
bearing only a few scars and tender spots, feel at ease with themselves, at
home – they respond safely and confidently to the world that addresses
them. Others show signs of collapse in places, or are hunched under the
weight of their burden; some feel numb, even paralyzed at times; others
bear deep scars which inhibit their movements in the world. Thus, for
instance,

Isabel literally could not reach out towards an object on the mantelpiece
besides her in my counselling room – wishing for anything for herself was so
paralyzing an experience. Besides, what was the point of wishing for anything?
It was useless... and "bad".

What felt impossible for Isabel, was no problem for Lisa. She could easily
reach out towards the mantelpiece, and directly in front of her with one hand or
even two; however, reaching up while looking up, evoked such intolerable, painful
yearning that she would begin to sob.

As to Carl, he could no more let go of the ball of string in his hands than
he could of all the old clothes, magazines and useless paperwork that cluttered
his flat.

Each of these three clients' basic, taken-for-granted body movements held
the emotional charge of a lifetime's history, experiences, meanings and beliefs.
Feeling ourselves into our habitual postures, observing our movements,
listening to what these are telling us, to the emotions and pain they may elicit,
can offer us greater understanding and a route to healing.

And as therapists too, it is of fundamental importance that we listen to our
own bodies: in everyday life, for the sake of our own understanding and well-
being, but also in relation to our clients, as we sit with them.

Bodily countertransference

There is a well-known phenomenon in the therapeutic relationship that
clearly illustrates the holistic aspect of understanding and the place of the
body within it. Known as 'countertransference' it refers to the embodied bias
of life experiences, ways of being, emotions, values and beliefs which the
therapist brings to the therapeutic encounter. It also refers to the therapist's
embodied response which a particular client, through their way of being,
elicits in them ('reactive countertransference'). Countertransference is of
crucial importance in therapy, both for its potential beneficial contribution to the therapeutic work and because of its potential detrimental effects

(*see Chapter 10 Mothers; Glossary 'transference'*). A therapist who is not mindful of the body language, issues, judgements, and other trigger buttons which they are bringing to their relationship with each client is in danger of sabotaging the therapy. And a therapist who does not use the information provided by their own response to their client is missing out on a highly important element of the therapeutic work.

Reactive countertransference can be quite an extraordinary experience. I not infrequently have physical reactions (tensions, heaviness, discomfort, twitchiness, pain, etc.) that replicate what is going on for the client. The first two occasions on which this occurred stand out for me as there had been no place for such countertransference, and hence no expectation of it, within the way I was taught Existential Therapy. Indeed, when I mentioned it to my then supervisor, she told me that it was pure coincidence.

The first occasion was when my client was telling me of sitting at home feeling numb and unable to cry the loss of her grandmother. As she spoke, I could feel my guts being wrenched incredibly painfully, as if someone were trying to squeeze the last drops out of a wet cloth. The following week, my client recounted going straight home from our session, into the bathroom and feeling a terrible, painful wrenching of her guts and then "crying her guts out". Had my experience been nothing but a coincidence? If not, what had happened and how? I have no answer to that, other than I believe something happened between us, (I call it 'mesopathy'), that facilitated her shift out of numbness and enabled her to cry.

The second occasion felt quite shocking:

As Belle spoke of having been seriously deceived and let down, I suddenly felt violently punched in the stomach. When I told her of my reaction, Belle went on to say that yes, she had felt "totally gutted" by the injustice of it, and then she stopped in her tracks... for tragically, she had ended up seriously ill in hospital, necessitating, quite literally, a 'gutting' operation. Telling her about my body's reaction had led Belle to articulate a possible link between seemingly disparate events. Her recent illness and the colectomy had overshadowed all else, but could they be separated, she now wondered, from the metaphorical 'gutting' of the elaborate deception she had experienced?

These two experiences of reactive countertransference astounded me and filled me with awe. They also taught me to question at times the theory I had been taught and not to discount out of hand what my body seemed to be telling me. The therapist's body may not always be right... but then neither are a therapist's reflections and interpretations!

Listening to the body: Conclusion

In the West, our view and experience of our body have been profoundly and variously influenced by the Church and Cartesian dualism. Still today, many regard the body as untrustworthy, sinful, corrupting – a remnant of the Christian view of the human condition as born *Inter faeces et urinam*. Society and the media offer us conflicting messages: both objectifying the body – suggesting we alter it surgically, shrink it, drastically 'detox' it, shave it, enhance it artificially, and at the same time asking us to take loving care of it and ourselves.

The first two decades of this millennium have seen an exponential interest in forms of therapeutic practices that focus on the embodied aspect of our existence (from psychotherapy and coaching to yoga and martial arts.) Language, in its own wisdom, has long recognized the body's wisdom. English reminds us that we can feel and know things 'in our bones', sometimes even 'with every fibre of our body'. And just as French recognizes the understanding of our *tripes* and German of our stomach, English has long realized the importance of our 'gut feelings'. This form of wisdom not only protects us from our enemies' guile, but can help us make decisions (not always good, it is true), even lead to great works of art and scientific discoveries. Indeed, the gut area is now known to be covered in a complex network of 500 million neurons connecting the gut, via the vagus nerve, to that part of the brain that mediates emotions, instinctive responses and decision making. From an existential perspective, this evokes Merleau-Ponty's 'chiasm' of criss-crossing, two-way connections between our sentient being and the world we sense – an invisible, intertwining network, co-creating the 'flesh of the world' of which we are a part. These concepts of science and philosophy may inspire awe by their complexity. Yet, equally awe-inspiring is the observation of our embodied experience in its everydayness and, with it, the realization that our body is the repository of ingrained beliefs and etched-in memories, of knowledge and skills, a repository of trauma but also a potential source of wise understanding, resourcefulness and healing.

Understanding through emotions

The question "And how does that make you feel?" has come to caricature counselling as a profession. And deservedly so, when uttered in a repetitive fashion, with a sentimental tone, head tilt and earnest expression. Yet, it is an extremely important question: it helps the therapist to understand the emotional charge and meaning which an experience carries for a particular client. Exploring emotions can also enlighten the client for, even if they are 'in touch' with their emotions, they may often not fully understand an emotion's complexities and what it is trying to say.

Just as embodiment and reflectiveness are intrinsic parts of being-in-the-world, so too is affectivity – the capacity to respond emotionally to ourselves and the world. Emotions add dynamics, tone and colour to our experience and therefore play a role in the way we interpret and understand the world, as well as our place within it. And when we feel devoid of any emotion, we know that this emotional nothingness – a flatness, blandness, numbness, indifference – is itself significant. Shining a gentle light on emotions, or the apparent lack of any, can help us resolve difficult interpersonal relations. It can help us to see inner conflicts and incongruences and try to understand their signifi-cance and origin. Emotions are a gateway to some of our beliefs about our-selves in-the-world, and this starts from babyhood.

I once met an acquaintance pushing her eight-month-old twin granddaughters in a pushchair. I started chatting to them: one was very smiley and responsive, the other rather grumpy. So, I directed greater attention towards the grumpy one and eventually she started smiling and becoming responsive. Meanwhile, her twin sister was displaying signs of agitation and annoyance – whether at getting less attention from me than her sister, or at her sister responding, I could not tell. Their grandmother remarked how unusual it was to see the other twin smile instead of being sullen.

Already at eight months, these twins' emotional engagement with the world was very different; and already, the very different responses they were receiving from others were informing their perceptions and beliefs about themselves and being-in-the-world. One twin was open to contact and exchange, and received stimulation and smiles; the other seemed to find contact and exchange dif-ficult and was less likely to be offered either. Already at eight months, these twins' familiar 'dispositions' and 'attunements', to use Heideggerian words, were different.

Heidegger emphasized that we are always emotionally 'disposed', 'attuned' in some way to ourselves, others and the world; it is an integral part of being-in-the-world. He assigned particular importance to a few specific emotions which he named fundamental attunements, such as anxiety, joy, boredom and despair. For not only do these colour the way we interpret and understand our whole being-in-the-world, but they pull us out of the comfort zone for which we yearn: they 'disclose' to us our mortality as well as our basic contingent nature, our 'thrownness' – the fact that we have no control over when, where, how we are born and much else. In this, these fundamental attunements differ from emotions about specific aspects of our day.

Heidegger was writing from a philosopher's perspective; as a therapist, I would like to suggest two other fundamental attunements, the first being com-passion.[4] A compassionate attunement can colour a whole existence across all dimensions of time: it can open up a different understanding of the past and encourage us to change our perspectives and take action for a more satis-fying present and future. Compassion colours our understanding of ourselves, others and our contextual situation: it bravely but gently discloses to us the various existential, and other, human limitations that impact on a situation. Awakening the attunement of compassion opens up paths to a wiser and kinder understanding and a path to 'authentic' action. 'Authentic' because, when com-passionately disposed, I can genuinely choose and own my actions and shoulder my responsibilities, within the broader context of my human existence (i.e. my contingent nature and my mortality) and my present situation.

I had considered adding 'deep shame' as another 'fundamental attunement'. For deep shame has the power to colour a whole existence and disclose its randomness and finitude. It can convey a fundamental sense of existential alienation and aloneness, yet it distorts this by conflating it with a sense of personal unworthiness and hopelessness. Where compassion is fair, shame is judgemental. Where compassion prepares for satisfying action, deep shame is paralyzing. Shame therefore does not meet the criteria of a fundamental attunement. Whereas compassion is able to disclose possibilities that lie even beyond the world of shame, including the possibility of feeling intrinsically worthy of belonging to the world.

In the counselling room, from the very first session, the client's emotions, or apparent lack of any, offer the therapist important clues and help to sketch a picture of the client's way of being-in-the world. The emotions that dominate the session, those in the background that vie for attention and those emotions for which there is no place can be enlightening; so can the manner in which emotions are expressed and how they fit with what is being said. The person who giggles after every statement, for instance, or else glances up coyly, scowls, or jokes as they speak, rings my alarm bells: I know these behaviours could reveal anxiety, great shyness, hurt, even a deep well of shame and self-loathing. The nature, articulation and congruence of emotions displayed all help to highlight possible areas for therapeutic exploration.

Rachel was smiling as she recounted her memories of holidays spent at her grandparents' farm. She spoke of the old wooden bridge, its planks half eaten away with fungus and moss and the wood beyond, where periwinkles grew. To this day she loved their unusual, triangular-shaped petals and their delicate shade of blue. And as Rachel was rememorating the scene, tears started to roll down her face, while she continued to smile.

I wondered what this rainbow of emotions signified.

L. *What is happening for you right now?*
R. *I can see myself with periwinkles all around me... and there is this sense of wonder... and freedom... And that hurts so much.* (And now the smile has gone and Rachel is crying openly.)
L. *That hurts so much?*
R. *Yes.*
L. *That sense of wonder and freedom hurt so much?*
R. *Mmm. It felt safe there.*
L. *It felt safe with the periwinkles all around you... Did the world not feel safe beyond the periwinkle wood?*
R. *The world was so terrifying.* Rachel shudders and holds herself tightly.
L. *So, terrifying?*
R. *Mmm.*
      ....
L. *And what did the young Rachel do to manage that terror?*
R. *She was always looking out for someone to protect her from it.... And I'm still doing it, aren't I?*

Through the emotions unexpectedly evoked by her memories of periwinkles in the woods behind her grandparents' farm, Rachel had gained a clearer understanding of the various choices of friends and partners she had made throughout her life.

As a therapist I am frequently faced with emotions that feel to me paradoxical, incongruent or dissonant: such as anger where I would expect sadness, crying that doesn't ring true, emotions that sit strangely together, blankness where the situation would ordinarily evoke a strong reaction. Usually, the emotion I would have expected was one that was either unsafe in that person's family or not allowed – whether explicitly or implicitly. The most common taboo emotions in families are anger, hurt and grief, though in some families it is pleasurable feelings, excitement and joy that are banned (*see Chapter 12, The Family Holy Book*). And there are those families where the adults' faces seldom register any emotions, offering a distorted mirror to their children, who learn to follow suit. In some families it is because showing one's emotions is not 'the done thing' within their social circle: parents, and their parents before them, priding themselves on their solemnity and 'stiff upper lip' that expressed a sense of social and moral superiority, grounded in impassivity and stoicism. This outdated, yet internationally famous characterization of Britishness, as portrayed in literature and mid-century films, comes at a cost: a stiff upper lip stifles not only the expression of emotions, but often their very experience. The socially elitist tradition of sending sons from a very young age to boarding school no doubt fostered the habits of compartmentalizing loved ones and cutting off feelings of homesickness; it also perpetuated this distorted ideal of stoic numbness. However, being 'cut off from' or 'out of touch' with one's emotions is not the prerogative of the British social elite alone. This form of cut-offness, where the person is 'not there', numb, not present to their experience, is most commonly the result of traumatic dissociation. And trauma does not look at nationality or social class.

Listening to numbness and dissonant emotions in therapy points to doors that are to be opened very slowly and gently, for behind them may live unspeakable pain. We can only hear emotions clearly as they express themselves. Some are vociferous and call out loudly, while others only feel able to whisper in the background. Others still have no words, not even a cry or a whimper. Yet, even these silent emotions can sign through facial expression, body posture and 'vibes' (for want of an accurate word). And when it feels safe enough to do so, the whispers will find a louder voice or the body, gently and mindfully addressed, will offer up the appropriate words to articulate the silent emotions.

Many training courses teach prospective counsellors not to break a client's silence. But silence in the therapy room (both the client's and the therapist's) is a complex phenomenon which deserves more than a theory-bound, dogmatic approach. A client new to counselling, who does not know that the therapist will not be the first to break a silence, may feel very anxious or frustrated. And the silence that some therapists maintain for most of their sessions may suit some clients, but it leaves others feeling confused, not 'held' and unsafe. Silence has different meanings for each of us: for some clients, silence is the luxury of some space for themselves, the feeling of being watched upon by a benevolent presence, or a time to feel witnessed as they drop into themselves to experience themselves differently or silently reflect. But to others, silence means abandonment, aloneness or anxiety, and can give rise to anger, terror and despair. To leave a client in silence without checking out whether they are all right with it may be leaving them to fall ever deeper into a dark hole. Clients usually come to therapy because their situation is painful and that pain needs to be met. Even if the client does not feel able to express the pain verbally, the therapist can seek to show, with or without words, that they are trying to meet it.

Naomi is sitting quietly in the armchair opposite me. By 'quietly' I don't simply mean 'in silence': her quietness is not just a lack of speaking, it seems a tentative way of being, a soft treading on the earth – lest she leaves any noticeable traces of her presence? Every so often she darts a glance at the second door in my counselling room.

L. *Are you worried about this door?* Naomi nods.
L. *There's no one there. The door is to a small washroom, would you like me to show you?* Naomi hesitates, then nods. I push the door open to show her. After a couple of minutes, I ask her:
L. *Would you like to tell me what's going on for you right now?*
     Naomi shakes her head from side to side, then, head bowed, she whispers:
N. *It's my cousin.*
L. *Your cousin?*
     Naomi nods and falls silent again.
     As she sits there, I try to get a feel of her; she feels very young, terrified and in great emotional pain, and I find myself stroking her hair (virtually, of course) in a soothing manner. After a little while, I ask:
L. *Naomi, you wanted to tell me about your cousin?*
N. *He is dead.*
L. *He is dead?*
N. *He was killed by a gang.*
L. *Oh! how terrible.*
N. *He was like my big brother.* (No wonder she had felt to me terrified and in great pain.)
L. *Did you grow up together?*
     Nods yes.

These early sessions with Naomi moved at a similarly slow pace for, it emerged, she had learnt the hard way that people were not to be trusted. But Naomi desperately needed someone in whom to confide her loneliness, terror and sorrow.

The expression of emotion is embedded within a relationship. The expression of difficult emotions requires trust that we will be heard, understood and not judged and, sadly, there are many who find that animals alone are able to hear and respond appropriately to their emotional needs. For many human beings can only pick up what is verbally articulated, many have great difficulty reading other expressions of emotions, let alone tuning emotionally into another person. And many have great difficulty listening to particular emotions (such as pain, sadness, or anger) and may themselves cut off or deflect from these. The gap between expressing emotions and being heard, listened to and responded to appropriately often lies at the heart of relationship problems, particularly between partners and between parents and children.

Alex' facial expressions and body language are so eloquent, he could lead a masterclass in how to communicate what he is feeling at any given moment. Unfortunately, based on his experience with Paul, his partner, he could also give a masterclass on the pitfalls of doing so. For he and Paul speak different languages. Paul tends to hear Alex' anxiety as "major panic" which gets all his alarm systems going; and he often mistranslates Alex' mild frustration with him as "flaming anger" or "fearsome criticism" and so shuts down completely and takes himself off. Although Alex is usually good at reading Paul's feelings, he seems to have a blind spot with reading Paul's "I love you, even when I take myself off for a while". So then Alex falls into a pit of despair.

Fortunately, though it may take a while, most times one of them is able to find a way out of their lonely predicament and help the other out of his.

In the counselling room, the way emotions reach me and I experience them is also significant. Just as I can experience bodily 'countertransference', physical reactions as a therapist to what a client is saying or the way they are saying it (*as with Belle above*), so too I can experience emotional countertransference. Whenever I experience anger, boredom, emotional blankness in a session, or at the thought of seeing a particular client, I consider these unusual feelings in my work to be highly significant. So too if I feel drawn to be jokey with a client (unless I have known them a long time), to feel sorry for them or look after them. I need to see whether something is happening with the client that is pushing my own particular buttons (and then I really need to explore those for myself) or whether that client is having that impact on many others.

When Jenny first started therapy, I found her extremely boring and had to fight to stay awake. She also seemed to bore many family members and various acquaintances (she had no friends). I think it was because when she spoke, and she spoke a lot, she herself was not in the picture. It is common for a client to spend large parts of a session speaking of a partner, child or colleague, but it is usually about the way that other impacts them. Not so Jenny: if she appeared in a story, it was as a cardboard character. And it is difficult to engage emotionally with cardboard. Then one day, as she was talking of a cousin's visit and of feeling sorry for him because of her family's bored reaction to him, I was able to bring her, emotions and all, into the picture. This resonance with her cousin's experience was the beginning of very fruitful work together and, twenty years on, I still remember her with great fondness.

The sleepiness which accompanied my boredom with Jenny felt different from instances of unexpected sleepiness – i.e. when I am neither tired nor bored. In such cases, all I need to say to a client is: *"you know, I've noticed that when I am not tired yet feel really sleepy with a client, like right now, it is usually because there is a strong emotion that is not being expressed, do you think that might be the case here?"* And immediately, a switch is turned on and usually we both re-engage.

Understanding through our emotions: Conclusion

Though this section has been about understanding through emotions, the above examples highlight once again how our emotions, the way we are attuned and respond to the world, cannot be separated either from the body that carries and expresses them, or from the thoughts and beliefs which they foster or express.

I would like to conclude this section by returning to two attunements that, from my therapist's perspective, I would add to a list of what Heidegger called 'fundamental attunements'. Compassion was my first addition. The other also underpins therapy and the possibility of satisfying change; what is more, it sustains life. I am speaking of hope. Not the unrealistic hope that lives in cloud cuckoo land. I mean the hope that keeps its feet fully on the ground, yet with an awareness of the infinite heavens above; the hope that 'discloses' realistic possibilities in full knowledge of the thrownness and finitude of human existence. I am tempted to give it a capital letter: Hope. Hope as a heartfelt, meaning-ful, embodied stance. Compare the feeling of sitting in a dejected or despairing pose with what happens when you imagine yourself engaging hopefully with the future. I suspect your spine lengthens, your head rises and you look ahead, there is a deeper intake of breath, the ground feels more supportive under foot, etc.

I have kept Hope for last, because such is its traditional place. You may remember that Pandora (Greek mythology's version of Eve), created by the Gods for Epimetheus, opened the jar, or 'Pandora's box', from which sickness and all evils escaped into the world. Only Hope remained within. There have been countless interpretations of this myth offering conflicting views as to whether hope itself, and keeping it within a jar, was a good or bad thing for human beings. Could I be a therapist if I could not hold some Hope for my clients, even in dire circumstances? I don't know. But I could not be a therapist if I did not firmly believe, from personal and professional experience, that Hope is a good thing.

Understanding through what is other than mind, body and emotions, yet inseparable from each and all of these

Psychotherapy, as I hope I have shown, needs to listen to the body (the therapist's and the client's) and to emotions, just as it needs to listen to the mind. As well as exploring possibilities and choices, deconstructing concepts, analyzing thoughts, motives and the use of language, and other such cognitive activities, psychotherapy needs the understanding which the body and the heart bring. In addition, psychotherapy needs to listen to the intuition and understanding of what is other than mind, body and emotions, yet is inseparable from them. Earlier in this chapter, when I mentioned the four-in-one aspect of understanding, I referred to this fourth element as 'spirit', a sufficiently general and vague term. For what are we to call this? 'Spirit', 'soul', 'the divine in us', 'life force', 'mystery'? Each of us will have a different word for our experience of it.

A spiritualist once came to me for therapy because, she told me, her "channels had become blocked and no longer let spirit through as before". We did not work directly on her spiritualist's channels – something that was quite mysterious and unfamiliar to me. However, I was fascinated to see that we both sensed at the same time when the work she wanted to do was done: for as I sensed that something about her had shifted significantly, she experienced a clearing of her channels that were now letting spirit through.

My work with end-of-life palliative care patients frequently faced me with that mysterious dimension of human existence. So too did my work with patients who had survived Intensive Care: many intensive care patients have very vivid dreams and hallucinations – so vivid that when they come round from their coma, they often cannot distinguish between dream and reality. Interestingly, even those patients who never knew that they had been admitted to Intensive Care, who had no conscious understanding of their situation, still had dreams that expressed their fight for survival. So, clearly, at some level – was it body, soul, spirit? – they had understood that they had to fight for their lives; and their dream scenarios, crafted by their unconscious mind and emotions, reflected that understanding.

We learn to develop 'antennae' and intuit about people and situations from the earliest age – we need to do so for our own safety – to sense danger, threat and hostility, as well as to select friends, mentors, partners and relate to them satisfactorily. These antennae also have an important place in the therapeutic encounter. Clients need them to detect whether they can trust the therapist; the therapist to get a fuller view of their clients. Intuiting involves a bodily-emotional-mental understanding of cues, but also an understanding that lies beyond these. I would argue that psychotherapy can only be 'good' if it encompasses all these modes of being and understanding.

There are numerous instances in which such an understanding is at play. I shall mention but two here:

'Reactive countertransference'

I mentioned above how, as my client spoke of her feelings of betrayal, I felt as if I had just been punched in the stomach, and how, mentioning that to her, had helped her verbalize how "gutted" she had felt (first metaphorically, but then quite literally). Another of my earliest experiences of reactive counter-transference felt most uncanny: I was watching a sexually dark production of the opera Don Giovanni, when a new client immediately sprung to mind. This very pleasant and intelligent young man did not bear any physical likeness to Don Juan, the anti-hero on stage before me, nor did the history he had given me point to any behavioural similarity, and there had been no sign of a par-ticularly sexualized or power-based way of being in the room with me. It was not until a month or so later that I began to hear about some of my client's sexual proclivities. (I hasten to add that these did not reflect a dark soul as in Don Juan's case.) So, what had I picked up, wherefrom and how? To speak of 'reactive countertransference' is simply to give these phenomena a name, it does not help us understand how they come about.

Systemic constellations offer another therapeutic setting in which some-thing other than mind, body and emotions is also at play.

Systemic constellations

There are times when a person's problem somehow does not make sense, does not feel as if it belongs to the person alone, or seems to be part of a broader picture. For instance, a person may have been feeling suicidal for years, without understanding why. Or else, a whole female line over three generations (mother, aunts, sisters, and female daughters) has suffered from debilitating, medically unrelated pain; while in another family, it is the men who, also over three generations, have suffered from severe, medically unre-lated breathing problems. It may be that among a set of four siblings, for no medically explicable reason, only the son has been able to have children. Such patterns may of course be viewed as coincidences and then part of the therapeutic work might be around accepting that some families do have strong painful or tragic repeating stories, quite coincidentally. Or else we can be curious about such coincidences. One way of being curious involves looking at the whole family system and its broader historical context. We may then hear that the suicidal person had a history of severe transgenerational trauma; that the great-grandmother of the above female line had long hidden a terrible, painful secret: her first-born twins born to a priest, had been torn away from her. We may learn that the four siblings' mother, throughout her life, carried a terrible guilt following a late abortion; while in the family of male lung sufferers, the great-grandfather had suffered severe lung damage in the First World War. Again, one may dismiss these facts as totally irrele-vant, since they do not belong within the realm of either physical causality or any rational explanation, especially in those cases where a descendant was unaware of their ancestor's fate. Yet, I personally believe that such seemingly unrelated facts and patterns deserve our attention, even if nothing is ever to come of it.

Systemic Constellations rely heavily on a dimension of understanding which is not of body-mind-emotion alone: at its heart, is the premise of a self-preserving system (e.g. a family or a work organization) with its own form of consciousness, inherent sense of order and balance, and the entanglements that, through loyalty, can develop between its members (*see Glossary*).

Systemic Constellations not only look at an issue from the perspective of the broader context (family, organization, country's history, etc.), they ask questions of a different order to those of therapy and common discourse, such as: has something happened to throw the system out of balance? How might it relate to the present issue? With whose fate am I entangled? Where does that strong emotion belong? Whose burden am I carrying?

One can get a certain feel for constellations and this other dimension of existence and understanding at home, alone, with a few props. For instance, imagine your same sex line and put cushions (or objects of your choice) in a line behind you to represent each generation – for instance, if you are a man, line up cushions for your father, paternal grandfather, great-grandfather, great-great-grandfather. Does adding each generational cushion feel better or worse? Or can you not notice any difference? Do your various male ancestors feel supportive and resourceful or do they feel threatening, collapsed, depressed, traumatized (e.g. by war, famine, slavery)? If you cannot derive any support from them, choose an object to represent a healthy, benevolent male ancestor and place it right at the back so that it holds your male line, and notice how that feels. Now, do you notice a difference? Then try with the men in your maternal male line – your maternal grandfather, great-grandfather, etc. You can also ask yourself, as you visualize those lines, what resource or quality these ancestors can offer you; and also, what burden of theirs you might still be carrying today, what task lies incomplete, and what you would like to make room for in your life. If you have felt this enlightening or resourcing in some way, was this physical, emotional, thought-provoking, and/or something different as well? If you have not felt anything at all throughout, ask yourself whether or not there is something anxiety-provoking for you personally about thinking about your ancestry, or about things outside the realm of rationality.

My first encounter with Systemic Constellations opened the floodgates to strange phenomena and experiences that were not explicable by scientific or rational understanding (unless by a sort of rationality and science still unknown to us). This first encounter also confirmed to me that there was so much that we human beings were able to intuit, understand and communicate through our very human presence and *being (in the strong verbal sense),* through body-mind-emotions-spirit (or whatever one wishes to call that additional, yet integral element). It also presented me with questions to which I had, and still have, no answers.

Constellations classically happen in a group (small or large) over a number of hours during which there will be a few constellations. In each constellation, the 'issue holder' (client) will sit next to the therapist in the circle and speak for about five minutes to the therapist in front of the group to lay out the issue and a few contextual facts. The issue holder might also be asked about their deep-felt wish, their 'heart's desire' and what a good resolution/outcome to this constellation might be or feel like. This may be anything from feeling more supported in their endeavour, more 'resourced', to having a different perspective on the issue, rather than hoping for it to be 'fixed'. Typically, the client will choose one person to represent themselves and one to represent the issue, both of whom they will place in the centre of the circle. Then, together with the therapist and the group, they will observe the relationship between these two representatives. So, for instance, the client and issue representatives might just stand there staring at each other, or one may feel weak at the knees, collapse, turn their back on the other, feel shivers down their legs or all sorts of strong emotions, or feel indifference, cut-offness, etc. The therapist, or 'constellator', is likely to ask the client to choose someone to represent their father and someone for their mother. Other representatives for siblings, grandparents, other ancestors or, more abstractly, for 'anxiety', 'illness', 'war' or a particular country may also be brought in, if the constellator intuits that they are required. A representative may pick up a feeling of loss, pain, or betrayal, they may sense where in the system a client's anxiety resides, or even suddenly experience intense stomach pains. Crucially, representatives *should not seek to play a role*, or think how they would/should behave in such a situation. Rather, they sense and behave as moved to do so – but 'moved' by what or whom? That is a question about which I am not prepared to speculate.

The representatives may be asked to give feedback, but it is important not to regard this as being the factual truth of the situation, nor view constellations as oracles. Yet, at the same time, one cannot ignore the phenomena. Uncannily, the grandfather may indeed have suffered/died from terrible stomach pains, as his representative was experiencing; or, unbeknownst to the client but subsequently confirmed by a parent, an older child was indeed born out of wedlock and excluded from the family – by fostering, adoption.; or else, as all the representatives looking down at a space on the floor in their midst seemed to indicate, there had been an unspoken, shocking death.

So, how are we to explain the mysterious phenomenon whereby a representative can pick up so much unspoken information about the client's family system? To adduce 'the collective unconscious' (Carl Jung), the 'flesh of the world' (Merleau-Ponty), 'morphic resonance'(Rupert Sheldrake), or General Systems theory (Bertalanffy), would be enclosing the mystery of the very real phenomenon within equally mysterious psychological, philosophical or scientific hypotheses and theories and would still beg the question of how this phenomenon emerges. To explain it as 'transpersonal' simply acknowledges that there is an observable and experienceable connection that goes 'beyond the person' to the systems within which human existence is embedded. Which is why I prefer to describe phenomenologically what I have observed and experienced with lay terms devoid of any scientific, philosophical or other pretension. There is a sense of allowing oneself to be open to the person or abstract thing one is representing, 'tuning into' something, I know not what, and allowing oneself to move, feel, sense, have thoughts accordingly. In collo-quial language it could be called 'picking up vibes'. It is easy to smile condes-cendingly at such new-agey-sounding stuff. It is far more difficult to dismiss the phenomena without closing ourselves to the possibility that some things are still beyond the understanding of our body-mind-emotions though insep-arable from them.

Although the optimum forum for Systemic Constellations is the group, I occasionally use cushions in my one-to-one work with clients, when exploring their broader family system, their workplace dynamics, or their need of resourcing.

In the Mothers chapter, you may remember, I recounted the story of David, whose mother, grandmother and great-aunt had survived the Holocaust.

For as far back as he could remember, David had felt guilt gnaw at him some-times for the most apparently trivial of things. After much exploration of guilt in his own life, we turned our attention to guilt in his broader family system, and in particular to his grandmother with whose sense of loss and guilt he had always felt strongly connected. I asked him one day whether he would like to try something out with cushions. Intrigued, he agreed. I suggested he choose one cushion for his grandmother and one for himself. Standing by his cushion facing his grandmother was emotional for David, especially when repeating the sentence which I had suggested for him: "out of loyalty to you, Grandma, I have carried this burden of guilt and pain for so many years." However, he was fascinated to see how difficult it was for him to add: "but this burden belongs to you, Grandma, and with love and respect, I hand it back to you." David realized the power of the fundamental loyalty, which, unbeknown to himself, he still felt towards his grandmother.

David also realized that some of his life was still spent in the company of his grandmother's old friends and relatives – dead friends and relatives, whom he himself had never known. Part of him was still back there, back then in "the old days", in a place, in a life that he had never known, that was never his own. David had always felt British, yet at the same time, he had always felt strongly that his roots belonged "back there" where his grandmother had come from. But the groundedness that this sense of roots gave him, also came with the pain of loss and of the dead that lived within him.

So, I asked David to select cushions to represent his life in the UK (parents, home, work, friends) and place them on the floor, which he did, half-surrounding himself with them in a semi-circle; then cushions for his grandmother's dead ancestors, which he placed behind his grandmother's cushion which he was still facing. It became clear that David found himself drawn so strongly to his dead ancestors that he wished to move over to be among them. But, as I pointed out to him, he belonged in the land of the living, while they belonged to the land of the dead. This was a factual divide.

This felt unbelievably painful to David. So, with the use of a scarf, we marked the boundary between the living and the dead.

D. *I still feel so drawn to cross that line, to be with them.*
L. *Yes, I know, but that is not where you belong. Can we try one more thing?*
D. *OK*
L. *Could you choose one suitable cushion to stand guard over your dead ancestors?*

David chose a beautiful large embroidered one and placed it at the head of all the other ancestor cushions.

As he faced them with this guardian cushion at their head, David was able to look at his ancestors with greater equanimity and without feeling the pull to be among them; having done so, he felt able to turn to face his present life and feel encouragement from his ancestors. The following session, David reported feeling something of a physical shift within himself and, amazingly, he felt ready to engage more fully with life.

Some may dismiss this use of cushions, scarf and sentence as too esoteric, yet, if observed phenomenologically, it enabled the expression of truths that David was able to experience: it highlighted the divide between the living and the dead; the way a person fate's can be entangled with that of another member, or members, of their family, dead or alive; how to their own detriment they can take up that person's burden or cause; and how they are likely to find it disloyal and painful to give it back. For David, handing back pain where it belonged, not in a spirit of blame or anger, but as a statement of fact, brought relief and a physical sensation of a shift within, a sudden, visceral change in understanding and being. It brought greater compassion for his grandmother and for himself; and, somehow, he felt, it gave her added dignity. For the burden had been given its rightful place in the family system; and its rightful owner had been acknowledged and honoured. He was also able to honour his ancestors, the lives they had lived, the deaths that were theirs. He was able to thank them for the roots they had given him and the contributions they had made to his understanding of himself in-the-world.

If David and the other examples of familial patterns above seem extreme, think how (grand)parent–child entanglements can be seen to strongly influence a child's life, e.g. through the carrying of anxieties, in particular death anxieties, for their parent or grandparent; in identification with a close relative, or vicarious living through a child or grandchild.

The concept of an entanglement of fates within a family line is found in different guises in a variety of cultures. Already in ancient times, Greek myths and tragedy depicted the cost of an ancestor's hubris on their own child and as it was handed down the generations: outrageous behaviour that broke the rules was punished by nemesis – opprobrium and the vengeance of the gods, as in the House of Atreus, or that of Oedipus. And in the Christian faith, the handing down of original sin was long a central tenet of Christian thought. Unlike these two traditions however, Systemic Constellations, respectfully returns the burden, or the responsibility, to where it belongs, freeing descendants from what is not theirs to carry.

Conclusion: The fourth dimension of understanding, other than mind–body–emotions, yet inseparable from them

As you may have experienced if you tried putting cushions for your same sex family lines, and as Systemic Constellations show, this dimension of understanding that connects us to our ancestral line connects us powerfully to our ancestors' engagement with survival, life quests and challenges. It offers us resources as we in turn engage with these.

This dimension of understanding is akin to the understanding which arises from the universal life force that sustains our lives. It is intimately connected with our sentient and thinking self: interwoven with emotions – with awe, gratitude, joy, it is felt in the depth of our heart. Interwoven with our body, it can be felt in every cell of our body, from the surface of our skin to our very core. And interwoven with the mind, it awakens and sustains our thoughts about the universe, life, human existence and that particular existence that is our own.

Latin had two words for the life force: *spiritus* and *anima* which have found their way into English 'spirit/spiritual' and 'animation'. Both *spiritus* and *anima* express the metaphor of the 'breath' of life. The human spirit's relationship to nature and the universe, coupled with our species' capacity for wonder and reflection, has awakened us to the great metaphysical and existential questions and to the perception of beauty. The human 'breath of life' has become 'soul' (French *âme* from Latin *anima*), opening us to the dimension of the sacred, the numinous, and all that which gives deep meaning to life. This connection between the breath of life and the spiritual dimension of existence can be found in other ancient languages: Greek (pneuma and psyche), Hebrew (ruach and nephesh) and Aramaic[5] (ruhau and napsha). These parallels partly arise out of attempts to translate biblical and other texts across these languages, but not solely since it exists outside the Graeco-judeo-christian tradition: for instance, Sanskrit has 'ātman', the word for 'breath' which comes to refer to the soul, the principle of life, the self and also to Brahma, the supreme ātman.

The life force, as breath of life, intricately connects all breathing beings with whom we share the cycle of life and death. And if our bodies, mind and emotions have evolved and developed from those of animals, should we assume any differently for the 'breath' of life, the 'spirit' that moves us? When Tortinette, our tiny tortoise, got what looked like runny nose syndrome and had to be quarantined, Tortie did not eat for five days until I had reunited them. In Tortie's sense of Tortinette's absence, his not eating, his letting himself waste away, can we truthfully say that we see no connection with the human understanding and experience of loss in all its dimensions? And without going down the path of anthropomorphism or zoomorphism, after reading recent research on trees and on fungi, can we still deny the vegetal world any form of possibly (pre-)instinctual 'animation'?

As I write, I am recalling my numerous conversations with my step-father in the last few years of his life. His radical views on immanence were a crucible for this stronger evolutionary understanding of the spirit/soul. His words still resonate in me:

> Animation nourishes animal instincts which, more than simple automatisms, are an integral part of their relationship to Nature and to that cosmic whole to which they too belong as part of the inexplicable adventure that is being... The human soul offers us no answers, however, it nourishes our coolly calculating and conceptualizing minds and connects us to eternity. Eternity, not in the sense of time as we know it, quantitatively prolonged to infinity, but as a qualitative dimension, eternity, where time as we know it is abolished; eternity as beyond time.[6]

I have chosen the following dream from one of my intensive care patients to conclude this section on understanding from the spirit/soul that *anima*tes us.

When Winston came for his follow-up post-Intensive Care Unit visit, he mentioned an abiding intensive care dream of a very large tree from his native Grenada. It was a rather unusual dream as intensive care dreams go, in that it was a static image, he could not recall any specific feelings and he was not doing anything in it. As I started asking him about his dream, it was clear, however, that it carried a strong emotional charge for him. There are of course myriad symbols attached to trees and parts thereof, from their roots to their blossoms and seeds via their trunks, sap and branches, but this was also a very personal tree from his homeland. He described the tree and its place in the village, and recalled his memories of his earlier life. I told him that I was loath to offer an interpretation to his dream, in the way that I would with most intensive care dreams (which tend to fall under a few themes), but that it was clearly very important and he ought to hold onto it. When I next saw him, a few weeks later, he told me, to my surprise, that the session had been extremely helpful. It turned out that he had taken me quite literally: he had visualized himself holding the tree and now he felt much better in himself.

By imagining himself putting his arms around the tree, grounded, deep-rooted and majestic in his home village, he was able to connect to his own ancestral roots and, intertwined with them, to something meaningful, life-sustaining and revitalizing for himself.

Understanding: Concluding remarks

Heidegger wrote that 'thinking is thanking'. While cognitive understanding alone lends itself to this word play, the same could be said of all sources of understanding, for they too are deserving of our awe and gratitude – whether or not we believe in a bestower.

The Graeco-Judeo-Christian heritage and centuries of Western philosophy have handed down to us traditions in which understanding of ourselves and our world belongs to the realm of the mind. They acknowledge that the spirit or soul may uphold faith and support the mind's conceptions of metaphysical matters and emotions may enhance this spiritual understanding. However, in their view, emotions, like the body, more often than not waylay the mind.

A focus on our embodied nature offers an alternative view in which the mind's understanding is interwoven with that of our emotions, body and spirit. In this way it is as an organic whole that, for each of us, our multidimensional understanding perceives and interprets our self, our existence, our world. Wisdom arises out of this organic, whole understanding, always in-the-world.

I suggested earlier that compassion was a disposition and movement towards the other person from a wise heart. If we attempt to extend this movement towards ourselves and all other living beings with whom we share the planet, under the same sun, we may begin to move towards an ecology of compassionate understanding.

Notes

1 On Systemic Constellations, *see below and Glossary*; on the physiology or trauma and the important concepts of dissociation, PTSD, and window of tolerance, *see Glossary.*

2 Interestingly, the psychology degree is a science degree (BSc/MSc) which leads many psychologists to believe they can start from a position of 'knowing'; while counselling and psychotherapy, for which the degree is usually an arts degree (BA/ MA) tend to start from a position of not-knowing.

3 When I write that 'the body' remembers or 'we' need to listen to our body, it might sound as if I am saying that there is an 'I' that is separate from my body. This couldn't be further from what I mean. I encounter and engage with the world as a whole person but cannot be aware of all aspects of my being and my world at all times. The capacity to direct awareness to each of these aspects separately is a privilege of the human condition; the difficulty of expressing the inseparable wholeness of human existence and its, world while speaking of its aspects, is one of its limitations.

4   It could be argued that 'compassion' is unnecessary as Heidegger has 'care' (*Sorge*), 'solicitude' (*Fürsorge*), and 'considerateness' (*Nachsicht*), but that would be a total misunderstanding of the meaning which Heidegger attaches to these concepts. *'Care'* defines the Being of human existence as inseparable from its relationship to the world; while *solicitude and considerateness* are universals that express modes of being-with, including 'deficient and Indifferent modes', even *'inconsiderate-ness'* (Heidegger, M. (1962 [1927]) *Being and Time*, trans. Macquarrie, J.R. and Robinson, E., Oxford: Blackwell pp. 121, 123).

5   I am indebted to Daren Messenger for drawing my attention to these semitic equivalents.

6   Cahen, C. (2011). *Appartenance et Liberté*, Paris: L'Harmattan, the translation here is my own.

Chapter 14

Heart

When I first started on this personal journey down the path set out by my dream, I did not imagine how fruitful it would prove for me personally and professionally, let alone that it would lead to my writing a book. When I began to consider writing, I visualized a very slim volume: for at one level, the heart of therapy, the heart of life, can be spoken so concisely it needs little space to house its truth. A nutshell would suffice.

One of my most treasured objects is my great-grandmother's small leather box in which she kept her 'treasures'; it was given to me by my grandmother when her mother died. Dark green, lined with dark green velvet, it contains a mother-of-pearl penknife no bigger than my little finger nail with three blades and a corkscrew; a miniature pack of cards; a silver thimble in a bucket; a tiny white dog; and, most wondrous of all to my child eyes, a hazelnut that opens in half and once held eight minute penknives with cork handles – now sadly down to four.

If the heart of therapy were enclosed within that nutshell and eight tiny penknives chosen to carve out a contented life, besides compassion, understanding, and boundaries, what would the other five be? The choice is a subjective one, so I don't expect you to choose the same as me. They say Love can be fickle, it can be blind and lead us astray. Still, to know what it means to be genuinely loved, and lovable, and to give genuine love, would have to be one of them for me. If I could have more choices, I would like to include gratitude, sense of humour, ability to connect to others, and to one-self – the ability to be alone, at one with oneself. However, as I only have four more choices, I shall name them: Openness (to others, to myself, to wonder and to the world), Courage (from Latin *cor* heart, as in 'take heart!'), and Meaningfulness. And, in its traditional place, last but paramount, Hope – not untethered cloud-cuckoo-land hope which promises that all our wishes will come true or that 'it will all be OK'. Rather a Hope which enables us to face the future with the grounded and grounding feeling that we can learn to deal with difficult and painful situations and try to make the best of them. I believe

DOI: 10.4324/9781003364504-15

that where these five coexist with compassion, understanding and boundaries, the others too can develop.

Therapists often say "you must trust the process". So too in life, we need to trust that there is some part of ourselves that is capable of leading us to a deeply satisfying life, provided life circumstances are not excessively constricting – and even then, some seem to manage. That part may feel very small, buried, or too painful still, yet, with compassion, understanding, good boundaries and Hope, it can begin to heal, emerge, and flourish.

Principal References

Rather than a full bibliography, I have listed works cited in the text and the principal books I have consulted while writing this book.

Bola, J. J. (2019). *Mask off, masculinity redefined*. London: Pluto Press.

Bourdieu, P. (2002). *La domination masculine* (2nd ed.). Paris: Seuil.

Bradshaw, J. (2005). *Healing the shame that binds you* (revised and expanded ed.). Florida: Health Communications.

Cahen, C. (2011). *Appartenance et liberté*. Paris: L'Harmattan.

Connell, R. (2005). *Masculinities* (2nd ed.). Cambridge: Polity Press.

Connell, R. (2021). *Gender* (4th ed.). Cambridge: Polity Press.

Dana, D. (2020) Foreword by Porges, S. W. *Polyvagal exercises for safety and connection, 50 client-centered practices*. New York: Norton.

Deane, B. (2014). *Masculinity and the new imperialism*. Cambridge: CUP.

Fuchs, T. (2018). *Ecology of the brain*. Oxford: OUP.

Gilligan, J. (2001). *Preventing violence*. New York: Thames and Hudson.

Hausner, S. (2011). *Even if it costs me my life*. Santa Cruz: Gestalt Press [Distrib. New York: Routledge].

Heidegger, M. (1962 [1927]). *Being and time* (J. R. Macquarrie & E. Robinson, Trans.). Oxford: Blackwell.

Heidegger, M. (1966 [1959]). *Discourse on thinking* (J. M. Anderson & E. H. Freund, Trans.). New York: Harper and Row.

Heidegger, M. (1980). In H. Feick & Ziegler (Eds.), *Index zu Heideggers Sein und Zeit* (2nd ed.). Tübingen: Max Niemeyer Verlag.

Heidegger, M. (1995 [1983]). *The fundamental concepts of metaphysics, world, finitude, solitude*. (lecture delivered 1929–30) (W. McNeill & N. Walker, Trans.). Bloomington: IUP.

Lawler, S. (2000). *Mothering the self: mothers, daughters, subjects*. London and New York: Routledge.

Lowen, A. (1985). *Narcissism, denial of the true self*. New York: Touchstone.

Maroda, K. J. (2013). *The power of countertransference, innovations in analytic technique* (2nd ed. revised and enlarged). New York and Hove, UK: Routledge.

McBride, K. (2013). *Will i ever be good enough, healing the daughters of narcissistic mothers*. New York: Atria paperbacks.

McConnell, S. (2020). Foreword by Schwartz, R. *Somatic internal family systems therapy, awareness, breath, resonance, movement, and touch in practice*. Berkeley, CA: North Atlantic Books.

Merleau-Ponty, M. (1945). *Phénoménologie de la perception*. Paris: Gallimard.

Merleau-Ponty, M. (1964). *Le visible et l'invisible*. Paris: Gallimard.

Minkowski, E. (1995 [1933]). *Le temps vécu, études phénoménologiques et psychopathologiques*. Paris: Quadrige, PUF.

Montagu, A. (2018). *Touching, the human significance of the skin* (3rd ed.). New York: Avon.

Moore, R., & Gillette, D. (1990). *King, warrior, magician, lover, rediscovering the archetypes of the mature masculine*. New York: Harper Collins.

Moretti, M., & Poggioli, D. (2017). *Handbook of individual family constellations* (V. R. Ferruci, Trans.). Original publ. Roma: Alpes Italia, ISBN-13: 978-1546964421.

Nathanson, D. L. (Ed.). (1987). *The many faces of shame*. New York: The Guilford Press.

Ogden, P., Minton, K., Fisher, J., Epstein, L., & Karelis, B. (2017a). *Sensorimotor psychotherapy for the treatment of trauma, affect regulation, survival responses and trauma regulation, training manual*. Boulder: Sensorimotor Psychotherapy Institute.

Ogden, P., Minton, K., Fisher, J., Epstein, L., & Karelis, B. (2017b). *Sensorimotor psychotherapy for the treatment of attachment injury, meaning making, emotional processing and relational memory, training manual*. Boulder: Sensorimotor Psychotherapy Institute.

Ogden, P., Minton, K., & Pain, C. (2006). *Trauma and the body, a sensorimotor approach to psychotherapy*. New York: Norton.

Rufo, M. (2009). *Chacun Cherche un Père*. Paris: Anne Carrière.

Sartre, J. P. (1943). *L'être et le néant, essai d'ontologie phénoménologique*. Paris: Gallimard.

Schneider, C. D. (1977). *Shame, exposure and privacy*. New York: Norton.

Schneider, J. R. (2007). *Family constellations, basic principles and procedures* (C. Beaumont, Trans.). Heidelberg: Carl-Auer.

Sieff, D. (2015). *Understanding and healing emotional trauma*. London and New York: Routledge.

Stolorow, R. D. (2009). *Trauma and human existence, autobiographical, psychoanalytic and philosophical reflections*. New York and London: Routledge.

Stolorow, R. D. (2011). *World, affectivity, trauma, heidegger and post-cartesian psychoanalysis*. New York and London: Routledge.

Turner, D. (2021). *Intersections of privilege and otherness in counselling and psychotherapy, mockingbird*. London: Routledge.

Wardi, D. (1992). *Memorial candles, children of the holocaust* (N.Goldblum, Trans.). London, New York: Routledge.

Wearing, D. (2005). *Forever today, a memoir of love and amnesia*. London: Doubleday.

Glossary

A personal summary of important concepts mentioned in this book

Being-in-the-world

This is Heidegger's characterization of human existence (*Dasein*). 'Being-in-the-world' is hyphenated to highlight the fact that all the elements belong together and cannot be understood in isolation.

'Being' is used in its verbal sense, rather than as a noun, to highlight the dynamic, ever-changing quality of existence.

The preposition -in- refers to the fact that we dwell within a web of interconnected meanings – rather like when we say we feel 'in' limbo, we are not referring to a place but to that particular way of being-in-the-world in which all is uncertain, in transition.

Human existence as being-in-the-world is always relational and always -in- a shared world of shared meanings. But at the same time, it is always -in- a private world of personal meanings (*see below Existential Therapy and Chapter 13*).

Boundaries

Boundaries are fundamentally connected to all areas of our lives, most intimately in relation to our bodies, our sense of personal space, identity, self-worth and security, but also in the way we live with the past, present and future dimensions of our lives.

Boundaries delineate the place we create and take for ourselves, as well as the place we give to others. So that in a myriad of ways, these boundaries affect our relationships with others around us and with anyone we encounter. However, interpersonal boundaries are not set in stone; they can be revisited at different moments of our lives. We can even revisit them in the absence of the other, for interpersonal boundaries are an embodied attitude involving all aspects of our being.

To feel unable to challenge the other's setting of boundaries, which we experience as overstepping our own, sets the scene for an abuse of power.

To believe unquestionably that we have no personal right to boundaries and feel "I do not deserve firmer boundaries, I am not worth it" indicates shame.

We also impose boundaries on the way we live time to delimit and ring-fence safe areas and to seek to defend and protect our well-being. We can set boundaries for ourselves that block off sections of time in an attempt to avoid a painful past, the anxiety of future change, or the intolerability of the present. Yet, we need to be able to travel to all areas of our life to gain a sense of both the ground beneath our feet and our mortality. Pretending some part of our life never existed or will never come to pass is one source of problems; not accepting that the past is past or taking up residence elsewhere than in the present is also problematic. *(see also Chapters 1-4 and Index)*

Brain, body, and basic physiology of trauma

The first premise of neurologically informed trauma therapies has emerged out of McLean's **'triune brain' theory**. The brain is viewed as having three distinct, yet intricately connected, structures that reflect and integrate its evolutionary history, from the reptilian to the mammalian and human stages. The oldest part of the brain, the 'reptilian' brain, consists of the brainstem and the cerebellum and governs our most basic physical functions such as our breathing and heart rate, as well as the basic survival responses of immobilization, fight and flight. The second structure, the 'limbic' part of the brain, is our mammalian heritage; it is involved in our emotional responses and in memory. It includes the amygdala, that part of the brain which, for all mammals, humankind included, sounds the alarm in dangerous situations and sends out messages to our body's various autonomic response systems. Capping them, the third, neocortical part of the brain is specific to humans and is involved in the more precise processing of the overall situation – making sense of it and of our experience. It also gives it a historical label – this incident took place at such a time.

When an animal senses a potential source of danger, it may orient towards it, then freeze so as to lessen the possibility of being noticed, its ears will prick up, its muscles tense up, it will prepare itself for action (if you try imitating an animal with pricked up ears, you will feel that tension throughout your body); then, it will follow the most appropriate response. It will seek protection, run away, stand firm and fight, show submission, or flop and feign death. *Every one of these responses is in itself valid and valuable*, as it is adapted to the situation as assessed at the time. So, for example, the feigned death response is, in itself, a valuable defence, because many animals do not like to eat meat from a prey which they have not killed themselves, as it may be rotting or poisoned. Also, in a 'flop' state, the prey, flooded with endogenous opioids, is numb and less likely to feel pain if it does get eaten.

When human beings find themselves in a situation that feels dangerous or threatening and the amygdala sounds the alarm, the specifically human, thinking part of the brain shuts down: humans therefore react like other mammals, with a hypervigilant stillness ('high freeze')[1], fight, flight, attach, or flop response. While other mammals characteristically shake themselves off after the threat has passed and generally return to a homeostatic state, humans do not tend to do so. We do not fully put a stop to the various physiological processes (nervous, hormonal, etc.) that have become activated. Trauma theory posits that the body therefore retains the trace of that traumatic experience, or as the titles of two of the most famous books in the field put it: *The body keeps the score*, *The body remembers*.

(See also below polyvagal theory, PTSD, trauma, and the window of tolerance)

Compassion

Compassion and understanding are intimately linked, for compassion is a disposition and a movement towards others, and ourselves, that comes from a wise and understanding heart.

Feeling 'compassion' is subtly but significantly different from 'feeling sorry for', 'feeling pity', 'empathizing'.

Self-compassion

When we look upon ourselves with compassion, we see ourselves as we would see a dear friend or loved one suffering our fate. We do not look down on ourselves nor judge ourselves.

Self-compassion does not mean exonerating ourselves of all wrong or responsibility. However, if we have done something we deem shameful or inexcusable, a compassionate understanding of ourselves will help us live better with the consequences of our actions.

Unlike self-pity which may draw us into a dynamic of victimhood and blame, self-compassion frees us from the emotions that hold us in their grip and opens us to change.

Compassion, towards ourselves and others, is key to healing *(see also Chapters 5, 6, 13 and index)*.

Defences

Like all animals, we have developed ways of defending ourselves against danger and enemies, but unlike other animals, we also have a highly developed ability to defend ourselves against ourselves.

We could not function in our everyday lives without the capacity to protect ourselves at times from strong emotions and toxic thoughts about ourselves. From our youngest infancy, we humans learn how to defend ourselves against getting emotionally hurt, whether by shutting down or else by covering up in any number of ways – e.g. through self-deprecatory remarks, jokes, or going on the violent offensive. We may later learn to self-medicate painful thoughts and feelings with alcohol or drugs, which further complicates matters, as well as adding to the sense of shame.

Defences often outlive their original use and gradually lose their efficacy and so we may feel the need to increase their level. Yet, if something is troubling us enough to necessitate such strong defences, it is unlikely to simply go away, it will continue calling out to us for attention.

This capacity of ours to protect ourselves deserves our admiration and awe. However, it comes to us at a cost. These defences may become so ingrained over the years that they prevent us from feeling spontaneity, equanimity, and joy, and from exploring the roots of our distress.

Developmental trauma

Therapy generally distinguishes between two broad forms of trauma: traumas such as accidents, violent assaults, witnessing a sudden death and other such specific experiences; and developmental trauma that arises from overwhelming, chronic experiences of neglect, violence, and/or terror at the hand of caregivers during childhood years. The two can coexist creating a complex trauma situation.

Developmental trauma may arise and develop in a number of ways.

For instance, a baby who has learnt that crying does not bring either comfort or milk, but might bring violent shaking, will give up crying. They begin to learn that there is no point in making any demands and that demands may even prove dangerous.

If a baby or young child is confronted with a parent's constantly depressed, terrified, scowling, furious, or zoned outlook, or their terrifying unpredictability, they are not going to think: "my mum/dad is not in a good place". They assume, or rather, since they cannot articulate it verbally to themselves, they absorb in every cell of their body the sense that they themselves are somehow at fault: that they are bad, frightening, unloveable... Besides, rather that than the alternative, namely that their parent is bad: at least by seeing themselves as the reason for their parent's harsh behaviour, a child still keeps alive the thought that by trying to be 'good' they will be looked after.

Similarly, a child who has learnt that any show of emotion will get them into trouble is likely to regard emotions as unacceptable, shameful even, and potentially dangerous. They are going to find a way to somehow block such emotions and stop feeling them.

As to the child who has been sexually abused by a caregiver, or someone close to them, unable to confide in anyone, their world is truly violated, betrayed, and desolate.

If seldom held emotionally and comforted when things feel overwhelming, children do not learn to integrate feelings of confusion, terror and rage within a fundamental sense of safety. They grow up feeling fundamentally insecure in a world that feels unsafe.

Tragically, such world-views die hard and many adults still carry from their earliest days the sense of their own 'badness' and/or of the world as threatening.

However, it is *vitally* important not to take a deterministic view, predicting only gloom and misery for a traumatized child's future. Freedom of choice and responsibility lie at the very heart of Existential therapy (*see Chapter 13*) and should, I believe, have a central place in trauma therapy. Freedom of choice and a non-deterministic perspective do not minimize the constricting, often crippling impact of childhood trauma on a person's being-in-the-world, rather they instil hope.

One should not confuse developmental trauma, the result of extreme parenting, with 'maladaptive attachment issues' which most of us have suffered and have inflicted on our own children to varying degrees. 'Maladaptive attachment' impacts on the way a child relates to their parents in an effort to feel loved, valued, and heard (e.g. by always being 'sweet', by learning how to get round them, by complying while toughing out rebuke, by working hard, etc.). Body-focused trauma therapies, informed by recent neuroscientific research, highlight how such learnt behaviour can, like trauma, become embodied in the child's nervous system and in their muscular–skeletal inter-action with the world. It can become, in the adult, a default way to position themselves (observable in their posture) and of being-in-the-world. However, again, it is important not to take a long-term, deterministic view of the impact of such parenting.

Dissociation

The term 'dissociation' is confusing as it refers to a number of very different phenomena: it can describe certain ways in which a person becomes in some sense dis-associated, i.e. separated; it can describe the ways in which they may somehow absent themselves from presence in the here and now.

One can encounter many instances of dissociation in everyday life, usually without recognizing them as such, for as with all human phenomena, these occur on a continuum from benign to very pronounced – when dissociation can have a highly detrimental impact on a person's life.

'Dissociation' can refer to that form of absence in which a person, suddenly, is no longer 'here': you can tell that they are 'elsewhere', in a cut-off state. And they themselves may describe having 'gone' somewhere or even speak of having 'left their bodies'. For some, it is a default mode of being that helps them when being 'here' feels too uncomfortable, painful, or somehow threatening.

Dissociative absences commonly develop out of a survival resource: during a traumatic event, in rape and sexual abuse for instance, where fighting back or running away are neither possible nor sensible options, numbing and 'leaving' the body enable the violated person to be somehow 'not here' and to experience what is happening less acutely (This is the equivalent of an animal's feigned death response. *See above, basic trauma physiology*). However, later, situations reminiscent of the original traumatic incident may trigger the same absenting response – in which case the person may be neither 'here', nor 'now' – they may be back there at the time of the original trauma (*see below, PTSD*), possibly feeling totally absent, 'dead to the world'. Such dissociation may become a default body-memory response to situations experienced as threatening.

If a dis-connection occurs between memory, cognition, emotions, and defences (hypervigilance, flight, etc.) as can happen in PTSD, there arises another form of dissociation, in which a person may recall every detail of the traumatic event without feeling any emotion, or vice versa want to drown in drink a pain of unknown origin. Similarly, they may feel constantly on their guard, even in their sleep, for no apparent reason.

Many are disconnected from parts of their lives in a way that makes them unable to give it a coherent timeline: it may feel to them as if the amnesia of dissociation has punched some gaping holes in the very fabric of their lives.

The dissociative response to a situation may also be such that the person can feel themselves depersonalized – looking at themselves through a distorted lens, or from out of their body. Depersonalization commonly goes hand in hand with derealization where the world no longer seems real. (From an existential perspective this is to be expected as our existence is inseparable from the world.)

As with all things human, classifications are not always clear cut: these different forms of dissociation can overlap and each can exist within a continuum.

However, 'dissociation' is often used as a shortcut for 'structural dissociation', which is now thought to reflect arrests in development, usually between the ages of two and nine. This is said to occur when the child cannot integrate overwhelming aspects of their existence, for instance when faced with extreme parental neglect or abuse at the hands of parents or strangers. Different aspects of the child's experience and personality, and later the adult's, come to split off from each other.

Of course, we all have different parts to ourselves that come to the fore in different areas and at different moments of our lives – anxious parts, organized and/or creative parts, parts that seek to protect us from what we do not want to confront, etc. Where it follows trauma, it seems that each part is trying to protect the person in its own way: as one part carries on functioning in the world while trying to be oblivious to the trauma, other protective parts have not realized that the trauma is over. In structural dissociation these parts are more distinct and fleshed out and may take on an existence of their own.

Structural dissociation itself covers a whole spectrum of ways of being: for some, one or more traumatized parts may take on life-managing roles very successfully (e.g. mother, high-flying professional), but, when triggered by specific, sometimes seemingly innocuous routine situations (e.g. making a bed), another part comes to the fore and takes over. Some live with fully-fledged multiple personalities that are aware of one another's existence; others have only one part that is conscious of some or all the parts *(see below Trauma and PTSD)*.

Embodiment

We are all embodied – this does not simply mean that we all have bodies, which is obvious, rather, it means we cannot but live, think, feel, relate through our bodies – we *are* body.

Existential therapy makes a distinction between the body we have and the 'body-we-are'. There are times when we need to objectify our body (e.g. for medical reasons). There are also times when we choose to treat it as an object, whether admiring it, finding fault with it, comparing it with that of others. Objectifying our body only becomes a problem when it is our default attitude towards it, for we then create a split within ourselves. And this will cut us off from the possibility of a truly satisfying experience of our embodied living.

Trauma can also shatter our relation to the body-we-are in a variety of ways *(see also Chapter 13 and index)*.

Existential therapy

Existential philosophy has the reputation of being gloomy, because of its strong focus on our 'thrownness' (the fact that we have no control on how, where and when we come into this world) and our mortality. Also, Existential philosophy asks us to question received opinions and deals with heavy concepts, such as freedom, responsibility and regret. Yet, because it links this all to meaning and asks us to consider what is most meaningful to us, to look at the possibilities that are open to us and to choose, as much as it is in our hands to do so, how we want to live our lives, I see the Existential perspective as freeing, empowering and hope-ful.

Existential Therapy is grounded in existential philosophy, and there are a variety of ways of practising it. As I see it, it is characterized by:

- a way of being towards the client that is open, genuine, warm, prepared to challenge yet does not judge the client as a person.
- a way of approaching issues: trying to understand without preconceived ideas what a specific issue means for that particular client and exploring its context (present and past) and its possible impact on the future *(see below Phenomenological)*.

- bearing in mind the universal existential issues which may offer a broader backdrop to the presenting issue (e.g. mortality) or open up vistas (e.g. freedom of choice) (see also *glossary: being- in- the- world, embodied, freedom, existential guilt, and Chapter 13*).

Existential guilt

This refers to the deep regret we may experience about the way we have been living our lives: e.g. drifting rather than making pro-active choices; not standing up for what is meaningful for ourselves; opportunities we did not dare to take, or else doors we shut for ourselves as we opened others, however worthwhile, etc.

Existential Guilt contains the sense of 'I owe it to myself' and can be a catalyst for change. *(on existential vs moral and neurotic guilt, see Chapter 6)*.

Family Holy Book

Most families have their own 'Family Holy Book'. This enshrines the rules, values and beliefs, both spoken and unspoken, which govern a family, and in particular the children, sometimes in the smallest details of their lives. It even governs which emotions are (un)acceptable.

Understanding the role played by the Family Holy Book in our childhood is an invaluable path to understanding the implicit beliefs and values we still hold and other constricting aspects of our adult lives. It is also a route to self-compassion that lies at the very heart of healing. *(see Chapter 12)*

Felt sense

We owe this important concept to Eugene Gendlin.

It refers to the pre-reflective, yet meaningful, bodily sense we can have of a situation or issue. Although pre-reflective, we can learn to bring our attention to it and later to reconnect to it.

Freedom

Freedom is often spoken of as an abstract entity that we either have or do not have. Freedom, as 'freedom of choice', is a very concrete concept of existential therapy where it is given a central place. It refers to that capacity that is ours to make choices and decisions and act upon them within the givens of our existence.

Freedom is an embodied stance which engages us in all aspects of our being-in-the-world – involving our values, beliefs, meanings, priorities and emotions.

Even where the context is restrictive in the extreme (e.g. totalitarian regime, imprisonment, serious degenerative illness) each person lives the situation differently, thus expressing their freedom of choice, underpinned by various personal traits, qualities and beliefs.

Freedom of choice discerns and opens up possibilities; it also comes with responsibility and may bring existential guilt (*qv*).

Hope

Hope is not a fantasy that promises that all our wishes will come true or even that 'it will all be OK'. Hope is a thought-ful, grounded and grounding, heartfelt, meaning-ful stance. As such, it is life-promoting and life-enhancing. It enables us to face the future with the sense that we can learn to deal with difficult and painful situations and try to make the best of them.

Implicit beliefs

Beside our explicit beliefs, we each hold some implicit beliefs about ourselves and the world that were formed in our early years. These are fundamental beliefs about our safety, about how welcome we are in the world, what we need to do to be accepted and valued, whether we can trust and ever depend on anyone, etc. (*see also Family Holy Book*)

'Mental health issues'

This phrase has entered everyday usage in recent years. While the term 'issues' is more inclusive and less stigmatizing than 'disorder', let alone 'illness' and 'hysteria', the term 'mental' is concerning. For 'mental' means 'pertaining to the mind' and hence should signify that these 'health issues' either manifest themselves in the mind or originate there; implying that they can be dealt with by dealing with the mind, or, a jump here, with the brain.

Yet, just consider the most commonly cited pair 'anxiety and depression'.[2] Anyone who has ever felt deeply depressed, or known someone who has, will know that the experience also manifests itself physically and emotionally, sometimes spiritually too, as well as in relation to others and to activities of everyday life. And it commonly arises elsewhere than in the mind e.g. out of experiences of loss (of a person, job, house, dream, purpose, faith, etc.). Similarly, anxiety is experienced in all dimensions of our being-in-the-world, and does not necessarily originate in the mind. In fact, trauma therapies highlight how many of our anxious states may arise as *physical* responses to physical or emotional triggers (*see basic physiology of trauma; polyvagal*).

So-called 'mental health issues' are therefore experiences that involve all dimensions of our existence; they may have their source in afflictions of body, mind, emotions or spirit, in relation to the world in which they are embedded.

Paying attention to the words we use it not simply pedantic. Language is powerful and using inaccurate words to describe an experience is confusing for all concerned and can have unfortunate consequences.

Phenomenological/Phenomenologically

To consider a person's life situation or way of being phenomenologically is to observe it, describe it without interpreting it and seek to understand what it means for that person, rather than approach these from preconceived theories or ideas. For instance, when I started as a cancer counsellor, I was told by my supervisor at the time that breast cancer was linked to unresolved grief; yet it soon became very obvious that while some people with breast cancer suffered from unresolved grief, others didn't, and some other cancer patients also did and many people with no cancer did as well. To start from such preconceived ideas ignores a person's specific life situation and, in bringing a strong bias, prevents genuine exploration.

The phenomenological method in therapy was developed out of the philosophical tradition of 'phenomenology' (Husserl, Heidegger, Merleau-Ponty, Gadamer, Ricoeur, etc.) and 'phenomenological' is often joined to 'existential' as it is the method of choice in existential therapy. However, it can be said of any form of therapy that adopts that approach.

Polyvagal theory

Polyvagal theory is a welcome newcomer to the trauma and interpersonal relations fields. Stephen Porges, its creator, revolutionized trauma therapists' understanding of the autonomic nervous system and its role in our responses to threat. He did so by replacing the old opposition between two neural pathways, a fight/flight defence pathway and a rest, recovery and growth one (innervated by the sympathetic nervous system and the parasympathetic nervous system respectively), with a more subtle, integrated system of three pathways.

In brief: he showed how the vagus nerve – the longest nerve in the body, which goes from the brainstem to the abdominal area and provides a calming influence on the heart, has a number of other roles besides rest and recovery. The vagus nerve has two branches: an ancient dorsal branch, which reaches down to the abdominal area, and which, Porges argues, is also responsible for the immobilizing[3] and dissociative responses in situations experienced as life-threatening. Porges goes on to argue that a more recent, mammalian, ventral branch of the nerve is linked to an area of the brainstem which controls various muscles of the face (eyes, ears and smile), as well as to the heart, thus creating a 'face-heart connection'. This has a predominant role, physiologically, in the conveying and receiving of emotion and intention. In that sense, from a physiological perspective, the ventral vagal nerve could be said to underpin our interpersonal engagement system, supporting our dual needs for connection and safety.

Porges describes a hierarchy of defences in challenging situations where friendly help is not at hand: first the newest system (ventral vagal) closes down and stops calming the heart; the sympathetic system is no longer inhibited and the fight/flight response becomes activated. And when the level of threat demands it, the sympathetic system in turn closes down and the most ancient immobilizing system takes over.

Polyvagal theory also highlights how, through neuroception, we constantly and unconsciously pick up the messages that both our environment and our own body send us. Our autonomic system then responds accordingly. Hence, if we cannot 'read' someone, if we experience a sense of confusion or panic, this can signal danger and trigger the sympathetic, fight/flight response. This resonates very strongly with a number of my clients or their partners. To realize that emotionally-charged reactions (one's own or one's partner's) can be physiologically triggered can be very comforting. Such an understanding can open the door to (self-)compassion. This does not mean that it absolves us of all personal responsibility in interpersonal relations. Rather, our responsibility can include in its focus a better understanding of physiological triggers and involve personal work on them.

Seen through a polyvagal theory lens, viewing ourselves and others with compassionate understanding is a way of being that, from a physiological perspective (by engaging the ventral vagus), develops a sense of safety that facilitates connection to others. On the other hand, shame engages our immobilizing dorsal vagal response, paralyzing us; while anger with ourselves may trigger our sympathetic nervous system as we 'beat ourselves up'.

However, we should not oversimplify explanations, as we need to remember that the brain and neural pathways are not independent of the person to whom they belong. *(see also basic physiology of trauma; dissociation)*.

PTSD *(see below the window of tolerance and PTSD)*

Rage

Rage is commonly associated with the violent acting out of anger, yet it is a life force. However, it is double-edged: it can be life-promoting or else bring about its destruction *(see Chapter 6)*.

Regret *(see existential guilt)*

Responsibility

Viktor Frankl famously said that facing the Statue of Liberty there should be a Statue of Responsibility.

Shame

Shame is an umbrella term for so many different experiences from a superficial feeling to a deep existential sense and belief, or a shocking, public humiliation. Shame is an embodied stance which makes us feel exposed, all eyes on us, singled out for what we feel is our intrinsic, personal ignominy.

Shame often camouflages itself in the neighbourhood of other, more acceptable emotions. A person may admit to feeling 'a bit embarrassed', 'upset', 'angry', or 'bad', when the dominant emotion is a shame that dare not speak its name.

The deep judgemental shame that we feel to our very core commonly goes with beliefs about ourselves developed in childhood. Whether these shaming beliefs stem from our family or from the society in which we may have felt ostracized growing up, we need to articulate these for ourselves and notice the extent to which we may have internalized them emotionally, cognitively, bodily, affecting our very life force. Compassionate understanding can help challenge them and develop a different embodied sense of ourselves. (*see Chapter 6*)

Systemic constellations

The theory of Systemic Constellations rests on three basic premises

1   When a system is out of balance in some way, it will try to rebalance itself.
2   When someone has been excluded or has excluded themselves in some way from a system (e.g. violent or premature death, estrangement) or doesn't have their proper place in the family (e.g. black sheep of the family; illegitimate or aborted child) or else has suffered a serious trauma, that system will become unbalanced – especially if the exclusion has been the subject of secrets and lies.
3   We may then find in the next generation or further down, the exclusion/ trauma/pain working itself out through one or more family members. For instance, a young adult who feels suicidal without quite knowing why, or who enjoys courting extreme danger, may be carrying 'out of loyalty' a burden that belongs to a grandparent or other member of the family system. That young person's 'fate' is then said to have become 'entangled' with their ancestor's. (*see Chapter 13 for examples*)

Transference/countertransference

Broadly speaking and very simplistically, transference refers to the way a client transfers onto the therapist feelings and thoughts that belong to their relationship to a significant other (commonly a parent). The concept of transference is central to psychoanalysis and psychodynamic therapy and much ink has been spilt on it in that literature. On the other hand, it has been given little or no place in many forms of therapy from Cognitive Behavioural Therapy (CBT) to Existential Therapy. Yet, there is no doubt that we commonly bring to a relationship beliefs, emotions and ways of being and reacting that belong elsewhere, learnt from previous relationships.

As with any therapy that is theory driven, there is a danger of misinterpreting what is going on in the room: a therapist who sees transference everywhere is in danger of missing the genuineness of the client's feelings (e.g. their love or anger); a therapist who denies the existence of transference flies in the face of phenomenal evidence and misses out on useful information.

Invariably, the therapist will bring their own experience to the therapeutic relationship. In addition, clients and their way of relating are likely to trigger something in the therapist. The lived bias of emotions, values, beliefs, as well as buttons that are easy to push, which the therapist brings to the therapeutic encounter, all affecting their response to the client, is known as counter-transference (*for examples of 'reactive countertransference', see Chapter 13; also, Chapter 3 Barry*).

Transgenerational trauma

'Transgenerational trauma' is said of a trauma that has occurred at some time in the past generation(s) and still has repercussions today. It can be applied to traumas on the grand scale, such as two of the greatest man-on-man inflicted traumas still affecting descendants to this day, slavery and genocide. Or else it can be specific to one family, where something traumatic that has happened to an ancestor is still being played out in some way today. (*see also Systemic Constellations and Chapter 13*)

Trauma

Saakvitne's definition of trauma is clear and helpful: 'Psychological trauma is the unique individual experience of an event, a series of events, or a set of enduring conditions in which: the individual's ability to integrate his or her emotional experience is overwhelmed [i.e. his or her ability to stay present, understand what is happening, integrate the feelings, and make sense of the experience] or the individual's experiences (either objectively or subjectively) a threat to life, bodily integrity, or sanity'. (Saakvitne et al. cited Sensorimotor Psychotherapy Institute training manual 1 January 2012)

This explains for instance how during the COVID pandemic, while all experienced lockdown, it was not traumatic for all. (*see Chapter 13*)

The experience of prolonged, repeated trauma is known as 'complex trauma'.

(See Chapter 13 Understanding through the body; and Glossary: body, brain, and basic physiology of trauma; developmental trauma; polyvagal theory; transgenerational trauma; window of tolerance; PTSD.)

The two triangles: The 'drama' or 'vicious' triangle and its 'virtuous' counterpart

Stephen Karpman's drama triangle consists of three points, 'victim', 'persecutor' and 'rescuer'; its beauty lies in its premise that if you are in one of those three positions in relation to someone, you can be sure that you will be at the other two as well. So, for instance, if we blame, e.g. our mother or our boss blindly (i.e. without trying to understand), we find ourselves oscillating between feeling 'victimized', 'persecutory' (angry, vengeful) and 'rescuing' (whether out of fear of conflict, need to fix, or hope for recognition). Though we may have default positions in which we are most likely to find ourselves, yet we still are involved in that dynamic. The drama triangle both normalizes the dynamic and appeals to our curiosity: where am I on it now and what shall I do about it? This appeal to our curiosity, to understanding with compassion and without judgement, is the key that unlocks the shift from the 'drama' or 'vicious' triangle, to the 'beneficial' or 'virtuous' triangle.

I do not know who devised the beneficial triangle, but theirs was a stroke of genius! These two triangles combined work like magic: as soon as you can move from feeling *victimized* to feeling *vulnerable* (or else to seeing the persecutor as vulnerable), you can feel, even physically, something shift in yourself and instead of *persecutory* you become able to be *potent,* as well as more *responsive* in the situation rather than *rescuing.* (You may ask what is wrong with rescuing? Rescuing is always in part for ourselves, and often not principally for the one we are trying to help, and hence it is often counterproductive.)

Understanding

We commonly ascribe greater validity to our mind's understanding over that of our emotions, spirit or body, yet all four have an important place in therapy, and in life, as we seek to understand the context of specific situations, actions or ways of being and relating.

The understanding that listens to mind, spirit and body and merges their insights with heart is compassionate and non-judgemental.

Compassionate understanding is capable of throwing a kind but powerful light on the values, implicit beliefs, triggers, transgenerational history and much else that all underpin the context of our lives. It can lift burdens of shame and guilt, open up possibilities and help to facilitate healing and change *(see Chapter 13)*.

The window of tolerance and post-traumatic stress disorder[4]

Window of tolerance (WOT)

In Existential therapy, it is commonly said that 'you need to sit with the anxiety', which is very fruitful when working with existential anxiety and the exploration of our life choices. Yet, there are certain overwhelming anxieties with which it is not helpful to sit, as they are likely to send us right out of our 'window of tolerance', into a state in which we are incapable of exploring anything.

In everyday life, we have varying degrees of tolerance to all sorts of stimuli (e.g. noise, smell, conflict situations) which may trigger a variety of sensations and emotions – irritability, claustrophobia, fear, grief. We can represent our levels of tolerance by drawing two horizontal parallel lines, with the space between those lines representing the 'window' within which we feel relatively comfortable. Our WOT to these every day stimuli is likely to vary according to situations: we may enjoy listening to loud music at a concert, but when it is our next-door neighbour in the middle of the night, night after night, our WOT to this same music is likely to be very narrow. We all have triggers, things that 'push our buttons' and make us feel uncomfortable, sometimes to the point of sending us out of our WOT. We might then have various strong reactions, such as exploding (going towards the upper edge or above the WOT) or retreating completely into our shells (going below the WOT).

Following a situation experienced as traumatic, our WOT to particular stimuli (e.g. a particular aftershave, the mention of 'lockdown', a woman shouting, the smell of burning tyres) may have been narrowed to the point of being paper-thin; this then lays us open to the phenomenon known as post-traumatic stress disorder.

Post-traumatic stress disorder (PTSD)

Following a traumatic experience, the body may react to situations that appear familiar in some way to the original traumatic situation: the amygdala will sound the alarm, setting off all the autonomic processes that arise in a threatening situation. Unless the person has been able to process the trauma in the meantime and can quickly distinguish between the past and the present situations ('that was then and now is now'), that stimulus will take them straight back there and they will find themselves *reliving* the traumatic event. This 'body memory' will send them into a defence response: it could be a high freeze, fight or flight response (i.e. upper edge or above the window of tolerance WOT), or else numbness, dissociation, depersonalization/derealization (lower edge of the WOT or beneath it).

The person whose WOT to stimuli reminiscent of the trauma is paper-thin will constantly receive Red Alert signals: the slightest smell of burning or the very sight of a man in a hoody will spell DANGER. Their defence system will become overwhelmed and disorganized: any one of the responses of hypervigilance, panic, fight, flight or feigned death may become exaggerated into default ways of being; and they may remain on emergency stand-by, creating a form of constant on-edge living. That person might be constantly scanning for danger, over-reacting unexpectedly strongly – whether violently 'flying off the handle' or shutting down and going completely numb; they may go to some lengths to avoid a place, group of people, or situation; they may be haunted by terrifying images, feeling or thoughts – or drink and 'self-medicate' to drown those.

Some people are all too aware of the original terrifying situation and the way it keeps making its reappearance (war veterans for instance); others are only dimly aware of the past that still somehow haunts them, as often happens with traumatic childhood events or with transgenerational trauma.

Some feel they had put the traumatic event well behind them, when suddenly decades later they find themselves behaving strangely and incomprehensibly: e.g. getting into a fight; dissociating; night after night waking from nightmares shaking with terror. And then there will be the realization that they had recently witnessed something on the news, or experienced something at work that had reactivated sensations, memories and emotions that had lain dormant for decades. For the body can carry the aftermath of a trauma for decades, unrecognized. Yet, it may have been manifesting itself in seemingly unrelated ways: patterns of tension in the body, breathing or digestive issues, involuntary spasms or shaking, a generalized sense of fearfulness or anxiety, etc.

Notes

1 It is important to distinguish between the high freeze of preparation for action and the low freeze of feigned death/flop: they are activated by different parts of the autonomic nervous system – the sympathetic and parasympathetic dorsal vagal, respectively, with different characteristic effects. There can also be a form of freeze, 'freeze 2', that is not a preparation for action as in the high freeze, but a paralyzing panic.
2 And using the noun 'depression' as a thing one can 'get', like measles, is another problem.
3 Though not the high freeze in the face of detected danger.
4 Since writing a brief critique of PTSD as a psychiatric diagnosis in *When Death Enters the Therapeutic Space*, a book I edited almost 15 years ago, my viewpoint has changed quite drastically. There were some interesting points, but overall, I now believe it was misguided as it ignored the contributions of much body-focused trauma therapy. This is rather embarrassing as I have seen my former views quoted, but I comfort myself with the thought that 'only fools don't change'!

Index

Ingram Content Group UK Ltd.
Milton Keynes UK
UKHW022201030523
421200UK00024B/185